WRITER AND AUDIENCE

Forms of Non-Fiction Prose

WRITER
AND
AUDIENCE

Forms of Non-Fiction Prose

Wilson Currin Snipes

Virginia Polytechnic Institute

HOLT, RINEHART and WINSTON, Inc.

New York   Chicago   San Francisco
Atlanta   Dallas   Montreal   Toronto

Copyright © 1970 by Holt, Rinehart and Winston, Inc.
All rights reserved
Library of Congress Catalog Card Number: 73—107438
SBN: 03-082995-x
Printed in the United States of America
1 2 3 4 5 6 7 8 9

Preface

Writer and Audience: Forms of Non-Fiction Prose begins with the writer writing first about himself and his surroundings—Part One: Writing from Experience, in the diary, letters, and autobiography; next writing about other individuals—Part Two: Writing about People, in the character sketches and biography; then, writing about subjects amenable to various audiences—Part Three: Writing for Audiences, in the editorial, informal and formal speeches and essays, the review; and, finally, writing critical examinations of man and his world—Part Four: Writing for Understanding in literary criticism and the research paper. In the process, the writer is introduced to the general characteristics of selected non-fictional literary forms, provided with examples of each, encouraged to analyze each form critically, and challenged to experiment with each form through its use in self-expression.

The introductions to the various sections, the selections, the questions, and the writing assignments are based on the following assumptions: first, in each written or oral expression, a writer chooses a primary intellectual purpose; second, he selects, unconsciously or consciously—preferably the latter—a literary form, governed generally by its own conventions, through which he may best express his thought and feeling; third, his self-expression originates in a complex of unstructured experience and progresses to purposeful, organized self-expression; fourth, he must be, at one and the same time, or in successive stages of composition, both creative and critical—creative in finding purpose, form, organization, and relevant detail for self-expression, and critical in analyzing, evaulating, and qualitatively revising his earlier creative efforts; and, finally, he must take himself, his subject, his audience, and his self-expression seriously.

In short, Writer and Audience: Forms of Non-Fiction Prose offers no short cuts to effective writing. Rather, it challenges the writer to discover for himself and to develop in himself, in the actual process of reading, thinking, and writing, his own abilities to write efficient, effective, meaningful prose.

Finally, I wish to express appreciation to the members of the Department of English at Virginia Polytechnic Institute for their valuable suggestions concerning the introductions and materials included, to Mrs. Carol Watson, Mrs. Gloria Dunlap, and Mrs. Sandra Lucas who typed and retyped the manuscript during its various stages, to Mr. Kenney Withers and Mr. Phillip Leininger for their encouragement and assistance, and to my family—Nita, Caroline, and Currin—the "without whom."

W. C. S.

Blacksburg, Virginia
January 1970

Contents

PART I

Writing from Experience

I

Diary, Journal, and Commonplace Book

The diarist maintains a personal, chronological record of his individual experiences: Samuel Sewall's *Diary* presents a picture of life in and around Boston during the late seventeenth and early eighteenth centuries; Cotton Mather's *Diary* records his spiritual states; Samuel Pepys noted, in great detail, aspects of his personal and public life at the time of the Restoration of the Stuarts to the throne of England; Anne Frank, in her *Diary*, reveals the developing maturity of an adolescent girl during the Nazi occupation of the Netherlands during World War II. Each diarist, for personal reasons, chooses to keep a diary of those daily matters that pass through his consciousness and take on special meaning for him. As distinguished from the professional diarist who writes for posterity, the personal diarist writes for himself to himself; his diary is an intimate record of the meaningful thoughts and events of his life.

Less personal and intimate are the journal and commonplace book. Ralph Waldo Emerson suggests the more intellectual character of the journal and its similarity to the commonplace book in his description of the purpose of his *Journal*:

> These pages are intended at their commencement to contain a record of new thoughts (when they occur); for a receptacle of all the old ideas that partial but peculiar peepings at antiquity can furnish or furbish; for tablet to save the wear and tear of weak Memory, and, in short, for all the various purposes and utility, real or imaginary, which are usually comprehended under that comprehensive title *Common Place Book*.

Some journals contain selected quotations from materials read, some contain observations about the surrounding society and environment, some include seminal ideas that may be used later in other forms of written expression; in most instances the writer anticipates a subsequent use he may make of the materials selected and recorded.

The writer of a diary, journal, or commonplace book normally adopts a personal point of view toward his subject, allowing himself a freedom of self-expression that he would not reveal were he writing to someone else or to a more general audience. His tastes, interests, and prejudices are intimately revealed through his choice of subject matter, and a kind of "no holds barred" treatment of subject matter; in fact, the writer may use his diary, journal, or commonplace book as a vehicle through which he may clarify his own thought concerning a debatable subject, or he may do little more than record passing impressions. The tone of the entries is that of the writer at the time he writes; the organization is primarily chronological, but may be thematic or governed by some other organizational principle; the ideas and details selected are relevant to the writer's values and life; the units of expression may be no more than one-word entries, phrasal entries, independent sentences, or extended paragraphs, depending in each instance upon the writer's specific purpose at the time the entry is made; the dictional choices may be quotational, paraphrase, or in the idiom of the writer.

The excitement of the diary, the journal, and the commonplace book is found in self-discovery, the act of seeking meaning and coherence in daily life, the joy of intellectual refinement, the process of keeping the memory alive, and the details of daily life selected for recording and for reflection.

FROM A WESTERN JOURNAL

Thomas Wolfe

Wed June 22.

Woke at 7:00 after sound sleep—water falling—girls voices, etc.— Breakfast—and good one at cafeteria—after that visited waterfalls took photographs, talked to people, visited swell hotel—sent post cards, etc, and then on way out—by the South Wawona entrance—then beautiful rockrim drive down through wooded Sierras to foothills—the brilliant leafage of scrub pine—then the bay-bright gold of wooded big barks—then the bay-gold plain and bay-gold heat—a crowded lovely road—and Clovis—lunch there—then the ride up to the mountains again—the same approach as the day before—the bay-gold big barks— then cupreous masses—then forested peaks—then marvelous and precipitous ride upward and the great view back across the vast tangle of the Sierras—then Gen. Grant and the great trees—the pretty little girls —then the 30 mile drive along the ridge

to the Sequoia—and Gen. Sherman—and the giant trees—then straight thru to other entrance then down terrifically the terrific winding road—the tortured view of the eleven ranges—the vertebrae of

the Sierras—then the lowlands—and straight highroad—no bends—
and Visalia—then by dark straight down the valley—to Bakersfield—
then East and desertwards across the Tehachapi range—the vertical
brightness of enormous cement plants—and now at 1:30 in Mohave
at desert edge—and tomorrow across the desert at 8:00 o'clock—and
so to bed—and about 365 miles today.

At Bakersfield—enormous electric sign—Frosted Milk-shakes—A
Drive-Inn—and girls in white sailor pantys serving drinks—I drank
Frosted Lime, Miller a Coco-Cola float, etc.

Sunday June 26, 1938.

Arose Bryce Canyon 7:30 dressed, walked with M to Rim and to observation house on point and looked at Canyon. Sky somewhat overcast
and no sunlight in the canyon, but it was no less amazing—looked
fragile compared to other great canyons "like filigree work", of fantastic loveliness   Great shouldering bulwarks of eroded sand going down
to it—made it look very brittle and soft—erodes at rate of 1 inch a year
—something the effect of sugar candy at a carnival—powdery—whitey
—melting away—Old man, roughly dressed, and with one tooth, and
wife, and daughter, surprisingly smart looking young female in pajama
slacks and smoked goggles talking geology—

the words came trippingly off her tongue—"erosion"—"wind erosion"
—"125 million years and so on"—There had been argument with
someone whether Canyon had been cut with water—"all canyons cut
with water" etc—M took pictures "Look out as if you're looking out"
—then quickly back through woods toward lodge and after last nights
rain brightly amazingly pungent, sweet and fragrant—smell of sage,
pine needles, etc—So breakfast in lodge and C as usual engrossed with
hotel manager haggling about prices, rates, cabin accommodations etc
—wrote

post cards and ate hearty breakfast and talked with waitress who was
from Purdue—studying "home economics" and dress designing and
hopes to be a "buyer" for Chicago store—observed the tourists—two
grim featured females—school-teachers—at table next—who glowered
dourly at everyone and everything with stiff inflexible faces and H. says
most of the tourists are women and many school teachers—So the
tourists rose to depart, and presently the sound of singing and the wait-
resses, maids, bell boys etc gathered in front of Lodge and by bus singing

"Till we meet again"—"Good-bye, ladies" etc—and one of the dour
looking school teachers dabbing furtively at eyes, and the bus departing, and emotional farewells, and the young folks departing back to

their work, and bragging exultantly "We got tears out of four of 'em this morning. Oh, I love to see 'em cry; it means business"—Then discussing hotel business again and the art of pleasing guests and squeezing tears from them

Saturday July 2.

Lay late, until 8:20—and C came in to build the fire, and in both of us quiet greetings, a feeling that our trip was almost done, and in me a sense of the tremendous kindness and decency and humanity of the man. He said: "Tom, look at the mountain!" I got up and looked; it was immense and terrific and near and cloud still clung to the Great

Cloudmaker at the side like a great filament of ectoplasm. C told me to sleep as long as I wanted, and went out but presently I got up and the room warm now and a brisk fire going in the stove and a basin of water and dressed and shaved, and walked over the packed and dirty snow to the Lodge, where joined C and Caderon at breakfast—and Caderon

a nice boy, doing his level best for us in everything, solicitous and good —the long face and teeth and loving agreeability of the Y.M.C.A. and Sunday School boy—he spoke frequently of his Sunday School Class —So M joined us, refreshed from sleep, and the Ranger and another Ranger, and so out to take pictures and to look at the Mountain—and the sun out now, the

mist ocean still below us—but the great mass of Rainer clearly defined now, save for the white sky-backwall—and the great mass faced up squarely and all its perilous overwhelming majesty, and with its tremendous shoulders, the long terrific sweeps of its hackling ridges, we stood trying to get its scale, and this

impossible because there was nothing but Mountain—a universe of mountain, a continent of mountain—and nothing else but mountain itself to compare mountain to. On this trip C's great love and knowledge of mountains has revealed itself—upon the summit of the pass at the Continental divide in Glacier the way he pointed out the little trees, the affection and reverence with which he spoke of them—the signs by which the

trees of timber-line could be observed and noted the Cloudiness at the Base etc—the little mountain flowers—now the astounding revelation that he had climbed Hood 225 times and Rainer 40—the quiet way he told of accidents and rescues—of the ice so hard that the axe bounds off and "ruins a man for life"

QUESTIONS

1.   The *Journal* is Wolfe's record of a thirteen-day trip to the national parks of eight western states. In the entry for Wednesday, June 22, Wolfe records the details of his daily life, his surroundings, and his impressions of Yosemite National Park, Sequoia National Park, and the drive to Mojave, California. Prepare a diary entry in which you meditate over several significant events of your life, such as the time you felt "rejected" by your family and society, the influence of a person on your life, or a turning point in your thinking about religion, politics, or morality.

2.   In Wolfe's *Journal* entry for Sunday, June 26, the many selected details reveal the author's perceptiveness: the way things looked, what people said, the appeals to the senses, and the cynicism of the young people. Contrast, in a diary entry, your attitudes as a college freshman with those you held as a high school senior, on a subject such as college. To what extent do the details of your contrast reveal your perceptiveness?

3.   According to the entry of Saturday, July 2, Wolfe looked at the mountain, Mt. Rainier, and "it was immense and terrific and near. . . ." Make a diary entry in which you explain some recent discovery you have made about yourself.

4.   Wolfe mentions his "sense of the tremendous kindness and decency and humanity of the man," one of his companions. Prepare a diary entry in which you comment on some admirable quality of one of your acquaintances.

5.   A common theme in much contemporary literature indicates that many teenagers and college students are concerned about their sense of alienation from society, their separation from family and traditional values, their individual emotional, intellectual, and spiritual isolation. Write a diary entry describing some recent, personal experience in which you felt you were separated from family, friends, or traditional values.

FROM A WRITER'S NOTEBOOK

Van Wyck Brooks

Whoever is accustomed to reading with a definite object in mind cannot long endure desultory reading. An object acts as a magnet attracting, in

From the book FROM A WRITER'S NOTEBOOK by Van Wyck Brooks. Copyright © 1958 by Van Wyck Brooks. Reprinted by permission of E. P. Dutton and Co., Inc.

all one reads, the facts and the ideas that are relevant to it, and this creates an excitement in the mind that makes all purposeless reading tame and insipid. And yet what a pity this is, for it is desultory reading that develops one's taste. It is fortunate that when we are young we are unfocussed.

———

Literature, properly speaking, has three dimensions,—breadth, depth and elevation. Most great writers have had these three dimensions, but few modern writers have more than two. Many have breadth, some have depth, and there are numbers who combine these two dimensions; but how very few at present have elevation! Three generations ago, this was perhaps the chief dimension of writers. Now the time has come round for it again, and I hope it will not be abused.

———

A publisher in England, advertising a new novel, says, "It contains no obscenities in the new American tradition," and I am wondering how long this tradition is going to last and why it thrives especially in our country. It is understandable that the modern mind requires discord with its harmony, that the beautiful must be "damned beautiful" to be mentioned at all, and I am aware of the prudery that dogged the American literary mind in the generation when I was growing up. But how long does this kind of reaction perform a real function?—and does one not feel now a kind of monotonous adolescence in our use of the cloacal word and the scene it evokes? When a character in a recent story, referring to the setting sun at sea, says it "looks like a big red behind being lowered into a bathtub," I think of some of the images that scene called up before Buck Mulligan spoke of the "snotgreen sea." In countless minds this phrase of Joyce deflated for all time the association of the sea with majesty and greatness that Homer had kept alive for two thousand years, and, while this may have been called for at the moment, deflation ever since has been virtually the rule in literary usage. And how tiresome is this flatness, this dull concentration on the mean,—as tiresome as the witless grin that seems to be obligatory in the photographs of public persons nowadays.

———

The writers who are to play a part in the rebuilding of civilization will share some of Schweitzer's reverence for life, the reverence that John Bartram revealed when this old naturalist was filled with compunction over the field-flowers that he had so carelessly mowed. They will understand the feeling of William James about vivisection, that he must somehow pay something back to life for every jet of pain that he was causing. Thomas Hardy wrote in *Tess* a chapter on the pheasants that were wounded to make sport for the English gentry,—after which, he said, the gentry cut him,—and Aldous Huxley and Bertrand Russell are vice-presidents of a society "to stop the sordid and ugly pastime of hunting foxes to death for fun." Pope's essay on the mistreatment of animals might convince one of his goodness of heart if it were not for his ridicule of the "dinnerlessness" and "rags" that he found so delightfully funny in the wretches of Grub Street.

"It has become a custom to call anyone a sentimentalist who is sufficiently civilized to be susceptible to the tender emotions." So says Lord David Cecil somewhere. But unless we cultivate tenderness, what will become of a human world that is now as red as nature in tooth and claw?

<hr/>

Whatever their conscious beliefs may be, Americans are instinctively believers in the freedom of the will. They may think they are determinists, but, when this is the case, they always turn out to be fatalists, and that is quite a different matter. William James made this clear in his *Principles of Psychology*: "The fatalistic argument is really no argument for simple determinism. There runs through it the sense of a force which might make things otherwise from one moment to another, if it were only strong enough to breast the tide. A person who feels the *impotence* of free effort in this way has the acutest notion of what is meant by it, and of its possible independent power. How else could he be so conscious of its absence and of that of its effects? But genuine determinism occupies a totally different ground: not the *impotence* but the *unthinkability* of free will is what it affirms."

In this sense, I say that all American fatalism assumes and, as it were, demands free will. It springs from a kind of disappointment, and this is our characteristic mood from Mark Twain and Henry Adams to Dreiser and Faulkner, whose people are generally defeated, like the people of Hemingway, Dos Passos, Fitzgerald and Farrell. Our world has not lived up to its expectations, and the single man feels helpless before the mass. Hence these tears, or this hard-boiled denial of the right to weep. But this does not argue that free will does not exist; it merely affirms that the will is not effective. It pays the highest tribute to the will, for it says that life is meaningless and empty precisely because of this negation. How many are the Americans, living or dead, for whom the will has not been the core of life, either in its operation or in its suspension?

The only unthinkable thing, for American minds, is that the will should not exist; and that is the reason why, when it is not effective, its impotence seems to Americans so overwhelming. One could never imagine an Asiatic writing as, for instance, Theodore Dreiser wrote. It takes long generations of disappointment, hundreds and thousands of years of disillusion to produce the deterministic frame of mind; or one might more truly say that the real determinist is one who has never known expectations. Fatalism presupposes hope, and any child can be a fatalist. Take away his kite or his train of cars, or lock him up in a closet, and he sees life stretching before him as a prison or a desert. We have lost so many kites, as Henry Adams pointed out, we have had to exchange so many nurseries for closets, that we have ceased to think of ourselves as the children for whom the world was one big vacant lot.

━━━━

The Irish poet James Stephens said that the trouble with American writers is, quite simply, that "they don't love words." I think there is some truth in this and I wonder if the reason is that, in the matter of words, we are so "scientific." How could we share, if we wished it, the fine careless rapture of the poets of prescientific times? For them words were laden with associations that we, with our semantics, are driven to reject.

A Swiss professor says that "a kind of language consciousness appears to be more generally developed in America than elsewhere," leading to an extreme awareness of the "errors of verbal suggestion" and the misunderstandings caused by "verbal trappings." But how can any intense wholehearted love of words survive this constant verbal scepticism? The love of words springs out of the unconscious. It comes from a long devotion to the language one inherits, and it cannot abide attempts to create new kinds of language or a too conscious scrutiny of the old kinds.

━━━━

The most serious charge that critics can bring against a writer nowadays is to say that he is naive, and yet something like naivety is rapidly becoming the one thing necessary for writers. Or perhaps the right word is ingenuousness, for I do not recommend the untutored, the too artless or the provincial. What I do mean is the opposite of the kind of sophistical knowingness that chokes so much of the writing of this generation. The literary mind of our day reflects the general urban mind in being, in all respects, overconscious, while the mass-influences of advertising, analysis, cosmetics and Kinsey reports have worn away its freshness and destroyed its bloom. In consequence it has lost the capacity for wonder that is so essential to the poet and the story-teller. What was it that accounted for Dylan Thomas's unique position among the younger poets of the time? Precisely that he had escaped the sophistication that has paralyzed the contemporary poetic mind. He seemed to be uniquely capable of both wonder and joy. The capacity for wonder presupposes a certain childlikeness that has lost its value today in both literature and life.

One of my correspondents wrote to me the other day that "the young writers of America are old and dangerous." From that frame of mind how can writing emerge? When no one speaks of the heart any longer except as a physical organ, and few seem to know the difference between love and sex, what becomes inevitably of natural feeling? And without natural feeling there can be no wonder, the kind of wonder that gave Theodore Dreiser, banal and material as he was, the sense that, in life and the world, he was "a guest at a feast." He found wonderlands on all sides, in newspaper offices, in factory buildings, in shop-girls brushing their hair at open windows, and for his readers too this wonder invested with magic the spectacle of everyday existence. It was this kind of ingenuousness that redeemed Dreiser,—the gift of being surprised by things, of looking at the world "with eyes wide open in wonder," as Ortega put it.

The painter's innocence of the eye belongs in this way to the writer too, and how right Amiel was in saying, "The novelist must be ingenuous, at least when his pen is in his hand." For this innocence is the spring of all clear perception, and the question is "how to regain the naive or innocent soul," as D. H. Lawrence said in one of his letters. "How to make it," he continued, "the man within the man,—your 'societal'; and at the same time keep the cognitive mode for defences and adjustments and 'work'." No one can tell how far writers are capable of this again until the gospel of knowingness has worn itself out, in criticism, in the general atmosphere that writers breathe. The ideal of the knowing man, which tends to dominate the modern writer, is altogether foreign to his true nature.

Mencius said that a wise man should somehow keep the childlike mind. What a rebuke that is to our tiresome American ideal of "sophistication."

The method of psychoanalysis in the writing of biography has, I think, a limited value, and I believe that, having once passed, it will not be used again. If one could accept for biography Georg Brandes's dictum that, while the romantic intellect is interested in the significance of things, the modern intellect is interested only in their causes, then one might say that the day of the Plutarchs has passed and that Freud is the master of the future. But, in fact, what concerns the biographer, whether "romantic" or not, is always the significance of things. Psychoanalysis serves the psychologist in the biographer by placing him in possession of certain facts which he cannot obtain so easily by other methods. But all a biographer's facts are useless until he has reconceived them in the light of his intuitive feeling for reality and proportion. This intuitive faculty is a different mental organ from the intelligence, which actually paralyzes its operation. It is not the causes that matter in biography, it is the character itself, which belongs to the moral and aesthetic sphere, a sphere that is quite apart from the sphere of causation. The attempt to turn biography into a science is as futile as it is with history.

In a word, owing to the avant-garde, a large part of our literature might be described as peripheral rather than central. It is the expression of a small closed world, walled in from the common world, which does not even wish to contribute to life, a semi-private art or game for which a great deal may be said but which is not a "literature fit for our occasions." (For what a role our literature might play in the emerging "planetary" world, the role that Whitman himself foresaw or dreamed of.) Will not our next phase restore this central literature, combining the great subject-matter of the "middle-brow" writers with the technical expertness bequeathed by the formalist critics, restoring in turn the notion of literature as a mirror and guide of society which is now discounted as journalistic?

One might well expect this, obvious as it must be that the avant-garde cannot produce this new departure, for, stifling both curiosity and independence, it does not permit the deviations that open new epochs. With its fanatical concentration on a few fashionable authors, it conveys no sense of the diversity of the history of letters, no feeling for the resources of the past that might breed fresh beginnings. For new departures one must look to the world outside the avant-garde, which inherits the exhaustion and despair of a diminished Europe, formed as it was under the spell of old-world writers for whom mankind had come to the end of its tether.

––––

Or might there be a coup d'état within the avant-garde restoring its lost tie with the main intellectual body, with those who have never been guilty of the "treason" to the cause of liberalism that Julien Benda and Toynbee have equally lamented? This would be the best conjuncture, for anything else might jeopardize the avant-garde machinery that has been a blessing, with its magazines and summer conferences, for the sensitive young, while the avant-garde only half answers the needs of American writers, who cannot feel deeply involved in the "decline of the West." No more than the Asiatics, whose own world is beginning anew, can they share truly the European mood of the moment, the *fin de siècle* mood of the post-war epoch; for their country is too vigorous for this and it has lost too little. So one might suppose the time has come to accept Melville's injunction that America should "set, not follow, precedents," speaking not for the country that is but for the country that promises to be, even if it always breaks its word.

QUESTIONS

1. Van Wyck Brooks, in the selections above from his *Writer's Notebook*, demonstrates an interest in and concern with reading, literature, naturalism, sentiment, free will, words, the capacity for wonder, biography, and the avant-garde. Prepare a series of "notebook" entries in which you discuss briefly your views on several subjects.

2. Brooks quotes the painter John Sloan: "Any man who speaks English with care is suspected of being a fairy nowadays." Write a notebook entry in which you support or attack this statement.

3. With certain individuals and groups today obscenities are in fashion. Brooks asks, ". . . does one not feel now a kind of monotonous adolescence in our use of the cloacal word and the scene it evokes?" Make an entry in your notebook in which you defend, excuse, or reject "sewer" language.

4.   Brooks repudiates "our tiresome American ideal of 'sophistication'." After thinking about the meanings this word has to you, as well as examples from your life that illustrate its meanings, write a notebook entry explaining its meanings to you.

5.   During the past year, much has been written about avant-garde student leadership, particularly about anti-establishment, anti-tradition, and anti-middle-class values. In a notebook entry clarify carefully and illustrate some of the values you consider invalid, outmoded, or useless.

II

Letters

By definition, a personal letter is a form of communication between two individuals, a form based on the human interrelationships existing between these persons. Other kinds of communication employing the letter form include social letters, business letters, literary letters, letters to the editor, letters of protest, letters of political support, and letters devoted to specific purposes. Usually a letter has little or no intrinsic value except to those involved in the correspondence, since its value rests upon the relationship between two people. Love letters, for example those written between George Bernard Shaw and Ellen Terry, or between Heloise and Abelard, are personal expressions of the genuine affection and respect that each lover held for the other; to posterity, the fascination of these letters is derived in great part from the human and historical importance of the people who wrote them. The letter as an art form, represented by Walter Savage Landor's *Letters of Pericles and Aspasia* or C. S. Lewis' *Screwtape Letters*, is written for contemporary society as a whole and for posterity. However, by far the letter most often written is a personal letter from one friend to another, "the most intimate of all forms of literature," as described by one student of letters.

The subjects of personal letters extend from what the writer had to eat at breakfast to detailed descriptions of his current love affair, from art to revolution, from the affairs of daily life to reflections on eternity. The writer writes about whatever matters to him. The "I" point of view predominates; the style is usually that of familiar talk, reflecting the personality, character, and tone of the writer; the organization of the letter may be loose, providing no more than an arbitrary enumeration of the events of the day, or it may represent an extended analysis of a current social, political, or religious issue; the sentence and dictional choices may be chatty and informal, close approximations to conversation, or they may be erudite and formal, depending upon the specific relationship between the correspondents at the time the letter is written.

In the letter form, the uninhibited personality of the writer manifests itself freely.

LETTER TO SCOTTIE

F. Scott Fitzgerald

[Metro-Goldwyn-Mayer Corporation]
[Culver City, California]

[Fall, 1938]

Dearest Scottie:

I am intensely busy. On the next two weeks, during which I finish the first part of *Madame Curie,* depends whether or not my contract will be renewed. So naturally I am working like hell—though I wouldn't expect you to understand that—and getting rather bored with explaining the obvious over and over to a wrong-headed daughter.

If you had listened when Peaches read that paper aloud last September this letter and several others would have been unnecessary. You and I have two very different ideas—yours is to be immediately and overwhelmingly attractive to as many boys as you can possibly meet, including Cro-Magnons, natural-born stevedores, future members of the Shriners and plain bums. My idea is that presently, not quite yet, you should be extremely attractive to a very limited amount of boys who will be very much heard of in the nation or who will at least know what it is all about.

The two ideas are *irreconcilable,* completely and utterly inverse, obverse and *contradictory!* You have *never* understood that!

I told you last September that I would give you enough to go to Vassar, live moderately, leave college two or three times during the fall term—a terrific advantage in freedom over your contemporaries in boarding school.

After four weeks I encountered you on a weekend. Here is how it was spent—God help the Monday recitations:

Friday—on the train to Baltimore
     Dance
Saturday—to New York (accidentally) with me
Sunday—to Simsbury to a reunion

The whole expedition must have cost you *much more* than your full week's allowance. I warned you then, as I had warned you in the document Peaches read, that you would have to pay for your Thanksgiving vacation. However, in spite of all other developments—the Navy game, the Dean's information, the smoking, the debut plans—I did not interfere with your allowance until you gave me the absolute insult of neglecting a telegram. Then I blew up and docked you ten dollars—that is exactly what it cost to

---

call you the day of the Yale-Harvard game because I could not believe a word you said.

Save for that ten dollars you have received $13.85 every week. If you doubt this I will send you a record of the cancelled checks.

There is no use telegraphing any more—if you have been under exceptional expenses that I do not know of I will of course help you. But otherwise you must stay within that sum. What do you do it for? You wouldn't even give up smoking—and by now you couldn't if you wanted to. To take Andrew and Peaches—who, I think you will agree, come definitely under the head of well-brought-up children—if either of them said to their fathers: "I'm going to do no favors for you but simply get away with everything I can"—well, in two minutes they'd lose the $25 a month they probably get!

But I have never been strict with you, except on a few essentials, probably because in spite of everything I had till recently a sense of partnership with you that sprang out of your mother's illness. But you effectively broke that up last summer and I don't quite know where we stand. Controlling you like this is so repugnant to me that most of the time I no longer care whether you get an education or not. But as for making life soft for you after all this opposition—it simply isn't human nature. I'd rather have a new car.

If you want to get presents for your mother, Peaches, Mary Law, Grandmother, etc., why not send me a list and let me handle it here? Beyond which I hope to God you are doing a lot about the Plato—and I love you very much when given a chance.

Daddy

P.S. Do you remember going to a party at Rosemary Warburton's in Philadelphia when you were seven? Her aunt and her father used to come a lot to Ellerslie.

QUESTIONS

1. The tone of a letter emerges from the relationship existing between the correspondents. In this instance a father, F. Scott Fitzgerald, is writing to his daughter, a freshman at Vassar. What is the dominant tone of the letter? Write a letter to a friend, in which you select details carefully to convey a specific tone.

2. In this letter, Fitzgerald contrasts the views of two generations toward boys. In a letter to a friend contrast your views and tone with those of your father, using a subject such as girls or boys, the church, the activist scene, or green power.

3. Obviously, Fitzgerald assumed that economic support of his daughter's education implied moral responsibility on her part. Attack or defend this position in a letter to your parents.

4. Fitzgerald speaks of "a sense of partnership" he felt with his daughter. Recently, students have frequently stated they did not want parents as pals, but as parents. In a letter to a relative, an aunt or uncle, explain what you think should be the parental relationship to college-age sons and daughters.

LETTER TO BARBARA CHURCH

Wallace Stevens

[Hartford, Conn.]
August 16, 1950.

Dear Mrs. Church:

You are probably in Germany or else just back. Are you going down to Auvergne? I ask because I sent for two new books by Henri Pourrat the other day: One on Socrates and his Demon, which appears to be an analysis of Socrates' smile, something which I never heard of before; and the other a collection of short stories, Tales of a Wood Cutter. What makes Pourrat precious is that he does not have a modern soul. In a way he is a Biblical figure, dynamic with spiritual vigor. When you first called my attention to him I felt rather languid about his love of humanity, his knowing way about life and the world. It did not take long to find that he has much more than all that. If you happen to see him, I should like to have two things: a good photograph and then a package of his paper, for which I should be glad to pay or if you paid him (for promptness), to reimburse you and if he did not want to be paid, I should be glad to make a donation for his work. He could make up a parcel and send it direct. I don't mean to trouble you about this. It would just be a happy experience for me.

Summer here drags along like the days of a woman without any taste regarding what she ought to wear. We have a bright day followed by a dreary one. A very recent Sunday was all east wind and clouds as if it was November. Today it is hot. Two days ago it was cold with the thermometer at 50 during the night. We ought to be in the midst of a long dry spell that is one of the classic features of August. In reality, it looks as though there was a storm coming on. The office keeps everything together for me. I have none of the disappointments of people who go to Maine and become lost in the fog or of people who go to the mountains of North Carolina and sit on the porch at the hotel watching it rain. We are as busy here as a group of one-armed paper hangers.

My book came out recently and I received the first few copies. It looks as smart as a new hat. And the typography and paper are good. Knopf

"Letter to Barbara Church." Reprinted with the permission of Alfred A. Knopf, Inc. from the *Letters of Wallace Stevens*, edited by Holly Stevens.

seems to have taken special pains with this book and I feel quite set up about the way it has been published. I should send you a copy except that it might be slow in transit and, certainly, you will not want to lug it around with you. It often happens that when I feel a bit low something of this kind comes along to pick me up. Yesterday was rather a poor day for me and yet before it was over I received a book from a friend of mine which gave me the greatest pleasure when I looked at it last night at home. I had, in fact, looked forward to a particularly busy summer running around all over Europe (in other people's shoes) because there are quite a number of people that I know over there this summer but they are not particularly communicative. Moreover, there has been too much to do to resort to such old relaxations as a day in New York now and then. I have thought of it once or twice and then decided it would be pleasanter to stay right here. Our neighborhood is as deserted as an attic and I like it that way, with all the children down at the seashore and with all the dogs apparently down with the children, so that if one wakes up at night there is neither breath nor sound. There is nothing to do except to fall asleep again. All this is discouraging. Going to bed at nine and getting up at six will soon appear to be great virtues, as no doubt they are.

Sincerely,

Wallace Stevens

QUESTIONS

1. Wallace Stevens provides us with a great many details, all revelatory of the quality of his daily life. Write a personal letter to a friend through which you convey a particular tone by your choice of details.

2. Any piece of effective writing must have a purpose, stated or implied. The purpose of Wallace Stevens' letter, his friendship for Mrs. Church, is both stated and implied. Write a second letter in which you provide a parent or friend with a detailed description of your daily life. Remember that the uniqueness of your specific experiences provides the material of your letter.

3. Our society places considerable emphasis upon certain conventional uses of language—spelling, punctuation, grammatical expressions, dictional choices—conventions which are taught in our public and private elementary and secondary schools. Yet good letter writers take great liberties with these conventions when they write personal letters. Write a personal letter in which you argue that the language conventions are essentially irrelevant insofar as effective expression is concerned. Then write a personal letter in which you follow the arguments you have advanced.

4. One way by which a letter writer reveals the uniqueness of his per-

sonality is through his particular way of phrasing and expressing ideas and feelings. Make a list of phrases or expressions which characterize Stevens. Then write a letter in which you attempt to express your personality through your particular way of phrasing and expressing yourself.

LETTER TO R. P. T. COFFIN
Robert Frost

24 February 1938 Gainesville

Dear Coffin,

It is my bad luck I am away off down here where I can't help you help me. I suppose you have nothing to call you even part way in this direction till you come to Baltimore for your lectures. I would venture some way into the cold but I mustn't come so far as to seem inconsistent to those with whom I have used the cold as an excuse to stay away from their platforms and dinner tables. A lot would come out in talk once you got me started with what you happened to remember of that Poetry Society affair. I'm terrible about my lectures. In my anxiety to keep them as long as possible from becoming part of my literary life, I leave them rolling round in my head like clouds rolling round in the sky. Watch them long enough and you'll see one near-form change into another near-form. Though I am sure they are hardly permissable on the platform, I continue to bring them there with no more apology than to a parlor or class room. Their chief value to me is for what I pick up from them when I cut across them with a poem under emotion. They have been my inner world of raw material and my instinct has been to keep them raw. That can't long retain their state however. The day approaches when they will lose their fluidity and in spite of my stirring spoon become crystal. Then one kind of fun will be over and I shall have to find another to take its place (tennis most likely or hoeing). I thought I was about ready to let them set when I accepted the Harvard invitation to deliver them in writing after delivering them by word of mouth. Something in me still fights off the written prose. The nearest I ever came to getting myself down in prose was in the preface to Robinson's *King Jasper*. That is so much me that you might suspect the application to him of being forced. It was really no such thing. We two were close akin up to a certain point of thinking. He would have trusted me to go a good way in speaking for him particularly on the art of poetry. We only parted company over the badness of the world. He was cast in the mold of sadness. I am neither optimist nor pessimist. I never voted either ticket. If there is a universal unfitness and unconformity as of a buttoning so started that every button on the vest is in the wrong button hole and the one empty button hole at the top and the one naked button at the bottom so far apart they have no hope of getting together, I don't care to decide whether God did this for the fun of it or for the devil of it. (The two expressions come to practically the same thing anyway.) Then again I am not the Platonist Robinson was. By Platonist I mean one who believes what we have here is an imperfect copy of what is in heaven. The woman you have is an imperfect copy of some woman in heaven or in someone else's bed. Many of the world's greatest—maybe all of them—have been ranged on that romantic side. I am philosophically opposed to having one Iseult for my vocation and another for my avocation; as you may have inferred from a poem called Two Tramps in Mud Time. You see where that lands me on the subject of Dante's Beatrice. Mea culpa. Let me not sound the least bit smug. I define a difference with proper humility. A truly gallant Platonist will remain a bachelor as Robinson did from unwillingness to reduce any woman to the condition of being used without being idealized.

But you didn't ask me to distinguish between myself and Robinson. I fell accidentally into a footnote to the *King Jasper* preface in self defence. What you asked for is any recollection I have of my recent talks. I may be able to bring some of them back in detail—give me time. What in the world did I say in New York. Was my subject "Neither or Both." Do you want to show me the notes you made? Is there time? I'm going to hurry this off tonight for a beginning and then if you say so try to tell you a little more. One of my subjects at Harvard was Does Wisdom Matter. I mean in art. Does it matter for instance that I am so temperamentally wrong about Beatrice. You can hear more if it is worth your while. Another subject was The Renewal of Words. Molly Colum had been saying the world was old, people were jaded and the languages worn out. My whole lecture was an answer to her defeatism, though I took good care not to name her—and don't you name her. Poetry is the renewal of words forever and ever. Poetry is that by which we live forever and ever unjaded. Poetry is that by which the world is never old. Even the poetry of trade names gives the lie to the unoriginal who would drag us down in their own powerlessness to originate. Heavy they are but not so heavy that we can't rise under them and throw them off.

Well well well ———

Sincerely yours   Robert Frost

Questions

1. Robert Frost explains to his friend Coffin why he has chosen not to commit his lectures to written form. Write a letter to your

parents or guardian in which you explain and defend a particular choice you have made. You may wish to explain and defend your choice of a departmental major, why you have joined a particular club or group, why you hope to enter a particular profession.

2.   Frost makes it clear that he is neither an optimist nor a pessimist in philosophy. Write a letter to a friend in which you present, clearly, one "faith" or belief upon which you are building your life; clarify the meaning of the belief through personal illustrations, such as times when your belief was in conflict with those around you.

3.   In the second paragraph Frost argues against the view held by Molly Colum, that "the world was old, people were jaded and languages worn out." Select one current view, most often expressed in cliché form ("Why go to college," "America is a dying nation," "the establishment doesn't understand us," "go find your bag"), explain the meanings of the cliché, and argue, in a letter to a friend, against the cliché.

4.   Today throughout the United States many individuals and groups are arguing the need for change, in foreign policy, in slum clearance, in education for the disadvantaged, in race relations, in the electoral college system, in management of the news by the news media and so on. Write a letter to your congressman, governor, mayor, or councilman in which you argue and support the need for a specific change.

III

Anecdotes

Originally an anecdote was an "unpublished" item, an interesting or striking incident, usually of a personal or biographical nature. Edmund Fuller, a celebrated collector of anecdotes, wrote, "Anecdotes are stories with points." But it should be added that anecdotes are usually personal narratives in form, such as one finds in "The Talk of the Town" in *The New Yorker* magazine or "Life in These United States" in *Reader's Digest*. Moreover, they are normally short, involving no more than a single incident, generally factual or authentic in content, and basically uncomplicated in plot line.

Recent celebrated anecdotists include Will Rogers, former Vice-President Alben Barkely, and Bennett Cerf; although their styles of delivering an anecdote differ greatly, each is a master of making a point through the vehicle of the anecdote. Their styles are illustrative; hence anecdotes appear most often as forms of social exchange, revelatory of some quality of character or personality of the speaker, or they form the germ of a more elaborate form such as a short story.

Many anecdotes, as told by raconteurs, have no greater purpose than providing a humorous moment to the hearer; yet an anecdote is not usually pointless humor for the sake of a laugh—it has a purpose. Moreover, an anecdote is based on fact. A joke is imaginative, fanciful, fictional; an anecdote, on the other hand, begins and ends in the authenticity of human life.

HAROLD ROSS IN HOLLYWOOD

James Thurber

I have no data at all on Ross as a swimmer, but ever fresh in Johnson's memory is a story of Ross at a moonlit swimming pool in Hollywood. During an evening party, twenty years ago, a lovely young blonde suddenly

---

"shucked," as Nunnally puts it, and ran out to the pool, naked as a Renoir nymph, only slenderer. One of the gentlemen also shucked and tore after the lady, and they were disporting like porpoises in the water when the male porpoise looked up and saw Dave Chasen viewing the antics with interest. Ross was there, too, but with his back squarely to the pool. He was trying to divert Dave's attention. The male swimmer heard him say, in his loud voice, "Where do you get your asparagus, Dave?" The swimmers dressed, all ardor spent, and the party was resumed in the living room, the embarrassed Ross nervously turning the conversation to a midnight probe of the parsley situation.

QUESTIONS

1. In *The Years with Ross* James Thurber creates a portrait of the celebrated editor of *The New Yorker*, Harold Ross. Among items in the book are recollections others have of Ross; in this anecdote, Thurber repeats an anecdote Nunnally Johnson tells concerning the *New Yorker* editor. What is the point of the anecdote? How did you determine the point? Write a personal anecdote in which you make a point; make a list of the problems you encountered in writing your anecdote.

2. Thurber is careful to distinguish between his own dictional choices and those Johnson provided in relating the episode. What particular advantages and disadvantages result from the repetition of an anecdote someone else has told? Write an anecdote that someone has told you; use the original phrasing, idiom, words as much as possible. In what way is the personality of the original storyteller retained; in what ways have you injected your own personality, attitudes, and idiom?

3. Figurative language is a means by which writers express meaning indirectly, state and imply comparisons, provide images, add suspense, and create greater effects, to mention some of the common uses of such language. Thurber uses the simile, an implied comparison, when he refers to the swimmers as porpoises. Write an anecdote in which you make use of metaphor, a stated comparsion (for example, "the fullback is a tiger") and the simile (for example, "they were disporting like porpoises"). Eric Partridge, an authority on the English language and author of such books as *Dictionary of Slang and Unconventional English*, *The World of Words: A Study of Language*, and *Shakespeare's Bawdy*, has stated that all language is metaphorical. Examine the language you used in your written anecdote; to what extent is Partridge's statement valid?

A QUIET ELDERLY COUPLE
Carl Sandburg

A quiet elderly couple had their home on the south side of Berrien west of Pearl. They had been there a year or two and we hadn't heard their name or what they lived on. When they sat on their front porch they might look at each other once in a while but they didn't speak to each other. When us kids passed by they didn't look at us. They just went on looking straight ahead at nothing in particular. They seemed to be living in a quiet world of their own. They looked quiet and acted quiet. They were so still and peaceable that we got to talking about how still and peaceable they were and we ought to do something about it. One boy said, "Let's give 'em the tin cans." It wasn't a case of hate. We didn't hate them. We were just curious about them and we thought maybe something funny would happen. Again we strung together a dozen cans on each of two ropes. We saw their light on, waited and saw their kerosene lamp go out, waited a while longer and then sent the two strings of cans slam-bang against the front door. We skipped across the street, three of us and each behind his own tree. We waited. Nothing happened. The door didn't open. Nobody came out. We waited a while wondering whether the man had gone out the back door and was circling around to surprise us. We picked up our feet and ran.

It was several months later that one of the boys went into a Main Street grocery and saw this couple. For how many bars of soap they wanted or how many pounds of butter, they held up their fingers, two fingers for two bars of soap and so on. They didn't say a word. They were deaf and dumb. When the three of us heard this we were honest with each other. We asked why we had done such a fool thing. "What the hell," said one boy as he turned his back to me and stooped, "kick me." I gave him a swift kick in the hind end, then stooped for him to kick me. Each of the three of us gave the other two a swift kick. Once later when I passed the house and saw the couple sitting quiet and peaceable on their front porch I looked straight at them and touched my hat. They didn't nod nor smile. They just went on looking ahead at nothing in particular.

QUESTIONS

1. An effective anecdote makes a point: what is the point of Sandburg's anecdote? Write an autobiographical anecdote through

which you wish to make a point concerning an opinion. Then write a brief paragraph explaining why you think the anecdote makes the point.

2.   In what way is the anecdote revelatory of Sandburg's character and personality? Is Sandburg's sense of honesty revealed? What can be said about his personality, based on his dictional choices, sentence structure, attitude toward the prank, and his subsequent reactions? Tell a personal anecdote through which you attempt to reveal some facet of your personality, as well as make a point. What techniques did you find helpful in projecting your personality?

3.   E. M. Forster, novelist and literary critic, distinguishes between a story and a plot: "The king died and then the queen died" illustrates a story; "The king died and then the queen died of grief" illustrates a plot. In the story, time-sequence provides coherence, whereas in the plot causality provides the primary coherence and "overshadows" the time-sequence. We ask "why" did something happen in a plot. Using Forster's distinction between story and plot, do you consider Sandburg's anecdote a story or plot? Write an anecdote in which you provide coherence through time-sequence—"and then," and a second anecdote in which you provide coherence through causality—"why?"

IV

Autobiography

As a writer of autobiography you commit yourself to writing about yourself. In one sense, you ask and answer the question, "Who am I?" Or you ask yourself questions about the meanings of your previous experiences, ideas, actions, conflicts, conversations, acquaintances. In an autobiography you may wish to develop the meanings of a trip you once took, of the influence of a particular person on your life, of a conflict with another person, of your love for the natural world, or of the value of a given idea.

Your point of view is personal, that is, the "I" point of view. Any reader of your autobiography is asked to view life through your way of looking at life. In choosing your material you use the criteria of relevance and meaning to you; you ask yourself about your experiences. Hence, autobiography is always based upon sustained introspection, your examining and re-examining of your past. However, oftentimes introspection—memory, reminiscences, diaries, records—is not enough. You may not recall exactly the context within which a given experience took place, you may not recall the name of the person you wish to mention, you may not remember the exact date of an event; research into these details may become necessary. Both Sandburg and Thurber found this procedure necessary when they wrote their autobiographies.

Autobiographies have other characteristics: the writer of an autobiography may follow a narrative line, but this line is not necessarily chronological; no dramatic principle is followed, leading from preliminary action through rising action to a climax and denouement; suspense is not necessarily an esthetic principle followed by the autobiographer; the emphasis throughout is on the truth of what the writer records about the facts of his life; much autobiography is based on showing rather than telling, involving the reader in the quality of an experience rather than moralizing about the experience; the autobiography may represent a writer's effort to recount the significant experiences of a lifetime, but more frequently the writer attempts to record those aspects of his life which he considers especially meaningful; obviously the writer of autobiography deals with his past life; the tone or tones of the autobiography emerge from the writer's attitudes toward himself, toward his past experiences, and toward his anticipated audience, depending upon the particular emphases the writer chooses; an autobiography will generally take an episodic form, involving progression from one meaningful experience to another, from youth through middle age to the time of the writing of the autobiography; among the techniques frequently used by autobiographers, dialogue (recollections of specific conversations) and digressions are used. No one autobiography necessarily includes all of these characteristics. But in general the writer of an autobiography will encounter each of these problems as he writes.

Leslie Stephen has called autobiography "the most fascinating branch of literature." If you find discovering the meanings of your life a fascinating project, then you too will agree with Leslie Stephen.

THINKING AS A HOBBY

William Golding

While I was still a boy, I came to the conclusion that there were three grades of thinking; and since I was later to claim thinking as my hobby, I came to an even stranger conclusion—namely, that I myself could not think at all.

I must have been an unsatisfactory child for grownups to deal with. I remember how incomprehensible they appeared to me at first, but not, of course, how I appeared to them. It was the headmaster of my grammar school who first brought the subject of thinking before me—though neither in the way, nor with the result he intended. He had some statuettes in his study. They stood on a high cupboard behind his desk. One was a lady wearing nothing but a bath towel. She seemed frozen in an eternal panic lest the bath towel slip down any farther; and since she had no arms, she was in an unfortunate position to pull the towel up again. Next to her, crouched the statuette of a leopard, ready to spring down at the top drawer of a filing cabinet labeled A-AH. My innocence interpreted this as the victim's last, despairing cry. Beyond the leopard was a naked, muscular gentleman, who sat, looking down, with his chin on his fist and his elbow on his knee. He seemed utterly miserable.

Some time later, I learned about these statuettes. The headmaster had placed them where they would face delinquent children, because they symbolized to him the whole of life. The naked lady was the Venus of Milo. She was Love. She was not worried about the towel. She was just busy being beautiful. The leopard was Nature, and he was being natural. The naked, muscular gentleman was not miserable. He was Rodin's Thinker, an image of pure thought. It is easy to buy small plaster models of what you think life is like.

I had better explain that I was a frequent visitor to the headmaster's

Reprinted by permission of Curtis Brown, Ltd. Copyright © 1961 by William Golding.

study, because of the latest thing I had done or left undone. As we now say, I was not integrated. I was, if anything, disintegrated; and I was puzzled. Grownups never made sense. Whenever I found myself in a penal position before the headmaster's desk, with the statuettes glimmering whitely above him, I would sink my head, clasp my hands behind my back and writhe one shoe over the other.

The headmaster would look opaquely at me, through flashing spectacles.

"What are we going to do with you?"

Well, what *were* they going to do with me? I would writhe my shoe some more and stare down at the worn rug.

"Look up, boy! Can't you look up?"

Then I would look up at the cupboard, where the naked lady was frozen in her panic and the muscular gentleman contemplated the hindquarters of the leopard in endless gloom. I had nothing to say to the headmaster. His spectacles caught the light so that you could see nothing human behind them. There was no possibility of communication.

"Don't you ever think at all?"

No, I didn't think, wasn't thinking, couldn't think—I was simply waiting in anguish for the interview to stop.

"Then you'd better learn—hadn't you?"

On one occasion the headmaster leaped to his feet, reached up and plonked Rodin's masterpiece on the desk before me.

"That's what a man looks like when he's really thinking."

I surveyed the gentleman without interest or comprehension.

"Go back to your class."

Clearly there was something missing in me. Nature had endowed the rest of the human race with a sixth sense and left me out. This must be so, I mused, on my way back to the class, since whether I had broken a window, or failed to remember Boyle's Law, or been late for school, my teachers produced me one, adult answer: "Why can't you think?"

As I saw the case, I had broken the window because I had tried to hit Jack Arney with a cricket ball and missed him; I could not remember Boyle's Law because I had never bothered to learn it; and I was late for school because I preferred looking over the bridge into the river. In fact, I was wicked. Were my teachers, perhaps, so good that they could not understand the depths of my depravity? Were they clear, untormented people who could direct their every action by this mysterious business of thinking? The whole thing was incomprehensible. In my earlier years, I found even the statuette of the Thinker confusing. I did not believe any of my teachers were naked, ever. Like someone born deaf, but bitterly determined to find out about sound, I watched my teachers to find out about thought.

There was Mr. Houghton. He was always telling me to think. With a modest satisfaction, he would tell me that he had thought a bit himself. Then why did he spend so much time drinking? Or was there more sense in drinking than there appeared to be? But if not, and if drinking were in fact ruinous to health—and Mr. Houghton was ruined, there was no doubt about that—why was he always talking about the clean life and the virtues of fresh air? He would spread his arms wide with the action of a man who habitually spent his time striding along mountain ridges.

"Open air does me good, boys—I know it!"

Sometimes, exalted by his own oratory, he would leap from his desk and hustle us outside into a hideous wind.

"Now, boys! Deep breaths! Feel it right down inside you—huge draughts of God's good air!"

He would stand before us, rejoicing in his perfect health, an open-air man. He would put his hands on his waist and take a tremendous breath. You could hear the wind, trapped in the cavern of his chest and struggling with all the unnatural impediments. His body would reel with shock and his ruined face go white at the unaccustomed visitation. He would stagger back to his desk and collapse there, useless for the rest of the morning.

Mr. Houghton was given to high-minded monologues about the good life, sexless and full of duty. Yet in the middle of one of these monologues, if a girl passed the window, tapping along on her neat little feet, he would interrupt his discourse, his neck would turn of itself and he would watch her out of sight. In this instance, he seemed to me ruled not by thought but by an invisible and irresistible spring in his nape.

His neck was an object of great interest to me. Normally it bulged a bit over his collar. But Mr. Houghton had fought in the First World War alongside both Americans and French, and had come—by who knows what illogic?—to a settled detestation of both countries. If either country happened to be prominent in current affairs, no argument could make Mr. Houghton think well of it. He would bang the desk, his neck would bulge still further and go red. "You can say what you like," he would cry, "but I've thought about this—and I know what I think!"

Mr. Houghton thought with his neck.

There was Miss Parsons. She assured us that her dearest wish was our welfare, but I knew even then, with the mysterious clairvoyance of childhood, that what she wanted most was the husband she never got. There was Mr. Hands—and so on.

I have dealt at length with my teachers because this was my introduction to the nature of what is commonly called thought. Through them I discovered that thought is often full of unconscious prejudice, ignorance and hypocrisy. It will lecture on disinterested purity while its neck is being remorselessly twisted toward a skirt. Technically, it is about as proficient as most businessmen's golf, as honest as most politicians' intentions, or—to come near my own preoccupation—as coherent as most books that get written. It is what I came to call grade-three thinking, though more properly, it is feeling, rather than thought.

True, often there is a kind of innocence in prejudices, but in those days I viewed grade-three thinking with an intolerant contempt and an incautious mockery. I delighted to confront a pious lady who hated the Germans with the proposition that we should love our enemies. She taught me a great truth in dealing with grade-three thinkers; because of her, I no longer dismiss lightly a mental process which for nine-tenths of the population is the nearest they will ever get to thought. They have immense solidarity. We had better respect them, for we are outnumbered and surrounded. A crowd of grade-three thinkers, all shouting the same thing, all warming their hands at the fire of their own prejudices, will not thank you for pointing out the contradictions in their beliefs. Man is a gregarious animal, and enjoys agreement as cows will graze all the same way on the side of a hill.

Grade-two thinking is the detection of contradictions. I reached grade two when I trapped the poor, pious lady. Grade-two thinkers do not stampede easily, though often they fall into the other fault and lag behind. Grade-two thinking is a withdrawal, with eyes and ears open. It became my hobby and brought satisfaction and loneliness in either hand. For grade-two thinking destroys without having the power to create. It set me watching the crowds cheering His Majesty the King and asking myself what all the fuss was about, without giving me anything positive to put in the place of that heady patriotism. But there were compensations. To hear people justify their habit of hunting foxes and tearing them to pieces by claiming that the foxes liked it. To hear our Prime Minister talk about the great benefit we conferred on India by jailing people like Pandit Nehru and Gandhi. To hear American politicians talk about peace in one sentence and refuse to join the League of Nations in the next. Yes, there were moments of delight.

But I was growing toward adolescence and had to admit that Mr. Houghton was not the only one with an irresistible spring in his neck. I, too, felt the compulsive hand of nature and began to find that pointing out contradiction could be costly as well as fun. There was Ruth, for example, a serious and attractive girl. I was an atheist at the time. Grade-two thinking is a menace to religion and knocks down sects like skittles. I put myself in a position to be converted by her with an hypocrisy worthy of grade three. She was a Methodist—or at least, her parents were, and Ruth had to follow suit. But, alas, instead of relying on the Holy Spirit to convert me, Ruth was foolish enough to open her pretty mouth in argument. She claimed that the Bible (King James Version) was literally inspired. I countered by saying that the Catholics believed in the literal inspiration of Saint Jerome's *Vulgate*, and the two books were different. Argument flagged.

At last she remarked that there were an awful lot of Methodists, and they couldn't be wrong, could they—not all those millions? That was too easy, said I restively (for the nearer you were to Ruth, the nicer she was to be near to) since there were more Roman Catholics than Methodists anyway; and they couldn't be wrong, could they—not all those hundreds of millions? An awful flicker of doubt appeared in her eyes. I slid my arm round her waist and murmured breathlessly that if we were counting heads, the Buddhists were the boys for my money. But Ruth had *really* wanted to do me good, because I was so nice. She fled. The combination of my arm and those countless Buddhists was too much for her.

That night her father visited my father and left, redcheeked and indignant. I was given the third degree to find out what had happened. It was lucky we were both of us only fourteen. I lost Ruth and gained an undeserved reputation as a potential libertine.

So grade-two thinking could be dangerous. It was in this knowledge, at the age of fifteen, that I remember making a comment from the heights of grade two, on the limitations of grade three. One evening I found myself alone in the school hall, preparing it for a party. The door of the headmaster's study was open. I went in. The headmaster had ceased to thump Rodin's Thinker down on the desk as an example to the young. Perhaps he had not found any more candidates, but the statuettes were still there, glimmering and gathering dust on top of the cupboard. I stood on a chair and rearranged them. I stood Venus in her bath towel on the filing cabinet, so that now the top drawer caught its breath in a gasp of sexy excitement. "Ah-ah!" The portentous Thinker I placed on the edge of the cupboard so that he looked down at the bath towel and waited for it to slip.

Grade-two thinking, though it filled life with fun and excitement, did not make for content. To find out the deficiencies of our elders bolsters the young ego but does not make for personal security. I found that grade two was not only the power to point out contradictions. It took the swimmer some distance from the shore and left him there, out of his depth. I decided that Pontius Pilate was a typical grade-two thinker. "What is truth?" he said, a very common grade-two thought, but one that is used always as the end of an argument instead of the beginning. There is a still higher grade of thought which says, "What is truth?" and sets out to find it.

But these grade-one thinkers were few and far between. They did not visit my grammar school in the flesh though they were there in books. I aspired to them, partly because I was ambitious and partly because I now saw my hobby as an unsatisfactory thing if it went no further. If you set out to climb a mountain, however high you climb, you have failed if you cannot reach the top.

I did meet an undeniably grade-one thinker in my first year at Oxford. I was looking over a small bridge in Magdalen Deer Park, and a tiny mustached and hatted figure came and stood by my side. He was a German who had just fled from the Nazis to Oxford as a temporary refuge. His name was Einstein.

But Professor Einstein knew no English at that time and I knew only two words of German. I beamed at him, trying wordlessly to convey by my bearing all the affection and respect that the English felt for him. It is possible—and I have to make the admission—that I felt here were two grade-one thinkers standing side by side; yet I doubt if my face conveyed more than a formless awe. I would have given my Greek and Latin and French and a good slice of my English for enough German to communicate. But we were divided; he was as inscrutable as my headmaster. For perhaps five minutes we stood together on the bridge, undeniable grade-one thinker and breathless aspirant. With true greatness, Professor Einstein realized that any contact was better than none. He pointed to a trout wavering in midstream.

He spoke: *"Fisch."*

My brain reeled. Here I was, mingling with the great, and yet helpless as the veriest grade-three thinker. Desperately I sought for some sign by which I might convey that I, too, revered pure reason. I nodded vehemently. In a brilliant flash I used up half of my German vocabulary.

"Fisch. Ja. Ja."

For perhaps another five minutes we stood side by side. Then Professor Einstein, his whole figure still conveying good will and amiability, drifted away out of sight.

I, too, would be a grade-one thinker. I was irreverent at the best of times. Political and religious systems, social customs, loyalties and traditions, they all came tumbling down like so many rotten apples off a tree. This was a fine hobby and a sensible substitute for cricket, since you could play it all the year round. I came up in the end with what must always remain the justification for grade-one thinking, its sign, seal and charter. I devised a coherent system for living. It was a moral system, which was wholly logical. Of course, as I readily admitted, conversion of the world to my way of thinking might be difficult, since my system did away with a number of trifles, such as big business, centralized government, armies, marriage. . . .

It was Ruth all over again. I had some very good friends who stood by me, and still do. But my acquaintances vanished, taking the girls with them. Young women seemed oddly contented with the world as it was. They valued the meaningless ceremony with a ring. Young men, while willing to concede the chaining sordidness of marriage, were hesitant about abandoning the organizations which they hoped would give them a career. A young man on the first rung of the Royal Navy, while perfectly agreeable to doing away with big business and marriage, got as red-necked as Mr. Houghton when I proposed a world without any battleships in it.

Had the game gone too far? Was it a game any longer? In those prewar days, I stood to lose a great deal, for the sake of a hobby.

Now you are expecting me to describe how I saw the folly of my ways and came back to the warm nest, where prejudices are so often called loyalties, where pointless actions are hallowed into custom by repetition, where we are content to say we think when all we do is feel.

But you would be wrong. I dropped my hobby and turned professional.

If I were to go back to the headmaster's study and find the dusty statuettes still there, I would arrange them differently. I would dust Venus and put her aside, for I have come to love her and know her for the fair thing she is. But I would put the Thinker, sunk in his desperate thought, where there were shadows before him—and at his back, I would put the leopard, crouched and ready to spring.

QUESTIONS

1. In the opening paragraph of "Thinking as a Hobby," Golding states his conclusion: as a boy he decided there were three grades of thinking, and as a man he concluded that he "could not think at all." To establish this conclusion he writes autobiographically about a series of youthful experiences. Select a series of personal experiences that illustrate a particular value you have learned and write a brief autobiography in which you develop the theme through recounting your experiences.

2. From his teachers, Golding learned "that thought is often full of unconscious prejudice, ignorance and hypocrisy." Prepare an autobiographical account through which you show the influence of a particular teacher on your life, or, preferably, your reactions to the teacher's character and personality.

3. According to Golding, the grade-two thinking asks, "What is truth?" The effective autobiographer must ask himself the same question about every detail he relates: is it true? Recreate in detail an episode from your life through which you *show* rather than tell the reader about the nature of your experience. Then critically examine every detail for accuracy, the truth to fact, feeling, and circumstance.

4. You reveal yourself, as Golding does, through the experiences you choose to relate, your attitudes toward these experiences, and your interpretations of these experiences. Relate an incident through which you attempt to reveal one aspect of your personality.

5. Golding uses the statuettes both as symbols and as means for conveying his understanding of their meanings. Choose a symbol from your past, such as a sycamore tree, a drinking cup, or a pair of shoes, and use this symbol to convey autobiographically the meanings of an earlier experience.

BIRTHDAY PARTY

Katharine Brush

They were a couple in their late thirties, and they looked unmistakably married. They sat on the banquette opposite us in a little narrow restaurant, having dinner. The man had a round, self-satisfied face, with glasses on it; the woman was fadingly pretty, in a big hat. There was nothing conspicuous about them, nothing particularly noticeable, until the end of their meal, when it suddenly became obvious that this was an Occasion—in fact, the husband's birthday, and the wife had planned a little surprise for him.

It arrived, in the form of a small but glossy birthday cake, with one pink candle burning in the center. The headwaiter brought it in and placed it before the husband, and meanwhile the violin-and-piano orchestra played "Happy Birthday to You" and the wife beamed with shy pride over her little surprise, and such few people as there were in the restaurant tried to help out with a pattering of applause. It became clear at once that help was needed, because the husband was not pleased. Instead, he was hotly embarrassed, and indignant at his wife for embarrassing him.

You looked at him and you saw this and you thought, "Oh, now, don't *be* like that!" But he was like that, and as soon as the little cake had been deposited on the table, and the orchestra had finished the birthday piece, and the general attention had shifted from the man and the woman, I saw him say something to her under his breath—some punishing thing, quick and curt and unkind. I couldn't bear to look at the woman then, so I stared at my plate and waited for quite a long time. Not long enough, though. She was still crying when I finally glanced over there again. Crying quietly and heartbrokenly and hopelessly, all to herself, under the gay big brim of her best hat.

QUESTIONS

1. In Brush's "Birthday Party" the "I" of the story, who is in a restaurant with another person or several people—identified as "us" in the second sentence—filters the descriptions and actions, and selects the details presented. At first glance, this episode appears to be about "a couple," but a second glance reveals the importance of the personal point of view and the interpretation of the incident provided by this point of view. Does the story actually reveal something about

the couple or the narrator? Write a short narrative in which you participate as an observer. To what extent does your participation color the narrative?

2.   Brush's "Birthday Party" is fictional rather than factual, imaginative rather than autobiographical. Did you know this? If so, how? Yet the point of view—in fiction called the "persona," or the identity the writer assumes in a story—is autobiographical. Write a brief narrative in which you adopt the role and point of view of another person. What difficulties do you encounter in making this adaptation?

3.   The reality of autobiographical episodes is dependent in great part on the specific detail selected. List the specific details that the narrator of Brush's story selected. What characteristics of the narrator are revealed by this list? For example, did the husband say "some punishing thing, quick and curt and unkind," or did the narrator imagine this? Prepare a first draft of an autobiographical episode in which you attempt to provide as much relevant detail as will be helpful toward a full understanding of the experience.

4.   Brush tells "Birthday Party" in past tense. What are the advantages of the past tense construction? Are there any advantages in telling the story in present tense? What are they? Which tense, present or past, is easier to use in representing time sequence? Prepare a second draft of your detailed autobiographical episode; experiment with the advantages and disadvantages of present and past tense.

5.   The secret to effective autobiography lies in showing, not telling, what happened. Examine your second draft: to what extent do you show and to what extent do you tell? Prepare a paper for submission, in which you attempt to remove all "telling" dictional choices and retain only "showing" words. What are the special advantages of "showing" above "telling"?

THE USE OF FORCE

William Carlos Williams

They were new patients to me, all I had was the name, Olson. Please come down as soon as you can, my daughter is very sick.

When I arrived I was met by the mother, a big startled-looking woman, very clean and apologetic who merely said, Is this the doctor? and let me in. In the back, she added. You must excuse us, doctor, we have her in the kitchen where it is warm. It is very damp here sometimes.

William Carlos Williams, *The Farmer's Daughters*. Copyright 1938 by William Carlos Williams. Reprinted by permission of New Directions Publishing Corporation.

The child was fully dressed and sitting on her father's lap near the kitchen table. He tried to get up, but I motioned for him not to bother, took off my overcoat and started to look things over. I could see that they were all very nervous, eyeing me up and down distrustfully. As often, in such cases, they weren't telling me more than they had to, it was up to me to tell them; that's why they were spending three dollars on me.

The child was fairly eating me up with her cold, steady eyes, and no expression to her face whatever. She did not move and seemed, inwardly, quiet; an unusually attractive little thing, and as strong as a heifer in appearance. But her face was flushed, she was breathing rapidly, and I realized that she had a high fever. She had magnificent blonde hair, in profusion. One of those picture children often reproduced in advertising leaflets and the photogravure sections of the Sunday papers.

She's had a fever for three days, began the father and we don't know what it comes from. My wife has given her things, you know, like people do, but it don't do no good. And there's been a lot of sickness around. So we tho't you'd better look her over and tell us what is the matter.

As doctors often do I took a trial shot at it as a point of departure. Has she had a sore throat?

Both parents answered me together, No . . . No, she says her throat don't hurt her.

Does your throat hurt you? added the mother of the child. But the little girl's expression didn't change nor did she move her eyes from my face.

Have you looked?

I tried to, said the mother, but I couldn't see.

As it happens we have been having a number of cases of diphtheria in the school to which this child went during that month and we were all, quite apparently, thinking of that, though no one had as yet spoken of the thing.

Well, I said, suppose we take a look at the throat first. I smiled in my best professional manner and asking for the child's first name I said, come on, Mathilda, open your mouth and let's take a look at your throat.

Nothing doing.

Aw, come on, I coaxed, just open your mouth wide and let me take a look. Look, I said opening both hands wide, I haven't anything in my hands. Just open up and let me see.

Such a nice man, put in the mother. Look how kind he is to you. Come on, do what he tells you to. He won't hurt you.

At that I ground my teeth in disgust. If only they wouldn't use the word "hurt" I might be able to get somewhere. But I did not allow myself to be hurried or disturbed but speaking quietly and slowly I approached the child again.

As I moved my chair a little nearer suddenly with one catlike movement both her hands clawed instinctively for my eyes and she almost reached them too. In fact she knocked my glasses flying and they fell, though unbroken, several feet away from me on the kitchen floor.

Both the mother and father almost turned themselves inside out in embarrassment and apology. You bad girl, said the mother, taking her and shaking her by one arm. Look what you've done. The nice man . . .

For heaven's sake, I broke in. Don't call me a nice man to her. I'm here to look at her throat on the chance that she might have diphtheria and possibly die of it. But that's nothing to her. Look here, I said to the child, we're going to look at your throat. You're old enough to understand what I'm saying. Will you open it now by yourself or shall we have to open it for you?

Not a move. Even her expression hadn't changed. Her breaths however were coming faster and faster. Then the battle began. I had to do it. I had to have a throat culture for her own protection. But first I told the parents that it was entirely up to them. I explained the danger but said that I would not insist on a throat examination so long as they would take the responsibility.

If you don't do what the doctor says you'll have to go to the hospital, the mother admonished her severely.

Oh yeah? I had to smile to myself. After all, I had already fallen in love with the savage brat, the parents were contemptible to me. In the ensuing struggle they grew more and more abject, crushed, exhausted while she surely rose to magnificent heights of insane fury of effort bred of her terror of me.

The father tried his best, and he was a big man but the fact that she was his daughter, his shame at her behavior and his dread of hurting her made him release her just at the critical times when I had almost achieved success, till I wanted to kill him. But his dread also that she might have diphtheria made him tell me to go on, go on though he himself was almost fainting, while the mother moved back and forth behind us raising and lowering her hands in an agony of apprehension.

Put her in front of you on your lap, I ordered, and hold both her wrists.

But as soon as he did the child let out a scream. Don't, you're hurting me. Let go of my hands. Let them go I tell you. Then she shrieked terrifyingly, hysterically. Stop it! You're killing me!

Do you think she can stand it, doctor! said the mother.

You get out, said the husband to his wife. Do you want her to die of diphtheria?

Come on now, hold her, I said.

Then I grasped the child's head with my left hand and tried to get the wooden tongue depressor between her teeth. She fought, with clenched teeth, desperately! But now I also had grown furious—at a child. I tried to hold myself down but I couldn't. I know how to expose a throat for inspection. And I did my best. When finally I got the wooden spatula behind the last teeth and just the point of it into the mouth cavity, she opened up for an instant but before I could see anything she came down again and gripping the wooden blade between her molars she reduced it to splinters before I could get it out again.

Aren't you ashamed, the mother yelled at her. Aren't you ashamed to act like that in front of the doctor?

Get me a smooth-handled spoon of some sort, I told the mother. We're going through with this. The child's mouth was already bleeding. Her tongue was cut and she was screaming in wild hysterical shrieks. Perhaps I should have desisted and come back in an hour or more. No doubt it would have been better. But I have seen at least two children lying dead in bed of neglect in such cases, and feeling that I must get a diagnosis now or never I went at it again. But the worst of it was that I too had got beyond reason. I could have torn the child apart in my own fury and enjoyed it. It was a pleasure to attack her. My face was burning with it.

The damned little brat must be protected against her own idiocy, one says to one's self at such times. Others must be protected against her. It is a social necessity. And all these things are true. But a blind fury, a feeling of adult shame, bred of a longing for muscular release are the operatives. One goes on to the end.

In a final unreasoning assault I overpowered the child's neck and jaws. I forced the heavy silver spoon back of her teeth and down her throat till she gagged. And there it was—both tonsils covered with membrane. She had fought valiantly to keep me from knowing her secret. She had been hiding that sore throat for three days at least and lying to her parents in order to escape just such an outcome as this.

Now truly she was furious. She had been on the defensive before but now she attacked. Tried to get off her father's lap and fly at me while tears of defeat blinded her eyes.

QUESTIONS

1.   The physician, the "persona" or narrator, tells the story of the "use of force." We view the occasion, the parents, the child, and the physician himself through the physician's reflections on the series of events, and his recollections of his own personal reactions to the parents, the child, and the behavior of all involved. What is the physician's opinion of himself? What did he learn from the experience? Recollect an experience in which you were a primary participant and retell the experience from your personal point of view.

2.   Williams makes little effort to recapture the exact speech idiom of the Olsons; instead, he only suggests speech patterns and usages: "Is this the doctor?" "it don't do no good," "we tho't you'd better look her

over." In your autobiographical recounting, incorporate comments and observations made by the participants, including yourself. To what extent is the dialogue revelatory of the speakers, and their attitudes and values in relation to the experience recounted?

3.   The autobiographer may draw conclusions from what he writes. In Bertrand Russell's *Autobiography*, for example, this great twentieth-century philosopher states that his life has been dominated by three great passions: the longing for love, the search for knowledge, and a pity for human suffering. In "The Use of Force" the physican does not overtly draw certain inevitable conclusions, but he has imbedded these conclusions in the story, from the title through the last line. Retell an experience in which you do not draw conclusions, but imbed them in the story; then retell the same experience and draw conclusions. As autobiography, which of the two ways is more effective in recounting an experience? Why?

4.   A portrait or embryonic character sketch of Mathilda Olson, the child, emerges as the physician recounts the story. She had "cold, steady eyes and no expression to her face"; she was "an unusually attractive little thing"; "she had magnificent blonde hair"; she was "one of those picture children . . . of the Sunday papers"; she not only refused to open her mouth but she struck out at the physician; after the attack the physician described her as a "savage brat," but one "he had fallen in love with"; then, after she screamed and shrieked that she was being hurt, she broke the wooden spatula the physician had forced between her teeth, and the physician physically overcame "the damned little brat," and examined her throat; finally she attempted physically to assault the physician. Write a brief reminiscence in which you imposed your will on another person. Include in the reminiscence your emotions at each stage of the experience.

PART II

Writing about People

V

Character Sketch

In many ways a character sketch lies half-way between an autobiography and biography. When the writer writes a narrative overview of his own life, he is preparing a character sketch of himself; when, on the other hand, the writer writes a narrative overview of another person, he is writing the commonly described character sketch. Thus James Thurber, for example, may have written a brief outline of his own life which would have been an autobiographical character sketch, whereas had he written an overview of the life of Harold Ross, the editor of *The New Yorker* for many years, he would have written a traditional character sketch.

The traditional character sketch is described by many names, each name bearing a slightly different meaning from the character sketch but resembling the character sketch more than other forms of literature. One will find profiles in *The New Yorker*, brief biographies in the encyclopedias, such as the *Britannica* and *Americana*, sketches in the *Dictionary of American Biography* and the *Dictionary of English Biography*, factual data outlines in *Who's Who*, and full-scale character sketches in *The New York Times Magazine* and *Saturday Review*; this list is by no means inclusive of the many character sketches found in biographies, histories, psychological case studies, and so on.

Character sketches are usually characterized by: 1) brevity, usually not exceeding fifteen double-spaced typewritten pages; 2) a narrative form, including the life of the individual from the time of his birth until his death; 3) a theme or guiding idea related to the life of the person being described as the basis for the sketch such as a character sketch of Lincoln which emphasizes his qualities as a statesman, one of Daniel Boone which highlights his adventuresome spirit, one of Washington emphasizing his character, or one of Jimmy Durante emphasizing his personality; 4) knowledge of facts about the individual's life, an analysis of these facts with the inclusion of those related to the theme, description of the environment in which the individual lived, such as political, social, or geographical factors, and some kind of evaluation of the quality and meaning of the life described; 5) the individual or unique qualities of the character, including such things as his physical appearance, special interests, way of life, peculiarities, and idiosyncrasies; 6) the character sketch being limited, sometimes, to a specific event in the life of the character described, such as a climatic moment or turning point in his life, as one finds in John Kennedy's *Profiles in Courage;* and, finally, 7) an attempt to present the character described as a living human being, individualized in terms of his life and time and place.

When someone asks your opinion of another person, you begin at the moment to develop a character sketch. You ask yourself, "What kind of person is Tom, or Jane, or Mr. Postlethwaite?" In answering the question you create a character sketch.

THEY MADE OUR WORLD . . . . GANDHI
Leo Rosten

INDIA—March 12, 1930. The wizened, toothless, half-naked little Hindu had walked 200 miles to the sea, enlisting volunteers for a Satyagraha ("insistence on truth") demonstration against British rule. Now, at the sea's edge, he picked up a pinch of dried salt—calmly breaking the law that made salt a government monopoly. As his followers surged forward, native policemen "rained blows on their heads with steel-shod *lathis*," reported Webb Miller. "Not one of the marchers even raised an arm to fend off the blows. They went down like tenpins. . . . The waiting marchers groaned, sucked in their breaths at every blow, [then] marched on until struck down. . . . The police kicked [them] in the abdomen and testicles. . . . Hour after hour, stretcher-bearers carried back a stream of inert, bleeding bodies."

This terrible scene climaxed but one more passive-resistance crusade led by the man millions called Mahatma, "Great Soul" or "man of God." To the British, he was a mystic rabble-rouser, a preposterous gnome in an immaculate white *dhoti* (a diaper, they sneered) who toured the engorged cities and squalid villages to preach love, self-purification and civil disobedience—leading a goat, whose milk, unlike the cow's or buffalo's, he drank. He was a strict vegetarian, befitting his caste, and lived on fruit and nuts. He addressed meetings of hundreds of thousands, or sat silent, cross-legged, on a platform before them—and they remained silent, too, transfixed.

This Gandhi held no office, commanded no soldiers, yet paralyzed India with a word: Men simply stopped work, crippling the offices, factories, mines, railways, ignoring the courts, paying no taxes, inviting arrest by tens of thousands, filling the jails until there was no room for more. The proud British *sahibs* imprisoned him again and again, but it did not help. "Jail is jail for thieves. . . . For me, it [is] a palace." He spent over 2000 days in prisons, reading, meditating, and drove the British frantic with his final, bloodless weapon: fasting. Nothing so haunted Whitehall as the nightmare of what might happen in this idolatrous land if the "seditious fakir," as Churchill called him, died in a protest fast.

India, this disease-ridden, clamorous, susperstitious, bursting Asian subcontinent, lived not by politics, but within a fantastic tanglement of rituals and demonologies before which Europeans stood bewildered or aghast. The doctrine of *karma* sanctified cows, birds, horses; an ant was a soul reincarnated. Young widows mounted funeral pyres to burn alive in a sacred suttee. The worship of Brahma, Vishnu and Siva, of Buddha, Allah, Krishna, mingled with fearful fealties to afreets and jinns of the air. In this mosaic of autistic commitments, the grinning little 'Mahatma exercised spiritual power such as "no ancient king or conqueror ever surpassed."

He was born Mohandas Karamchand Gandhi, in 1869, and was married off by his parents at 13. Excruciatingly shy, intensely sensuous, he studied law in London, then went to South Africa as a barrister. He suffered insults and humiliations because he was "colored," and urged his despised, disenfranchised compatriots to unite for peaceful disobedience, which he had learned from reading Thoreau. He told them to end the ancient rancors that split Hindu from Moslem, Parsee from pariah; to be clean of body, no less than spirit; to set a moral example to their overlords by absolute truthfulness. ("Not even for the freedom of India would I resort to an untruth.") He led 2000 Indians from Natal across the Transvaal border, defying the law that forbade Asians to immigrate; returned by force to the coal mines, they refused to work. Beaten, starved, they held fast. Fifty thousand joined the *Satyagraha*, until the hamstrung government passed the Indian Relief Bill.

Gandhi set up an *ashram* (retreat) of ascetics devoted to prayer and meditation, in a search for godliness. Later, he left his lucrative law practice, returned to India and established a Tolstoyan retreat to which he admitted untouchables—horrifying even his Hindu wife, who warned that a place so defiled would fail. When funds finally ran out, Gandhi said "We shall go to live in the untouchable quarter." He was often stoned, vilified, almost lynched.

His moral severity alienated his four sons. He set out to become a *Brahmachari* ("godlike") and at 37 took a vow of celibacy. He held the New Testament as sacred as the *Bhagavad Gita* and regarded all men as equal. India's future lay in education, sanitation, self-discipline: "It is not so much British guns that are responsible for our subjection as our . . . cooperation." He angered his countrymen by denouncing the caste system and child marriages, and by advocating birth control through continence. Converts flocked to him from all India, Europe, America. To them, he was a Mohammed or Jesus. To gibes that he was a saint meddling in politics, Gandhi replied, "I am a politician trying . . . to be a saint."

He asked his disciples to love those who hated them: "It is not non-violence if we merely love those that love us." He long refused to call the British enemies, because he admired them for "ideals [I] love . . . If we are just to them, we shall receive their support." Despite the religious and caste hatreds that split India into impassioned and irreconcilable fragments, he became its undisputed leader. "All India is my family."

His influence declined as his hours of meditation, his economic panaceas (the use of crude spinning wheels to make homespun and boycott British cotton), even his fasts came to seem ineffectual. He refused to help Britain against the unspeakable Nazis, talked on the edges of subversion, was interned once more.

With Jinnah, the Moslem leader, and Lord Mountbatten, he framed India's independence in 1947, desperately opposing partition into Hindu and Moslem (Pakistan) states. When hideous fighting broke out, he toured the Bengal villages, pleading for an end to bloodshed. At a great prayer meeting in New Delhi, he was assassinated—by a Hindu fanatic who blamed him for India's partition. The irony was as supreme as the injustice. His ashes were strewn into the sacred river Ganges at Allahabad, and his great disciple Nehru said, "The light has gone out of our lives, and there is darkness everywhere."

This ugly, skinny, fearless little man was "a moral genius," a triumph of sheer character and will. He sounded the death knell of colonialism. Soon, dark-skinned masses in Africa and the Middle East and Mississippi were using their bodies as unprotesting instruments of protest—in marches, boycotts, sit-ins—acting out a Hindu-Christian drama that still disorients the modern world, refuting power with the ageless dream of dignity and freedom blind to color.

QUESTIONS

1. The first step involved in writing a character sketch—of your father, your roommate, or a community or national leader—requires the gathering of facts: date and place of birth, parents, schooling, hobbies, organizational activities, military and educational experiences, marriage, children, vocational and professional careers, special recognitions, and time and place of death. But this chronology of facts provides no more than the skeleton of a character sketch; as a writer of a character sketch you must recreate a living person; to do so you must humanize the facts. In Rosten's sketch of Gandhi, the Mahatma's strength of will, self-discipline, sense of purpose, and love for mankind and for India are revealed through selected details. Prepare a chronology of facts concerning the subject of your character sketch. (This first step may involve an extended interview, during which you record detail, or may require considerable research among the resources of the library, including newspapers, periodicals, and books.)

2. By definition a character sketch is usually brief. Therefore the writer must focus on a primary quality of character, as did John Kennedy in *Profiles in Courage* when he focussed on specific moral decisions made by prominent American political leaders. Rosten did not attempt to present a detailed life of Gandhi; instead, he chose to emphasize certain qualities of Gandhi's character. Once you have gathered the facts, you, too, must focus and humanize these facts without dictating the character and personality of your subject. Prepare an outline illustrative of the theme you intend to develop.

3. Rosten describes Gandhi as "excruciatingly shy, intensely sensuous." These are judgments Rosten makes on the basis of observations and commentaries on Gandhi's behavior in various situations. Search through the material you have gathered for details that are revelatory of the character of your subject.

4. Rosten introduces his theme by selecting a specific action as illustrative of Gandhi's character, an instance in which Gandhi defied a British mandate, an action in keeping with the Mahatma's basic philosophy of "passive resistance," a cornerstone of his philosophy of life. Select an episode illustrative of the theme you have selected and write an opening paragraph through which you show, rather than announce or state, your theme.

5. At the end of the character sketch Rosten summarizes his interpretation of Gandhi's life, his strength of character, and the influence of his character on the modern world. Prepare a final paragraph in which you summarize the meanings you have developed in your character sketch. Revise and submit a final draft.

THE DISCOVERY OF KENTUCKY
William Carlos Williams

There was, thank God, a great voluptuary born to the American settlements against the niggardliness of the damming puritanical tradition; one who by the single logic of his passion, which he rested on the savage life about him, destroyed at its spring that spiritually withering plague. For this he has remained since buried in a miscolored legend and left for rotten. Far from dead, however, but full of a rich regenerative violence he remains, when his history will be carefully reported, for us who have come after to call upon him.

Kentucky, the great wilderness beyond the western edge of the world, "the dark and bloody ground" of coming years, seemed to the colonists

William Carlos Williams, *In The American Grain*. Copyright 1925 by James Laughlin, 1933 by William Carlos Williams. Reprinted by permission of New Directions Publishing Corporation.

along the eastern North-American seaboard as far away, nearly, and as difficult of approach as had that problematical world itself beyond the western
ocean to the times prior to Columbus. "A country there was, of this none
could doubt who thought at all; but whether land or water, mountain or
plain, fertility or barrenness, preponderated; whether it was inhabited by
men or beasts, or both or neither, they knew not." But if inhabited by men
then it was the savage with whom the settlers had had long since experience sufficient to make them loth to pry further, for the moment, beyond
the securing mountain barrier.

Clinging narrowly to their new foothold, dependent still on sailing vessels for a contact none too swift or certain with "home," the colonists
looked with fear to the west. They worked hard and for the most part
throve, suffering the material lacks of their exposed condition with intention. But they suffered also privations not even to be estimated, cramping
and demeaning for a people used to a world less primitively rigorous. A
spirit of insecurity calling upon thrift and self-denial remained their basic
mood. Opposed to this lay the forbidden wealth of the Unknown.

Into such an atmosphere, more or less varied, more or less changed for
better or worse in minds of different understanding, was born Daniel
Boone, the foremost pioneer and frontiersman of his day. A man like none
other about him Boone had for the life of his fellow settlers, high or low,
no sympathy whatever. Was it his ancestry, full of rural quietness from
placid Dorset or the sober Quaker training of his early associations that
bred the instinct in him, made him ready to take desperate chances with
his mind for pleasure, certainly he was not, as commonly believed, of that
riff-raff of hunters and Indian killers among which destiny had thrown him
—the man of border foray—a link between the savage and the settler.

His character was not this. Mild and simple hearted, steady, not im-
pulsive in courage—bold and determined, but always rather inclined to
defend than attack—he stood immensely above that wretched class of men
who are so often the preliminaries of civilization. Boone deliberately chose
the peace of solitude, rather than to mingle in the wild wranglings and
disputings of the society around him—from whom it was ever his first
thought to be escaping—or he would never have penetrated to those secret
places where later his name became a talisman.

Three years the junior of George Washington, Boone was taken while
still a child from his birthplace on the upper waters of the Schuylkill River
near Philadelphia to the then comparatively wild country of western Pennsylvania. Here he grew up. Soon a hunter, even as a boy men stepped back
to contemplate with more than ordinary wonder the fearlessness with
which he faced the fiercer wild beasts that prowled around. It was the early
evidence of his genius. At eighteen, with his love of the woods marked for
good, and his disposition for solitude, taciturnity and a hunter's life determined, the family moved again this time from the rapidly settling country

of Pennsylvania to the wild Yadkin, a river that takes its rise among the mountains that form the western boundary of North Carolina.

With his arrival on the Yadkin, Daniel Boone married a neighbor's daughter, Rebecca Bryan, and together the young couple left the world behind them. Boone at once traversed the Yadkin Valley at a point still more remote from the seaboard and nearer the mountain; here he placed his cabin. It was a true home to him. Its firelight shone in welcome to the rare stranger who found that riverside. But he was not to remain thus solitary! The lands along the Yadkin attracted the notice of other settlers, and Boone, at thirty, found the smoke of his cabin no longer the only one that floated in that air. These accessions of companionship, however congenial to the greatest part of mankind, did not suit Boone. He soon became conscious that his time on the Yadkin was limited.

The fields for adventure lay within his reach. The mountains were to be crossed and a new and unexplored country, invested with every beauty, every danger, every incident that could amuse the imagination or quicken action, lay before him, the indefinite world of the future. Along the Clinch River and the Holston River hunting parties pursued their way. As they went, the mysteries of forest life grew more familiar. Boone learned even better than before that neither roof, nor house, nor bed was necessary to existence. There were, of course, many things to urge him on in his natural choice. It was the time just preceding the Revolution. The colonial system of taxation was iniquitous to the last degree; this the pioneer could not fathom and would not endure. Such things Boone solved most according to his nature by leaving them behind.

At this point Boone's life may be said really to begin. Facing his first great adventure Boone was now in his best years. His age was thirty-six. He is described by various writers as being five feet ten inches high, robust, clean limbed and athletic, fitted by his habit and temperament, and by his physique, for endurance—a bright eye, and a calm determination in his manner. In 1769, John Finley returned from a hunting trip beyond the mountain. He talked loud and long of the beauty and fertility of the country and Daniel Boone was soon eagerly a listener. It touched the great keynote of his character, and the hour and the man had come.

"It was on the first of May, in the year 1769, that I resigned my domestic happiness for a time and left my family and peaceful habitation on the Yadkin River in North Carolina, to wander through the wilderness of America, in quest of the country of Kentucky, in company with John Finley, John Stewart, Joseph Holden, James Monay, and William Cool. We proceeded successfully and after a long and fatiguing journey through a mountain wilderness, in a westward direction on the seventh day of June following, we found ourselves on Red River, where John Finley had formerly been trading with the Indians, and from the top of an eminence, saw with pleasure the beautiful level of Kentucky."

Thus opens the so-called autobiography, said to have been written down from Boone's dictation, late in his life by one John Filson. But the silly phrases and total disregard for what must have been the rude words of the old hunter serve only, for the most part, to make it a keen disappointment to the interested reader. But now, from everything that is said, all that Boone is known to have put through and willingly suffered during the next two years, there ensued a time of the most enchanting adventure for the still young explorer. For a time the party hunted and enjoyed the country, seeing buffalo "more frequent than I have seen cattle in the settlements, browsing on the leaves of the cane, or cropping the grass on those extensive prairies, . . . abundance of wild beasts of all sorts through this vast forest; and the numbers about the salt springs were amazing." Here the party practised hunting till the twenty-second day of December following.

"On this day John Stewart and I had a pleasant rambel; but fortune changed the scene in the close of it. We had passed through a great forest, Nature was here a series of wonders and a fund of delight, and we were diverted with innumerable animals presenting themselves perpetually to our view. In the decline of the day, near the Kentucky River, as we ascended the brow of a small hill, a number of Indians rushed out of a thick canebrake upon us and made us prisoners." Escaping later the two returned to their camp to find it plundered and the others of their party gone.

But now, by one of those determining chances which occur in all great careers Squire Boone, Daniel's brother, who with another adventurer had set out to get news of the original party if possible, came accidentally upon his brother's camp in the forest. It was a meeting of greatest importance and unbounded joy to Daniel Boone. For a short time there were now four together, but within a month, the man Stewart was killed by Indians while Squire Boone's companion, who had accompanied him upon his quest, either wandered off and was lost or returned by himself to the Colonies. Daniel and Squire were left alone.

"We were then in a dangerous and helpless situation, exposed daily to perils and death amongst the savages and wild beasts—not a white man in the country but ourselves. Thus situated and many hundred miles from our families, in the howling wilderness, I believe few would have equally enjoyed the happiness we experienced. We continued not in a state of indolence but hunted every day, and prepared to defend ourselves against the winter's storms. We remained there undisturbed during the winter. . . . On the first day of May, following, my brother returned home to the settlement by himself, for a new recruit of horses and ammunition, leaving me by myself, without bread, salt or sugar, without company of my fellow creatures, or even a horse or a dog.

"I confess I never was under greater necessity of exercising philosophy and fortitude. A few days I passed uncomfortably: The idea of a beloved wife and family, and their anxiety upon the account of my absence, and exposed situation, made sensible impressions on my heart. A thousand dreadful apprehensions presented themselves to my view and had undoubtedly disposed me to melancholy if indulged. One day I undertook a tour through the country, and the diversity and beauty of nature I met with in this charming season expelled every gloom and vexatious thought. Not a breeze shook the most tremulous leaf. I had gained the summit of a commanding ridge, and looking around with astonishing delight, beheld the ample plain, the beauteous tracts below. All things were still; I kindled a fire near a fountain of sweet water and feasted on a loin of a buck which a few hours before I had killed. Night came and the earth seemed to gasp after the hovering moisture.————" But only impatience is kindled by the silly language of the asinine chronicler.

But when Filson goes on to declare Boone's loneliness "an uninterrupted scene of sylvan pleasures" it is a little too much to bear. Constant exposure to danger and death, a habitation which he states had been discovered by the savages, the necessity of such stratagems as the resort to the canebreak rather than to take the risk of being found in his cabin, have nothing of sylvan pleasures in them. Boone had too much strong sense to feel anything but patience amidst the scenes of his solitude. And yet, having sounded the depth of forest life, and having considered and weighed all it had to offer, he felt secure enough to brave the perils of an exploring tour. He saw the Ohio, and unquestionably, from the results of this excursion, strengthened his determination to establish himself in such a land of delight.

For three months he was alone. It was an ordeal through which few men could have passed. Certain it is that nothing but a passionate attachment of the most extraordinary intensity could have induced even him to undergo it. If there were perils there was a pleasure keener, which bade him stay on, even in solitude, while his day was lasting. Surely he must have known that it was the great ecstatic moment of his life's affirmation.

By instinct and from the first Boone had run past the difficulties encountered by his fellows in making the New World their own. As ecstasy cannot live without devotion and he who is not given to some earth of basic logic cannot enjoy, so Boone lived to enjoy ecstasy through his single devotion to the wilderness with which he was surrounded. The beauty of a lavish, primitive embrace in savage, wild beast and forest rising above the cramped life about him possessed him wholly. Passionate and thoroughly given he avoided the half logic of stealing from the immense profusion.

Some one must have taken the step. He took it. Not that he settled Kentucky or made a path to the west, not that he defended, suffered, hated and fled, but because of a descent to the ground of his desire was Boone's life important and does it remain still loaded with power,—power to strengthen every form of energy that would be voluptuous, passionate, possessive in that place which he opened. For the problem of the New World was, as every new comer soon found out, an awkward one, on all sides the same: how to replace from the wild land that which, at home, they had scarcely known the Old World meant to them; through difficulty and even brutal hardship to find a ground to take the place of England. They could not do it. They clung, one way or another, to the old, striving the while to pull off pieces to themselves from the fat of the new bounty.

Boone's genius was to recognize the difficulty as neither material nor political but one purely moral and aesthetic. Filled with the wild beauty of the New World to overbrimming so long as he had what he desired, to bathe in, to explore always more deeply, to see, to feel, to touch—his instincts were contented. Sensing a limitless fortune which daring could make his own, he sought only with primal lust to grow close to it, to understand it and to be part of its mysterious movements—like an Indian. And among all the colonists, like an Indian, the ecstasy of complete possession of the new country was his alone. In Kentucky he would stand, a lineal descendant of Columbus on the beach at Santo Domingo, walking up and down with eager eyes while his men were gathering water.

With the sense of an Indian, Boone felt the wild beasts about him as a natural offering. Like a savage he knew that for such as he their destined lives were intended. As an Indian to the wild, without stint or tremor, he offered himself to his world, hunting, killing with a great appetite, taking the lives of the beasts into his quiet, murderous hands as they or their masters, the savages, might take his own, if they were able, without kindling his resentment; as naturally as his own gentle son, his beloved brother, his nearest companions were taken—without his rancor being lifted. Possessing a body at once powerful, compact and capable of tremendous activity and resistance when roused, a clear eye and a deadly aim, taciturn in his demeanor, symmetrical and instinctive in understanding, Boone stood for his race, the affirmation of that wild logic, which in times past had mastered another wilderness and now, renascent, would master this, to prove it potent.

There must be a new wedding. But he saw and only he saw the prototype of it all, the native savage. To Boone the Indian was his greatest master. Not for himself surely to be an Indian, though they eagerly sought to adopt him into their tribes, but the reverse: to be *himself* in a new world, Indian-like. If the land were to be possessed it must be as the Indian possessed it. Boone saw the truth of the Red Man, not an aberrant type, treacherous and anti-white to be feared and exterminated, but as a natural expression of the place, the Indian himself as "right," the flower of his world.

Keen then was the defeat he tasted when, having returned safe to the Colonies after his first ecstatic sojourn, and when after long delay having undertaken to lead a party of forty settlers to the new country, his eldest son, among five others of his own age, was brutally murdered by the savages at the very outset. It was a crushing blow. Although Boone and others argued against it, the expedition turned back and with his sorrowing wife Boone once more took up his homestead on the Yadkin. And this is the mark of his personality, that even for this cruel stroke he held no illwill against the Red Men.

Disappointed in his early hopes and when through subsequent years of battle against the wild tribes, when through losses and trials of the severest order, he led at last in the establishment of the settlers about the fort and center of Boonesborough, he never wavered for a moment in his clear conception of the Indian as a natural part of a beloved condition, the New World, in which all lived together. Captured or escaping, outwitted by or outwitting the savages, he admired and defended them always, as, implacable and remorseless enemy to the Red Man that he proved, they admired and respected him to the end of his days.

You have bought the land, said an old Indian who acted for his tribe in the transaction which now made Kentucky over to the white man, but you will have trouble to settle it. It proved true. An old lady who had been in the forts was describing the scenes she had witnessed in those times of peril and adventure, and, among other things, remarked that during the first two years of her residence in Kentucky, the most comely sight she beheld, was seeing a young man die in his bed a natural death. She had been familiar with blood, and carnage, and death, but in all those cases the sufferers were the victims of the Indian tomahawk and scalping knife; and that on an occasion when a young man was taken sick and died, after the usual manner of nature, she and the rest of the women sat up all night, gazing upon him as an object of beauty.

It was against his own kind that Boone's lasting resentment was fixed, "those damned Yankees," who took from him, by the chicanery of the law and in his old age, every last acre of the then prosperous homestead he had at last won for himself after years of battle in the new country.

Confirmed in his distrust for his "own kind," in old age homeless and quite ruined, he must turn once more to his early loves, the savage and the wild. Once more a wanderer he struck out through Tennessee for "more elbowroom," determined to leave the young nation which he had helped to establish, definitely behind him. He headed for Spanish territory beyond the Mississippi where the Provincial Governor, having gotten wind of the old hunter's state of mind, was glad to offer him a large tract of land on which to settle. There he lived and died, past ninety, serving his traps as usual.

In the woods he would have an Indian for companion even out of preference to his own sons, and from these men, the Indians, he had the greatest reverence, enjoying always when afield with them the signal honor of disposing them in the order of the hunt.

Too late the American Congress did follow him with some slight recognition. But that was by then to him really a small matter. He had already that which he wanted: the woods and native companions whom, in a written statement of great interest, he defends against all detractors and in that defense establishes himself in clear words: the antagonist of those of his own blood whose alien strength he felt and detested, while his whole soul, with greatest devotion, was given to the New World which he adored and found, in its every expression, the land of heart's desire.

QUESTIONS

1.   The writer of a character sketch makes a series of judgments concerning the character and personality of the person being presented in the sketch. The basic judgment involves the selection of the theme or central idea of the sketch. Is Williams' central idea the discovery of Kentucky or Daniel Boone? Interview an acquaintance, during which you gain as much information as possible concerning the background, interests, schooling, and activities of the acquaintance. Based on this interview and your observations of the person and his surroundings, write a central statement or guiding idea around which you will build a character sketch; then prepare, in sentence outline form, the major statements you will use to support your central idea.

2.   A character sketch is based on a narrative principle, time-sequence. In the sketch of Daniel Boone the author uses such statements as the following to indicate the age in which Boone lived and the passage of time in Boone's life: "Three years the junior of George Washington," "at eighteen," "the time just preceding the Revolution," "His age was thirty-six," "In 1769," "the next two years," "for three months." Prepare a paragraph outline, enlarging the sentence outline prepared above in question one, of a character sketch you wish to write; include in it the pertinent sentences, words, phrases or clauses that indicate the passage of time.

3.   Williams utilized John Finley's "so-called autobiography" of Boone as a source of information. Gather detailed information from a number of sources, apart from the interviewee, and incorporate these details in the outline prepared above.

4.   A writer of a character sketch attempts selectively to recreate the environment—natural, social, political, economic, domestic—of the subject of the sketch. Does Williams recreate the eighteenth-century American environment of Western North Carolina and Kentucky? Incorporate in your outline selected specific details of the environment of the subject of your sketch—home, place of work, city or town, social currents, religious context, and political forces.

5.   Using the outline you have prepared, write a first draft of a charac-

ter sketch. Re-examine the draft critically to determine whether or not the central idea is clearly developed and supported, the character emerges as a living human being or a wooden puppet, the selection of details presents an accurate and honest portrait of the individual, the coherence of ideas and time are clearly reflected, and important details have not been excluded. Write a second draft in which you attempt to overcome the critical objections your analysis suggested. Then copy this final draft for submission.

VI

Biography

In 1683 John Dryden, a seventeenth-century poet-critic-dramatist, first used the term "biography" to describe "the history of particular men's lives." Today biography is generally described in terms of subject as factual or fictional, in terms of method as artistic or inartistic, and in terms of the biographer's approach as historical, philosophical-critical, biographical, and psychological. Hence we read and write what is broadly described as "factual" biography and fictional biography; in the former instance the biographer is limited, in what he may say about the subject of the biography, to the letters, autobiography, anecdotes, speeches of the subject himself, to the genealogical facts of history, and to the reminiscences and statements of those who knew the subject; the biographer still must sift through these materials to discover the chronology of the subject's life, to sort fact from hearsay, and to establish the reality of the subject's life. The writer's problem is well illustrated by the many lives of Shakespeare or those of Robert E. Lee; in the first instance a reconstructed life is developed from small factual detail; in the latter instance most of the biographies of Lee emanate from the writers' emphases. Abraham Lincoln was both a politician and a statesman; the biographer must show both qualities.

The artistic or inartistic qualities of a biographer are particularly evident in the principles of selection he observes, in the quality of the construction of the narrative, and in the level of style he employs. As a branch of literature, many biographies include enormous detail concerning the daily life of the subject, as James Boswell, in his *Life of Johnson*, included immediate recordings of conversations, opinions, dress, meals, conduct, and actions; others, particularly those written from the perspective of history, the more typical type of biography, are committed by circumstance to selection of relevant and documented facts, usually drawn from the primary resources of the subject's own writings and those of persons who knew him well.

In the event you write a historical biography, you are confronted with the problem of showing the reality of the life of the subject in his age, showing the subject's place in history, or ignoring these preconceptions and concentrating on the life of the subject as he lived it. Usually the concentration on the life of the subject leads the biographer to make some evaluation of the subject's place in his age and in history, but such an evaluation is not essential to sound biography. Other biographers wish to write philosophical-critical biographies in which they show the evolution of the subject's thoughts and actions, or his place in the history of a type of biography such as political or literary biography. Still others attempt to penetrate the psychological characteristics of the subject; for example, John Livingston Lowes attempted, in *The Road to Xanadu*, a study of the germination of Samuel Taylor Coleridge's poem "Kubla Khan." The successful biographer will steep himself in the materials available and bring his biography to fruition through an inductive approach.

Certain characteristics are to be found in the art of biography: 1) a biographer attempts to recreate a flesh and blood human being, a lifelike person, one who reveals himself through his character, personality, accomplishments, and actions; 2) the biographer who seeks to recreate a living person endeavors to adopt an impersonal and objective point of view, permitting the reader to draw his conclusions from the selected details; 3) the biography is built around the chronology of the subject's life, with careful attention devoted to the sequence of events, thoughts, and details; 4) in the process of humanizing the subject, the biographer frequently uses meaningful allusions, quotations, conversations, excerpts from letters and other written works, and actions that reflect the living experience of the subject.

William Roscoe Thayer in *The Art of Biography* said, "as little as possible of the writer should intrude in the biography"; this statement summarizes a good starting point for a biographer.

EUGENE'S FIRST YEAR AT THE UNIVERSITY

Thomas Wolfe

Eugene's first year at the university was filled for him with loneliness, pain, and failure. Within three weeks of his matriculation, he had been made the dupe of a half-dozen classic jokes, his ignorance of all campus tradition had been exploited, his gullibility was byword, he was the greenest of all green Freshmen, past and present: he had listened attentively to a sermon in chapel by a sophomore with false whiskers; he had prepared studiously for an examination on the contents of the college catalogue; and he had been guilty of the inexcusable blunder of making a speech of acceptance on his election, with fifty others, to the literary society.

And these buffooneries—a little cruel, but only with the cruelty of vacant laughter, and a part of the schedule of rough humor in an American college—salty, extravagant, and national—opened deep wounds in him, which his companions hardly suspected. He was conspicuous at once not only because of his blunders, but also because of his young wild child's face, and his great raw length of body, with the bounding scissor legs. The undergraduates passed him in grinning clusters: he saluted them obediently, but with a sick heart. And the smug smiling faces of his own classmen, the wiser Freshmen, complacently guiltless of his own mistakes, touched him at moments with insane fury.

"Smile and smile and s-mile—damn you!" he cursed through his grating teeth. For the first time in his life he began to dislike whatever fits too snugly in a measure. He began to dislike and envy the inconspicuous mould of general nature—the multitudinous arms, legs, hands, feet, and figures that are comfortably shaped for ready-made garments. And the prettily regular, wherever he found it, he hated—the vacantly handsome young men, with shining hair, evenly parted in the middle, with sure strong middling limbs meant to go gracefully on dancefloors. He longed to see them commit some awkward blunder—to trip and sprawl, to be flatulent, to lose a strategic button in mixed company, to be unconscious of a hanging shirt-tail while with a pretty girl. But they made no mistakes.

As he walked across the campus, he heard his name called mockingly from a dozen of the impartial windows, he heard the hidden laughter, and he ground his teeth. And at night, he stiffened with shame in his dark bed, ripping the sheet between his fingers as, with the unbalanced vision, the swollen egotism of the introvert, the picture of a crowded student-room, filled with the grinning historians of his exploits, burned in his brain. He strangled his fierce cry with a taloned hand. He wanted to blot out the shameful moment, unweave the loom. It seemed to him that his ruin was final, that he had stamped the beginning of his university life with folly that would never be forgotten, and that the best he could do would be to seek out obscurity for the next four years. He saw himself in his clown's trappings and thought of his former vision of success and honor with a lacerating self-contempt.

There was no one to whom he could turn: he had no friends. His conception of university life was a romantic blur, evoked from his reading and tempered with memories of Stover at Yale, Young Fred Fearnot, and jolly youths with affectionate linked arms, bawling out a cheer-song. No one had given him even the rudimentary data of the somewhat rudimentary life of an American university. He had not been warned of the general taboos. Thus, he had come greenly on his new life, unprepared, as he came ever thereafter on all new life, save for his opium visions of himself a stranger in Arcadias.

He was alone, he was desperately lonely.

But the university was a charming, an unforgettable place. It was situated in the little village of Pulpit Hill, in the central midland of the big State. Students came and departed by motor from the dreary tobacco town of Exeter, twelve miles away: the countryside was raw, powerful and ugly, a rolling land of field, wood, and hollow; but the university itself was buried in a pastoral wilderness, on a long tabling butte, which rose steeply above the country. One burst suddenly, at the hill-top, on the end of the straggling village street, flanked by faculty houses, and winding a mile in to the town centre and the university. The central campus sloped back and up over a broad area of rich turf, groved with magnificent ancient trees. A quadrangle of post-Revolutionary buildings of weathered brick bounded the upper end: other newer buildings, in the modern bad manner (The Pedagogic Neo-Greeky), were scattered around beyond the central design: beyond, there was a thickly forested wilderness. There was still a good flavor of the wilderness about the place—one felt its remoteness, its isolated charm. It seemed to Eugene like a provincial outpost of great Rome: the wilderness crept up to it like a beast.

Its great poverty, its century-long struggle in the forest, had given the university a sweetness and a beauty it was later to forfeit. It had the fine authority of provincialism—the provincialism of an older South. Nothing mattered but the State: the State was a mighty empire, a rich kingdom— there was, beyond, a remote and semi-barbaric world.

Few of the university's sons had been distinguished in the nation's life —there had been an obscure President of the United States, and a few Cabinet members, but few had sought such distinction: it was glory enough to be a great man in one's State. Nothing beyond mattered very much.

In this pastoral setting a young man was enabled to loaf comfortably and delightfully through four luxurious and indolent years. There was, God knows, seclusion enough for monastic scholarship, but the rare romantic quality of the atmosphere, the prodigal opulence of Springtime, thick with flowers and drenched in a fragrant warmth of green shimmering light, quenched pretty thoroughly any incipient rash of bookishness. Instead, they loafed and invited their souls or, with great energy and enthusiasm, promoted the affairs of glee-clubs, athletic teams, class politics, fraternities, debating societies, and dramatic clubs. And they talked—always they talked, under the trees, against the ivied walls, assembled in their rooms, they talked—in limp sprawls—incessant, charming, empty Southern talk; they talked with a large easy fluency about God, the Devil, and philosophy, the girls, politics, athletics, fraternities and the girls—My God! how they talked!

QUESTIONS

1. In "Eugene's First Year at the University" Wolfe defines the meanings of that first year to Eugene Gant in the opening sentence:

"Eugene's first year at the university was filled for him with loneliness, pain, and failure." In the remainder of the opening paragraph and in the subsequent paragraphs, Wolfe describes, without developing the specific incidents, some of the causes of Eugene's "loneliness, pain, and failure." Interview a fellow student concerning his first week at your college or university; ask him to recall in detail the significant events of this week and his reactions to these events. Include the interviewee's background and special interests, orientation sessions, lectures, the physical characteristics of the campus, registration, dates, "bull sessions," fraternities and sororities, professors, parents, new acquaintances, roommates, the dormitories, athletics, the town, townspeople, and first class meetings. Write a central idea statement, such as Wolfe's, and prepare a topic outline of the biography.

2.   As a biographer, your objective is the creation of a flesh and blood human being. Write a brief biography, based on the outline developed above. Insofar as possible show, as Wolfe did, what kind of person the biographee is. Wolfe showed Eugene's innocence, gullibility, and "greenness" of university life through references to Eugene's behavior, such as his listening to a sermon given by sophomores, his studying for an examination on the contents of the university catalogue, his preparing and delivering an acceptance to a pseudoliterary society.

3.   Wolfe shows, through Eugene's private responses to the treatment he had been given at the university, the biographee's indignation, hurt, and sense of humiliation. Rewrite the biography, prepared above, placing the greatest emphasis on the biographee's reactions to what he found and experienced at the university.

4.   To provide the context in which Eugene found himself, Wolfe provides a general description of Pulpit Hill and Eugene's reactions to the university environment. Include a paragraph devoted to the university environment in your biography.

5.   The effective biographer, in his efforts to humanize his subject, frequently includes dialogue, allusions, comments by friends and teachers, and excerpts from letters, diaries, and notes. Write a final version of the biography in which you attempt to create a lifelike human being.

THOMAS WOLFE

Malcolm Cowley

During his early days in New York, Wolfe used to write in bound ledgers opened on top of the icebox, so that he stood at his work like a factory hand. Later he wrote at a table, using ordinary sheets of manuscript paper, but more of them than anyone else with good eyesight, for ninety of his penciled words filled a sheet. He wrote at top speed, never hesitating for a word, as though he were taking dictation. The moment a sheet was finished, he would push it aside without stopping to read it over or even to number it. In the course of filling thousands of sheets with millions of words, he developed a wart on the middle finger of his right hand "almost as large and hard," he said in a letter, "but not as valuable, as a gambler's diamond."

He was not so much an author of books as a member of that much less familiar species, the writing man, *homo scribens*. His life was spent in conjugating a single verb in various tenses—*scribam, scripsi, scriptum est*—with the result that his working habits and problems are even more interesting to study than the works themselves. Indeed, they reveal the works in a rather unexpected light and help to explain why their real virtues were achieved at an inevitable cost to the writing man and his readers.

The first of his problems was how to maintain a steady flow of words from the vast reservoir of his conscious memories to the moving tip of his pencil. Before the flow could be established he would go through weeks or months of self-torture, walking the streets of Brooklyn at night, fleeing to Europe, staying drunk for days on end. Once the flow started, it might continue for months, during which his pencil sprayed out words like water from a hose. "You forget to eat, to shave, to put on a clean shirt when you have one," says Wolfe's autobiographical hero George Webber in *You Can't Go Home Again*. "You almost forget to sleep, and when you do try to you can't—because the avalanche has started and it keeps going night and day. . . . You can't stop yourself—and even if you could you'd be afraid to because ther'd be all that hell to go through getting started up again."

Revision formed part of his system too, but not the usual sort of revision that consists in making interlinear changes, then having the draft retyped. "When he was dissatisfied with a scene or character," says his friend Edward C. Aswell, who had watched him working, ". . . he would put it aside, and rewrite it some different way from start to finish." In other words, he had to start the flow over again and continue until he had reached the end of an episode. He would remember new details and incidents the second time, so that his rewritten manuscripts were longer—often several times longer—than the first drafts. After being copied by a typist, they were tied in a bundle and put away in the big pine packing box that stood in the middle of his parlor. Then, in the same frenzy of production, he might go to work on another episode, often one remembered from a different period of his life.

His friends wondered how it was that he could reach into the packing box and, after a little fumbling, produce the desired episode, even if it had been written months or years before. I think the answer must be that he had his own filing system, chronological by subject matter. If the episode belonged to his boyhood, it would go below the episodes relating to his studies at Harvard, which in turn went below his years of teaching at Washington Square College and his love affair with Aileen Bernstein, which went below his struggles to write a second novel. All were parts of "the book" into which he planned to transcribe all his life, his world and time, in a continuous flow of memories. His ambition, announced by George Webber, was "To use myself to the top of my bent. To use everything I have. To milk the udder dry, squeeze out the last drop, until there is nothing left."

Unfortunately the book of his life was too big to be published or even to be written. His memories would have to be divided into separate books, or novels, and each of these would have to be something more than a chronological series of events; it would also have to possess its own structure and controlling theme. That was the problem of changing flow into form, which always puzzled him and for which he found a solution only in his first novel, as if without trying.

Look Homeward, Angel had a natural unity because, as Wolfe said in a letter to Mrs. Margaret Roberts, his English teacher in Asheville, it was "the story of a powerful creative element"—that is, Eugene Gant, or the author as a boy—"trying to work its way toward an essential isolation; a creative solitude; a secret life—its fierce struggles to wall this part of its life away from birth, first against the public and savage glare of an unbalanced, nervous, brawling family group, later against school, society, all the barbarous invasions of the world." As always it was a book of memories, but they were shaped and controlled by a theme close to the author's heart, the familiar theme of a young artist in a hostile environment. It had a natural beginning, which was the artist's birth, and a natural end, which was his escape from the environment.

But what could he do after writing *Look Homeward, Angel?* "I've got too much material," George Webber tells his friend Randy Shepperton. "It keeps backing up on me . . . until sometimes I wonder what in the name of God I'm going to do with it—how I'm going to find a frame for it, a channel, a way to make it flow. . . . Sometimes it actually occurs to me that a man may be able to write no more because he gets drowned in his own secretions." Then after a pause George says, "I'm looking for a way. I think it may be something like what people vaguely mean when they speak of fiction. A kind of legend, perhaps."

In 1930, the year after the publication of *Look Homeward, Angel,* Wolfe was looking for a legend into which he could fit everything he had felt and seen after leaving Asheville. Since he was in Europe at the time, and since his strongest emotion, outside of the passionate desire to write another book, was longing for the home he had lost—irretrievably, so he thought, for Asheville people had threatened to lynch him if he came back

—he fixed upon the Antaeus legend of the giant born from the marriage of earth and water. He gave the legend a special turn, however, to fit his circumstances. In a letter to Maxwell Perkins, his editor at Scribner's, he explained that the argument of the new book would be:

> . . . of the Lybyan giant, the brother of Polyphemus, the one-eyed, and the son of Gaea and Poseidon, whom he hath never seen, and through his father, the grandson of Cronos and Rhea, whom he remembereth. He contendeth with all who seek to pass him by, he searcheth alway for his father, he crieth out: "Art thou my father? Is it thou?" and he wrestleth with that man, and he riseth up from each fall with strength redoubled, for his strength cometh up out of the earth, which is his mother. Then cometh against him Heracles, who contendeth with him, who discovereth the secret of his strength, who lifteth him from the earth whence his might ariseth, and subdueth him. But from afar now, in his agony, he heareth the sound of his father's foot: he will be saved for his father cometh!

Of course the giant born of earth was Eugene Gant again, or Wolfe in person. His brother Polyphemus was intended to stand for the sterility that hates life; probably he was to be represented by Francis Starwick, the homosexual dramatist who appears in *Of Time and the River*. Gaea or Earth was to be introduced in the same novel as Mrs. Esther Jack, but the manuscript chapters about her were omitted from the published book and filed away; later they would figure in *The Web and the Rock*. Heracles the antagonist was to be the city of New York. As for the father, Wolfe's plan was that he should never be seen. But in a final chapter called "Pacific End"—later Wolfe thought of it as a final complete book, though he never got round to writing it—Antaeus was to hear "the thunder of horses on a beach (Poseidon and his horses); the moon dives out of clouds; he sees a print of a foot that can belong only to his father, since it is like his own; the sea surges across the beach and erases the print; he cries out 'Father' and from the sea far out, and faint upon the wind, a great voice answers 'My Son!' "

It was a magnificent conception, if slightly overblown; the trouble was that Wolfe was psychologically unable to carry it through. Like Eugene Gant he was gripped by an obsessive desire to say everything, with the result that "all ordered plans, designs, coherent projects for the work he had set out to do . . . were burned up in a quenchless passion, like a handful of dry straw." Soon the Antaeus legend got mixed with others, and the hero —without ceasing to be Thomas Wolfe—was called upon to play the successive parts of Orestes, Faustus the student, Telemachus, Jason, and Faustus in love. The more he worked on the book, the farther he seemed from its "Pacific End." By the beginning of the fourth year after the publication of *Look Homeward, Angel*, he had written a million new words, on his own estimate, and the great conception was not so much burned up as buried like Herculaneum under a flow of lava. It was Perkins who saved him, by suggesting how he might make a novel out of one segment of the material, saving the rest for other books. Even then almost half the segment had to be pared away before *Of Time and the River* was published in 912 pages.

The plan he evolved for a third novel was less Wagnerian. As he described the book in a letter to Aswell, who had become his editor after Wolfe left Scribner's, "It is about one man's discovery of life and the world, and in this sense it is a book of apprenticeship." The hero's name would be changed from Eugene Gant to George Webber, and his height would shrink from six feet five to five feet nine; Wolfe was looking for a protagonist whose angle of vision didn't quite duplicate the author's, so that his world could be treated more objectively. Webber would be the eternal innocent on his painful way to knowledge—another Candide or Wilhelm Meister—and the lessons he learned in a succession of adventures would be summed up in the title, *You Can't Go Home Again*.

It was a conception better suited to Wolfe's writing habits than that of his second novel had been, for it was loose enough so that one episode after another could be fitted into the scheme. But already, as he worked on it, the episodes had proliferated and some of them had grown almost to the length of separate books. His immense store of memories was imposing its pattern on the narrative, or its lack of pattern. The bandylegged figure of George Webber was being presented less and less objectively until it became indistinguishable from the author's figure; George seemed to grow taller as one looked at him. By the spring of 1938 Wolfe had once again written more than a million words, which he turned over to Aswell before leaving for the West. Most of the words—too many of them—were published in three volumes after his death. No one can say how Wolfe himself would have finished the novel, or group of novels, or in how much time, or how and whether, if he had lived, he could have brought himself to relinquish all that private wealth of words.

But although he was incapable of solving the larger problem of form, he did solve a lesser problem in a way that is often overlooked. Wolfe's unit of construction was the episode, not the scene or chapter or novel. He always had trouble connecting the episodes, many of which were complete and strikingly effective in themselves. Two of the best are "The Web of Earth" and "A Portrait of Bascom Hawke," both of which were printed in *Scribner's Magazine*, although the "Portrait" was afterward taken apart and fitted into *Of Time and the River*. Other fine episodes are the long passage about the death of Old Gant, written for inclusion in the same novel while Wolfe and Perkins were revising it; the account of the students in Professor Hatcher's (or Baker's) famous course in the drama; the disintegration of Francis Starwick; the story of Nebraska Crane (partly in *The Web and the Rock* and partly in *You Can't Go Home Again*); and the visit to Nazi

Germany called "I Have a Thing to Tell You." If these had been published separately, from the text of the original manuscripts—as *The Story of a Novel* was published—Wolfe might have gained a different reputation, not as an epic poet in prose, but as the author of short novels and portraits, little masterpieces of sympathy and penetration. But with his mania for bigness, one can't be sure that he would have enjoyed that other kind of fame.

Most of Wolfe's faults as a writer were closely and fraternally connected with his virtues; both resulted from his method of composition. Take for example the fault most frequently and justifiably urged against him: that he was unable to criticize his own work, that he couldn't distinguish what was good in it from what was absurd or pretentious, and that he wouldn't take criticism from others. Wolfe acknowledged the fault even when he was a very young man; at twenty-two he said in a letter to George Pierce Baker, "I admit the virtue of being able to stand criticism. Unfortunately it is a virtue I do not happen to possess." It wasn't that he was lacking either in humility or in critical talent. One couldn't talk with him about books for ten minutes without finding that he was perceptive and discriminating about other people's work, if he had read it. He didn't apply that sort of discrimination to his own work not through inability to do so, as he sometimes said, but chiefly as a matter of policy.

In a sense he chose to be only half of an author. The usual author is two persons or personalities working in partnership. One of them says the words to himself, then writes them down; the other listens to the words, or reads them, and then silently exclaims. "This is good, this is what you wanted to say, but *this!* Can't you say it again and say it better?" A result of the dialogue between the writer and the reader within is that the usual manuscript moves ahead spasmodically—a sentence or two, a pause while another sentence is phrased and rejected and rephrased, then a rapidly written paragraph, then another pause while reader and writer argue silently (or even aloud) about what has been said, then the sound of a page crumpled and dropped into the wastebasket, then a day's interval, perhaps, then another page that goes better. . . .

With time always pressing him, Wolfe couldn't afford to stumble ahead by a process of inner dialectic. There had to be that uninterrupted flow of memories from mind to paper; if he once questioned the value of the memories or changed the words that came to him, the flow halted for the day or night or perhaps for weeks. The solution he found instinctively, but later supported with arguments, was to suppress the critical side of his nature, or at least to keep it silent until an episode was finished; then if the inner critic objected to what he had written, he would do it over from the beginning, again without allowing the critic to interrupt. It was an effective system for producing words—very often accurate and truly inspired words—but it involved a great deal of wasted effort for the writer and wasted time for the reader of his published work.

Another fault urged against him is his use of formulas, including stock phrases, paired nouns or verbs where only one is needed ("grief and anguish," "sneered at and derided"), as well as the inevitable and therefore useless epithet. Here again the fault results from his system of writing and is closely connected with virtues that it helped him to achieve. Wolfe composed his novels, or rather the episodes that went into his novels, much as ancient bards, standing before a company of warriors, composed their epic poems. Like them, if for different reasons, he had to maintain an unbroken flow of words, with the result that there had to be moments when his pencil moved automatically while his mind was preparing the next powerful effect.

I couldn't help thinking of Wolfe when reading a passage in Moses Finley's illuminating book, *The Word of Odysseus*:

> The repeated formula [Finley says] is indispensable in heroic poetry. The bard composes directly before his audience; he does not recite memorized lines. In 1934, at the request of Professor Milman Parry, a sixty-year-old Serbian bard who could neither read nor write, recited for him a poem of the length of the *Odyssey*, making it up as he went along, yet retaining meter and form and building a complicated narrative. The performance took two weeks, with a week in between, the bard chanting for two hours each morning and two more in the afternoon.
>
> Such a feat makes enormous demands in concentration on both the bard and his audience. That it can be done at all is attributable to the fact that the poet, a professional with long years of apprenticeship behind him, has at his disposal the necessary raw materials: masses of incidents and masses of formulas, the accumulation of generations of minstrels who came before him.

Wolfe was perhaps the only American author of this century who could have duplicated the feat of the Serbian bard. That was because he had the same sort of equipment: partly an enormous store of characters and incidents (drawn from his own experience, not from the traditions of the race), and partly a supply of epithets, metaphors, and synonyms (remembered from his early reading) that could be applied to any human situation. His writing was a sort of chant, like the declamation of a Homeric bard.

Poetry of a traditional sort can be written faster than prose, and Wolfe kept falling into traditional poetry. His books, especially *Of Time and the River*, are full of lines in Elizabethan blank verse:

Were not their howls far broken by the wind?

huge limbs that stiffly creak in the remote
demented howlings of the burly wind,

and something creaking in the wind at night.

Page after page falls into an iambic pattern, usually a mixture of pentameters and hexameters. Other passages—in fact there is a whole book of them called *A Stone, A Leaf, A Door,* selected from Wolfe's writing by John S. Barnes—are a rather simple kind of cadenced verse:

Naked and alone we came into exile
In her dark womb
We did not know our mother's face.

Often there are internal rhymes and half-rhymes: "October is the season for *returning:* the bowels of youth are *yearning* with lost love. Their mouths are *dry* and bitter with *desire:* their hearts are *torn* with the *thorns* of spring." Again there are phrases almost meaningless in themselves, but used as musical themes that are stated and restated with variations, sometimes through a whole novel. "A stone, a leaf, a door" is one of the phrases; others are "O lost" and "naked and alone," in *Look Homeward, Angel,* and "of wandering forever and the earth again," repeated perhaps a hundred times in *Of Time and the River.* All these patterns or devices—cadence, meter, rhyme, assonance, refrains—are those into which the language naturally falls when one is trying to speak or write it passionately and torrentially. They are not the marks of good prose—on the contrary—and yet in Wolfe's case, as in that of a few other natural writers, they are the means of achieving some admirable effects, including an epic movement with its surge and thunder. They also help Wolfe to strike and maintain a *tone,* one that gives his work a unity lacking in its structure, a declamatory tone that he needs for his effort to dignify a new race of heroes and demigods, to suffuse a new countryside with legend, and to bring new subjects into the charmed circle of those considered worthy to be treated in epic poems.

His persistent immaturity—still another fault that is often urged against him—was not so much a weakness of character as it was a feature of his literary policy. He had to play the part of an innocent in the great world. He had to have illusions, then lose them painfully, then replace them with others, because that repeated process was the story he wanted to tell. He had to be naïve about his emotions in order to feel them more intensely and in order to convey the impression—as he does in his best work —that something as commonplace as boarding a train or writing a book is being experienced not only for the first time in the author's life but for the first time in history. If he had learned from the experience of others, he would have destroyed that sense of uniqueness. If he had said to himself with the wisdom of middle age, "There must be a catch somewhere," in his exultation, or, "You'll feel better about it tomorrow," in his bottomless despair, he would have blunted the edge of both feelings and made them less usable as memories.

God said in the proverb, "Take what you want and pay for it." That might have been the motto and moral of Wolfe's collected works and of his private life as well. Determined as he was to find words for every experience, he denied himself many of the richest experiences because they might have interfered with his writing, or simply because he had no time for them. He never had a real home after he was seven years old; he never owned so much as a square foot of the earth he loved (even his grave is in a family plot); he never planted a tree or a garden, never married, never fathered a child. Much as he loved good company, he spent most of his time alone in dingy lodgings or roaming the streets at night. He played no games, took part in no sports, displayed no social accomplishments. Indeed, he had few amusements: eating and drinking were the first two, and afterward came travel, making love, and conversation, in about that order of importance. He didn't enjoy music, or much enjoy art (except the paintings of Breughel and Cranach); he stopped going to the theatre after his quarrel with Mrs. Bernstein; and though he liked to talk about books, I suspect that he did comparatively little reading after he left Harvard. His real avocation was the physical act of writing; his one preoccupation was preparing for the act. He said in a letter to Mrs. Roberts, written a few months before his death:

> . . . There is no rest, once the worm gets in and begins to feed upon the heart—there can never after that be rest, forgetfulness, or quiet sleep again. . . . After this happens, a man becomes a prisoner; there are times when he almost breaks free, but there is one link in the chain that always holds; there are times when he almost forgets, when he is with his friends, when he is reading a great book or poem, when he is at the theatre, or on a ship, or with a girl—but there is one tiny cell that still keeps working; even when he is asleep, one lamp that will not go out. . . .
>
> As far as I am concerned, there is no life without work—at least, looking back over my own, everything I can remember of any value is somehow tied up with work.

The price Wolfe paid in his life was not the price of his debauches, which were intense while they lasted, like all his other activities—once he landed in jail and another time in a German hospital with a broken head, richly deserved—but which were occasional or intermittent. He paid more for his one great virtue than for all his vices. He paid for his hours of steady writing, for his sleepless nights, for his efforts to remember and interpret everything that happened, to find a key to it all, to give form to his memories. The price was partly in terms of health, for he was drawing sight drafts against his constitution without stopping to ask whether there was still a credit balance.

But there was also a price in mental health that most of his critics have been too considerate to mention, even long after his death. His alternating moods of exuberance and despair became more extreme; especially the periods of despair were longer and deeper. Many physicians would say that in his last years he was a victim of manic-depressive psychosis.

He also developed paranoid symptoms, as manic-depressives often do. There were ideas of reference and delusions of persecution and grandeur.

At times he thought the whole literary world was leagued in a conspiracy to keep him from working. "As for that powerful and magnificent talent I had two years ago," he wrote to Perkins in January, 1937, "—in the name of God is that to be lost entirely, destroyed under the repeated assaults and criminalities of this blackmail society under which we live? Now I know what happens to the artist in America." His farewell letter to Perkins was a magnificent piece of sustained eloquence—130 of his manuscript pages—but in places it was a crazy man's letter. One fine sentence is often quoted: "And I shall wreak out my vision of this life, this way, this world and this America, to the top of my bent, to the height of my ability, but with an unswerving devotion, integrity and purity of purpose that shall not be menaced, altered or weakened by any one." But the following sentences, which reveal his state of mind, are usually slurred over:

> I will go to jail because of this book if I have to. I will lose my friends because of it, if I will have to. I will be libeled, slandered, blackmailed, threatened, menaced, sneered at, derided and assailed by every parasite, every ape, every blackmailer, every scandalmonger, every little Saturday Reviewer of the venomous and corrupt respectabilities. I will be exiled from my country because of it, if I have to. . . . But no matter what happens I am going to write this book.

That is impressive as eloquence, but not as a statement of the facts. Wolfe was planning to write a book that might have hurt a few persons, notably Mrs. Bernstein and some of the staff at Scribner's, but not so much as some of his neighbors in Asheville had been hurt by *Look Homeward, Angel*. Nobody was trying to keep him from writing it. For the author it would involve absolutely no danger of prison, blackmail, ostracism, or exile. "I am a righteous man," he said in the letter, with an undertone of menace, "and few people know it because there are few righteous people in the world." There are many with delusions of righteousness, which they use as an excuse for being unjust to others. Wolfe was becoming one of them, as he must have realized in part of his mind—the Dr. Jekyll part, as he sometimes called it. At this point, as at some others, he was losing touch with reality.

It had better be made clear that his fits of despair were not the "down" phase of a manic-depressive cycle. There was no loss of appetite or vigor, no moping in silence; on the contrary there were quarrels, broken furniture, and a torrent of spoken and written words. The fits did not recur at regular intervals and they were not induced by mere pretexts; on the contrary they had understandable causes, usually connected with his work. As Wolfe said to Alfred S. Dashiell of *Scribner's Magazine* in one of his many letters of apology:

> The effort of writing or creating something seems to start up a strange and bewildering conflict in the man who does it, and this conflict at times almost takes on physical proportions so that he feels

he is struggling not only with his own work but also with the whole world around him, and he is so beset with demons, nightmares, delusions and bewilderments that he lashes out at everyone and everything, not only people he dislikes and mistrusts, but sorrowfully enough, even against the people that he knows in his heart are his friends.

I cannot tell you how completely and deeply conscious I have been of this thing and how much bloody anguish I have sweat and suffered when I have exorcised these monstrous phantoms and seen clearly into what kind of folly and madness they have led me.

It had all started so boyishly and admirably with his gift for feeling joys and sorrows more deeply than others. He chose to cultivate the gift because it helped him in his writing, and gradually it had transformed his character. At first he was proud, if in a rather sheepish fashion, of sometimes losing control of himself. He wrote to his sister Mabel in May, 1929, "Don't be afraid of going crazy—I've been there several times and it's not at all bad." It was indeed an almost normal state for a romantic artist forcing himself, provoking himself, beyond the natural limit of his emotions. Soon he began to feel the sort of dismay he expressed in the letter to Dashiell, but it was becoming too late to change his professional habits. There were always occasions in the literary life for those fits of manic exultation and, increasingly, of despair—the sense of loss on publishing a book, the insults of a few reviewers (notably Bernard DeVoto), the strain of getting started again, the fatigue that followed months of steady writing, the disappointment when Perkins felt that his latest work wasn't quite his best, the injustice of a suit against him for libel—and all these hurts became more painful as he brooded over them in solitude or drank to forget them, until at last he couldn't help interpreting them as signs that his talent was threatened by a vast conspiracy. His psychosis, if we call it that, was not organic or toxic, nor was it functional in the usual sense of being an illness due to unsolved emotional conflicts. Like the oversized wart on the middle finger of his right hand, it was a scar he had earned in combat, a professional deformation.

Questions

1. In "Thomas Wolfe" Malcolm Cowley attempts to present a psychological portrait of the novelist. In doing so he traces Wolfe's habits of working from "his early days in New York," in the first paragraph, through a letter written to Mrs. Roberts, "a few months before his death." Obviously, Cowley selected carefully the details he presents. Write a brief psychological portrait of an acquaintance, based on a careful selection of details.

2. The structure of Cowley's brief psychological biography follows the traditional pattern of introduction, body, and conclusion. In the

introduction, Cowley states his purpose: to examine Wolfe's "working habits and problems." In the body of the biography he examines specific problems Wolfe encountered: initiation of a "flow of words," the habit of revision, filing system, "changing flow into form," the discovery of conceptions, arguments, and new forms for his material, and the problem of units of construction. This is followed in turn by an examination of Wolfe's "faults as a writer," including his uncritical approach to his own work, his sensitivity to the criticism of others, "his use of formulas," his habit of using the traditional patterns of poetry, and his "persistent immaturity." In the final paragraphs, Cowley offers an interpretation of Wolfe's mental state in the last years of the writer's life. Prepare an outline, in preparation for writing a biography of an acquaintance, in which you analyze and interpret the strengths and weaknesses of the acquaintance.

3. Write a brief psychological portrait, based on the material above.

4. Cowley believes poetic techniques and devices are "not the marks of good prose." He rejects, specifically, lines of blank verse, the iambic pattern, cadenced verse, internal rhymes and half-rhymes, refrains, and assonance. Examine each of these poetic techniques carefully and write a brief paper in which you agree or disagree with Cowley's statement.

5. The emotional power of Cowley's prose is manifest in his evaluation of Wolfe's life and works. Study carefully the paragraph beginning, "God said in the proverb, 'Take what you want and pay for it'." What is the strength of Cowley's enumeration of fact? Write a paragraph, about a classmate or acquaintance, in which your enumeration of fact propels the reader toward an emotional response. What techniques did you find especially helpful?

C. G. JUNG

Anthony Storr

Jung, who died in June 1961 at the age of eighty-five, was the last survivor of the great trio of European psychiatrists whose names are household words. Freud, Jung and Adler were all, in their different ways, pioneers; each contributed ideas that have had a powerful influence, not only upon psychiatry, but upon the general conception that twentieth-century man has of his own nature.

Of the three contributions, that of Jung is the least generally appreciated. Adler, during his lifetime, exerted considerable personal influence.

Reprinted from *The American Scholar*, Volume 31, Number 3, Summer, 1962. Copyright © 1962 by the United Chapters of Phi Beta Kappa. By permission of the publishers.

His ideas were easy to grasp, and expressed in a style so popular that they are liable to be undervalued by the sophisticated. Freud's work has been widely accepted; and, although his originality and iconoclasm at first made him enemies, he wrote with such admirable clarity that his books have long been familiar to educated people. But Jung remains unread, and this is not altogether surprising. For the man who picks up a book on psychology usually does so in the hope of finding some illumination of his personal problems, and if he turns to Adler or Freud he will inevitably find something that applies to himself. But if he happens to light on Jung he is likely to be nonplussed. For he may well find that he is confronted by an erudite discussion of the Trinity, or by an excursion into Chinese Yoga, or by a disquisition on medieval alchemy. What possible relevance can such esoteric subjects have to the day-to-day problems of living for which the average person seeks advice? It is understandable that some conclude either that Jung is too deep for them, or else that he is a crank who has deserted science for some crazy mixture of religion and speculative philosophy.

That this is not so it is the purpose of this article to demonstrate. Jung's point of view is, in some ways, unusual, and during the latter part of his life he was chiefly concerned with patients who differed from the common run of psychiatric cases. But the fact that Jung's viewpoint has not won more general appreciation is not because it is intrinsically bizarre, but because he himself had some difficulty in communicating it. As a talker Jung was superb; anyone who has heard him in private conversation or who has read the verbatim record of his seminars must realize that he was a tough, realistic thinker who could not be dismissed as a crank. But his writings are often obscure, and nowhere did he himself make an adequate summary of his ideas, as did Freud, for instance, in his *Outline of Psychoanalysis*. Jung's influence has been both wide and deep; but his ideas have penetrated by a process of diffusion rather than as a result of detailed study of his actual writings. As he himself said: "I have such a hell of a trouble to make people see what I mean."

Jung's work can best be appreciated by way of an outline of the development of his thought. He was the son of a Swiss pastor, brought up in the country, and as a child somewhat isolated, since his sister was nine years younger. Quite early he developed an interest in the past and originally wanted to be an archeologist. But the family did not have the money for him to pursue a purely academic career, so he turned to medicine as a second choice. At the time when Jung qualified as a doctor, psychiatry was a specialty of negligible importance; but Jung embraced it eagerly, since he saw that in the study of the mind he could combine both his interest in natural science and his extensive knowledge of philosophy and the history of ideas. He obtained a post in the Burghöelzli mental hospital in Zurich, where he worked from 1900 to 1909.

During this time he produced a great deal of original work, including the studies in word-association in which he introduced the word "complex," and his famous book on *The Psychology of Dementia Præcox*. By the end of 1900 Jung had read Breuer and Freud's *Studies on Hysteria*, and Freud's *The Interpretation of Dreams*. He at once perceived the value of Freud's conceptions and became his enthusiastic advocate. *The Psychology of Dementia Præcox* was the first attempt to apply psychoanalytic ideas to the study of insanity, and one of the first in which it was demonstrated that there was a hidden meaning in the apparently incomprehensible words and gestures of the insane. Jung sent this book to Freud, and the two men first met in 1907 when Jung went to Vienna at Freud's invitation.

There followed a period of some six years of collaboration, during which Jung was Freud's favorite lieutenant. But a certain intransigence, characteristic of genius, precluded Jung from remaining *in statu pupillari*; with the publication in 1913 of his next book, *The Psychology of the Unconscious*, communication with Freud came to an end. There were many reasons for the break. The temperamental gulf between the two men was a wide one, and there was a considerable difference in age. But, in addition to this, their training and experience were quite dissimilar. Freud's interest, in his early days, was centered upon neurosis; his original theories of mental structure were based upon the study of hysteria. He never worked in a mental hospital for more than a brief period and had little experience of psychotic patients. It was natural enough that his views should derive from the study of repressed, infantile patterns and the tangle of early interpersonal relationships, since this is the material that comes to light in the analysis of neurotic patients.

Jung, on the other hand, was fascinated by schizophrenia, and remained so until the end of his life. While accepting Freud's theory of repression as applied to neurosis, he came to the conclusion that it was inadequate to explain the extraordinary depth and richness of the material produced by patients suffering from schizophrenia. Psychotic phantasies, and many dreams of both normal and abnormal people, could not, he concluded, be explained in terms of the vicissitudes of infancy. There must be a deeper region of the unconscious mind which lay below the level of personal repression; this region Jung named the collective unconscious. Because of his interest in the past, Jung already had a considerable knowledge of the myths of primitive people; he was thus able to demonstrate remarkable parallels between the dreams and phantasies of his patients and recurrent patterns of myth from all over the world. The variations on these mythological themes might be infinite but the underlying patterns remained the same; to these patterns and the figures that appeared in them Jung gave the name of archetypes. In *The Psychology of the Unconscious* Jung took the phantasies of a patient who later became psychotic and showed, with a wealth of detailed parallels, that the production of phantasy was governed not only by the personal experiences of childhood, but also by determinants that the individual shared with all mankind, even with peoples who might be remote both geographically and in time from himself. In Jung's view the child was not born into the world with a mind like a sheet of blank paper on which anything could be imprinted. The child was already predisposed to feel and think along the same lines as his ancestors had done since the beginning of time. The unconscious could not be regarded simply as a part of the mind to which unpleasant emotions were banished. It was the very foundation of our being, and the source not only of mental disturbances but also of our deepest hopes and aspirations.

Freud could not accept this view, and the two men parted. But it is interesting to record the fact that, in one of his last works, Freud reached a similar conclusion about the nature of the unconscious. "Dreams bring to light material which could not originate either from the dreamer's adult life or from his forgotten childhood. We are obliged to regard it as part of the archaic heritage which a child brings with him into the world, before any experiences of his own, as a result of the experiences of his ancestors." Jung's concept of the collective unconscious, common to all mankind, was, therefore, not so controversial as it at first appeared: many Freudians accept something of the kind. The rift between Jung and Freud, like all such rifts, was surely based on personal conflict, not simply on theoretical differences; and it is time that curiosity about this ancient controversy was replaced by an objective appraisal of the great contribution that each man has made to our understanding of the mind.

The conflict with Freud had, however, one positive result. It set Jung thinking about how it happened that he, Freud and Adler studied the same material and yet produced such different points of view about it. From his reflections sprang the idea for which he is best known to the general public, the idea of differing psychological types. Jung saw that men approached the study of the mind, and indeed life in general, from different basic preconceptions, of which they were not always aware. The extravert valued the outer world, the relation to external objects, whereas the introvert gave his chief esteem to the world he discovered within himself. Both attitudes were necessary for a full comprehension of reality, but men were usually one-sided and tended toward one or the other extreme. Adlerian psychology, with its emphasis on power, was the product of an introvert, for Adler was concerned with exalting the subject at the expense of the object, as if the object were a threat that might overwhelm the subject. Freudian psychology, on the other hand, was an extraverted construction since Freud regarded sexuality as paramount and it is in the sexual relationship above all others that the object is most highly valued.

Jung's further subdivision of both types into thinking, feeling, sensation and intuition has not been generally accepted; but his original terms "extravert" and "introvert" have become part of everyday speech. For, as he rightly perceived, this particular dichotomy reflects something fundamental in human nature; many other psychologists, including William James, Kretschmer, Eysenck and Melanie Klein, have found a similar classification valuable. Jung regarded himself as predominantly an introvert, in whom thinking was the best developed function. His difficulty in communicating his ideas is characteristic of the introverted type who is often, as Jung said of himself, "at variance with the reality of things" and thus may not realize what it is that prevents other people from understanding him. A gross example of this is the misunderstanding that led to the accusation that Jung was antisemitic and a Nazi sympathizer, a slander that has already been refuted by his Jewish pupils and need not detain us here.

The next step in Jung's thought follows naturally as a result of combining his view of the unconscious with his typology. Neurosis, Jung concluded, was due to a one-sided development of consciousness which certainly had its roots in earliest childhood, but which was chiefly manifested in a lack of adaptation to the present situation. The extravert's danger was that he might lose himself in the press of external affairs; the introvert ran the risk of failing to maintain contact with the outer world. The ideal man would be equally well adapted to the reality of both inner and outer worlds; but such perfect adaptation was a goal toward which to aim rather than a reality that was ever completely achieved. It seemed to Jung that there was a reciprocal relationship between conscious and unconscious, and that the unconscious compensated for a one-sided attitude of consciousness. Hence neurotic symptoms were not simply unpleasant relics of the repressions of childhood, but were also abortive attempts on the part of the mind to remedy its own lack of balance. The psyche, in other words, was a self-regulating entity; and dreams, phantasies and other derivations of the unconscious could not be regarded solely as childish wish-fulfillments, but often as revelations of latent potentialities and as pointers toward the future development of the individual.

The idea that the mind is a self-regulating system is valuable in clinical practice. It is, moreover, a conception that accords well with modern ideas in physiology and cybernetics. The body itself is self-regulating; there are within it numerous devices that serve the purpose of keeping the internal environment constant, so that each cell may function at its optimum efficiency. Such devices, for example, regulate the hormonal system, the acid-base equilibrium of the blood, and body temperature. Automation existed within himself before man ever applied it to machines; and the checks and counterchecks that prevent the internal environment of the body from straying too far from an ideal balance are more complex and more subtle than those in any automatic factory.

It is surprising that Jung's theory of the self-regulating psyche has not attracted more attention. Of all his hypotheses it is the easiest to substantiate with clinical evidence; it is in line with physiology and thus scientifically respectable; it is borne out by the experience of everyday life. We are all familiar with the tough writer who at heart is a sentimentalist; with the frail, emotional woman who is actually ruthless; with the office tycoon who, at home, is a dependent child; with the hard-bitten rationalist who suddenly succumbs to the allure of an outlandish creed. Men are all a mixture of opposites; and the more extreme a person's conscious attitude, the more certainly will one find its opposite within. Jung concluded that the aim of man's development was the integration of the personality, which he conceived as a balance between opposites, between inner and outer reality, between reason and emotion, between extraversion and introversion. The individual who achieved integration was one who had succeeded in reconciling the opposites within himself and making a whole out of the disparate elements of his personality. It was not possible for a man to attain complete integration, any more than it was possible for an artist to create a perfect work of art; but this appeared to be the goal of human life toward which the unconsciously directed process of development was tending.

In Jung's view this search for integration and wholeness was characteristic of the second half of life; it is in dealing with the problems of older patients that Jung's analytical psychology comes into its own. Freud and his followers tended to assume that a man's development was complete with the achievement of freedom from parental ties and the establishment of sexual maturity: psychoanalysts have generally been reluctant to treat patients of middle age and over. Jung, however, found that his practice largely consisted of such patients. They were often people who had achieved both sexual maturity and professional success and who did not fit into the usual categories of neurosis. Nevertheless, they had come to a point at which they felt "stuck," and at which life seemed arid and without significance. The study of such people convinced Jung that at about the age of thirty-five or forty a change took place, at least in the people who consulted him. It was a time at which the individual might find that the pursuits of his youth had palled and that many of the activities that used to give him pleasure were no longer enthralling. At such a time the study of the products of unconscious phantasy is often particularly rewarding: Jung found that, in some people, a process of development seemed to be taking place that could be followed both in dreams and in the paintings, poems and other works of the imagination that he encouraged his patients to produce. This sequential development Jung called the individuation process; its study became the chief preoccupation of his own latter years.

Having formulated the idea that there was, in the second half of life, a psychological process of development tending toward the integration of the individual, Jung started to look about for historical parallels. For he believed that man's essential nature did not alter much in the course of time, and he therefore felt that there must be evidence in the past of men seeking the same integration for which his patients were looking in the present.

He found his parallel in alchemy. Those who are unfamiliar with Jung's thought have found it hard to understand why he should preoccupy himself with such matters as the alchemist's quest for the philosopher's stone. Alchemy, like astrology, which was also one of Jung's interests, has long been discredited by science. Of what possible interest can it be today?

The explanation of Jung's interest is simple. Alchemy is interesting psychologically just because there is nothing in it scientifically. It is equivalent to the projection tests that psychologists use in the assessment of personality. Like a Rorschach inkblot, alchemy contains nothing objective, and, since it is far removed from external reality, it provides an admirable field for the study of unconscious processes. The alchemists were searching for something that had no existence in the outside world, but that nonetheless seemed to them of extreme importance. Like Jung's patients, they were looking for integration and wholeness: the symbolism in which they described their quest was remarkably similar to the symbolism that Jung found in the dreams and phantasies of his patients.

In essential terms the alchemical quest was a search for salvation, but one that could not be contained within the framework of conventional religion. Jung found that many of his older patients were also attempting to find a meaning in life in a way that could only be described as religious, although most of them could not accept any orthodox creed. If a man were to attain his full stature as an individual it would seem that he must acquire some philosophy of life, some view as to the meaning of his own existence. As Jung himself said: "Man cannot stand a meaningless life."

It was not only in alchemy that Jung found evidence of the individuation process. He made wide-ranging researches into the fields of comparative religion, Chinese philosophy, Yoga and other arcane subjects; in doing so, he incurred the suspicion of scientists who, without understanding what he was doing, felt that he had abandoned science for mysticism. But the truth is that the less a subject is based on external reality, the more fruitful a field is it likely to be for the study of unconscious processes; Jung's later researches follow logically from his original premises.

Jung has been generally recognized as one of the great original minds of the twentieth century. Freud's psychoanalysis and Jung's analytical psychology have sometimes been regarded as incompatible; but in many respects the two approaches are complementary, and it is only the fanatics of either school who cannot see any value in the other's point of view. Freud's contribution to psychology took a generation to establish. It will probably take at least as long for the full impact of Jung's thought to be assimilated. But Jung's influence has been felt in many fields outside psychiatry, and his place in history is already assured. The concept of the collective unconscious, for instance, has been used by the writer J. B. Priestley in his book *Literature and Western Man*, by the historian Arnold Toynbee in *A Study of History*, and by the physicist W. Pauli in his work on the astronomer Kepler. Sir Herbert Read has acknowledged his debt to Jung in his writings on art, and many creative artists have felt that Jung understood their aims in a way that no previous writer on psychology had been able to do.

Although he was the first to demand that the analyst himself be analyzed, Jung was reluctant to have his teaching codified, and for many years he resisted the setting up of an institute to train pupils in his methods. He believed that his ideas were no more than a preliminary venture into a new field of research and referred to them as a subjective confession. Science takes a long time to catch up with intuitive genius; so far, there have been only a few experimental investigations based on Jung's later concepts. But it should be possible to formulate a series of propositions in such a way that his findings can be objectively demonstrated. A start has already been made in the study of dreams.

Jung maintained that our ignorance of ourselves is profound. He considered that man's most urgent task today is to deflect his gaze from the further conquest of the material world toward the study of his own nature. In a world in which opposites are so far divided that they threaten each other with mutual annihilation, we should do well to listen to Jung's counsel.

QUESTIONS

1. Storr states his purpose at the beginning of the third paragraph: ". . . it is the purpose of this article to demonstrate" that Jung is neither too deep nor is he a crank who deserted science. Using Al Capp, Bill Mauldin, or some other American humorist as your biographical subject, write a purpose statement in which you make a judgment concerning the humorist.

2. In "C. G. Jung," Storr presents the organization of his study at the beginning of the fourth paragraph: "Jung's work can best be appreciated by way of an outline of the development of his thought." After making a careful study of the works of the humorist you have selected, prepare an outline, based on chronological order, to support your purpose statement.

3. A biographer must use the terminology of the field or profession of the subject. For example, any discussion of a humorist, such as Al Capp, involves an understanding of Capp's particular sense of humor, the concept of the comic, meanings of social and political satire, and humorous idioms. Storr employs the terminology of psychology and psychoanalysis in his discussion of Jung: "complex," "neurosis," "schizophrenia," "repression," "collective unconscious," "myths," "psychotic," "phantasies," "extravert," "introvert," "dreams," "consciousness," "self-regulating psyche." Rewrite your sentence outline, providing supporting detail and careful distinctions between and among the terms you will use in explaining your purpose statement.

4. Storr distinguishes among the points of view of Adler, Freud, and Jung. Each had "studied the same material and yet produced such different points of view about it." Write a second purpose statement, which differs significantly from the earlier purpose statement, and prepare a sentence outline based on this second point of view. Which of the two outlines is better? Why?

5. Write a brief biography of the humorist you selected. Pay special attention to the inclusion of relevant supporting detail.

PART III

*Writing
for
Audiences*

VII

Editorial

An editorial is the expression of a newspaper's policy; in fact, many newspapers, such as the Jacksonville *Times-Union*, include daily summary statements of the general editorial policy followed by the publishers and editors of the paper. As a free enterprise institution in a democratic society, the editorial press does not attempt to remain impartial and objective, but attempts to lead the public to adopt its editorial viewpoint. Hence, on a subject such as American politics, an editorial policy frequently includes the endorsement of various candidates and specific political programs, as well as persuasive repudiations of other candidates and political viewpoints. In one sense an editorial represents a form of public leadership, persuasion, and argumentation. Other editorials may be devoted to human interest stories, eulogies of outstanding leaders of the community, or descriptions of the seasons of the year or groundhog day or the blooms on the apple trees, or to subjects of community, state, and national interest, such as conservation of natural resources, the powers of the Atomic Energy Commission, the need for better transportation services in the community or state, the importance of highway safety, or the significance of education.

An editorial is usually brief, with an average length of 300 to 1200 words. It follows no specific structure, since it may be a logical argument in support of a primary idea, a narrative human interest story, an enumeration of the accomplishments of a community leader, or an examination of the causal factors leading to a specific urban or rural condition; however, each editorial is governed by a dominant idea, a positive tone, a wide use of reference materials for facts, a clear but impersonal style, and a strong conclusion. It is addressed to the "average man," with considerable attention devoted to "proof" in support of the editorial position. In general the editorial "we" has been abandoned by the leading editorial writers in the United States.

As a writer of editorials you should remember that you are committing yourself to a critical examination of specific current issues before you write. Hence you must have a command of the facts involved before you commence writing.

SERVANT OF THE PEOPLE

Editor, *New Republic*

The worst servant of a democracy is the man who obeys the people because he fears them. In his deference to the opinion of others he surrenders his own, and if his example were followed by everyone, the opinion of a democracy would degenerate into little more than timid conventionality. The true democrat does not obey the people; he regards himself as one of the people, with the democratic privilege of having a mind of his own. He never pretends that the majority is necessarily right; he knows that courageous minorities are the very soul of a democracy.

This is why there has arisen the curious paradox that many of the best leaders of democracies have had to fight the majority all their lives. Had they not done so, they would have been little more than sheep, and a flock of sheep is not the symbol of a free people. It is the man who stands against the dead uniformity of opinion and breaks it up with some fresh current of ideas, who really creates a situation in which real opinion is possible. A mob cannot think; a nation of one mind may well be a nation of no mind at all, as the terrible intellectual inertia of Europe shows. This is why discerning people place so high a value on courage like that of Governor Slaton's of Georgia. They recognize in it the virtue on which democracies rest—the ability to think independently, the willingness to defy the weight of fixed beliefs, and a loyalty to ideals that cannot be deflected by the anger of a crowd. A democracy is damned when its leaders are slaves; it is safe when its leaders are not afraid to be free.

QUESTIONS

1. In the opening sentence of "Servant of the People," published in 1915, the editor states the dominant idea of the editorial: "The worst servant of a democracy is the man who obeys the people because he fears them." Write a carefully-phrased dominant idea for an editorial.

2. "Tone" is first a matter of the weight or value or significance you give to specific ideas. Hence, in general, ideas are presented in particular relationships: main ideas, coordinate ideas, subordinate ideas, parenthetical ideas, and interrupters or indirectly related ideas. To support the purpose statement, the editor presented certain coordinate ideas. What are these ideas? Write a sentence outline in which you list coordinate ideas in support of your purpose statement.

3. The editorial from *The New Republic* is based on the idea of the relationship of the one to the many, the leader to the crowd, the minority to the majority. Examine every sentence in the editorial for the presence of this basic idea. Re-examine the outline you have prepared for your editorial: what basic assumptions underlie it?

4. The editor believes "the best leaders of democracies have had to fight the majority all their lives." Examine the supporting arguments. Revise your outline by including specific supporting arguments.

5. Write your editorial, and then revise it by adding specific supporting data, such as examples, statistics, statements by authorities, observations and experiences, and factual information. Prepare a final draft for submission.

THE WIND RETURNETH

Vermont Royster

We live in such times of toil, trouble, and despair as the world has never known—or that anyway is the burden of the lament in the newspapers, magazines, TV documentaries, novels, poetry, sermon, and song. You can scarce escape the refrain.

Wars, riots, and strikes. Revolutions abroad. At home, violence in the streets. A decay of manners and morals. Economic tribulations. Racial hostility. Rebellion and delinquency among the young; a disregard of law among their elders. Disillusionment with the dream of the parliament of man. And so, in fact, it goes *ad infinitum*.

Ah, well; the indictment can hardly be dismissed. Still, it is only the young who can soak themselves in the romantic view of history, although sometimes the middle-aged cling to it, that everything is new, different, and worse than in some halcyon day of yore.

For old men the antidote is memory; if you were born before the turn of the century you may have the queer feeling that you've been here before, although that is perhaps small comfort. For the young, or for those too busy with middle age to have time for memories, the only antidote is a bit of browsing through the history books. Not the solemn history of kings and foreign policy, albeit that too is instructive. It's more curative, and much more delightful, to spend an hour among the volumes of Mark Sullivan's *Our Times*, which were mainly our grandfathers' times, or the *Only Yesterday* of Frederick Lewis Allen, who recounts the days of our youth.

Or lacking these musty volumes you can turn with as much delight,

---

Reprinted by permission of *The Wall Street Journal*, "Talking Things Over," August 15, 1966.

and equal instruction, to the newest of Doubleday's Mainstream of America series in which Jonathan Daniels brings both research and recollection to *The Time Between the Wars*. It's just plain nostalgic for those lucky enough to have been there, instructive for those with the misfortune to miss it all.

All that ancient history, that interlude of peace between two global wars. And was it, then, a quiet time with no wars, riots, or strikes? No revolutions abroad, and at home no violence in the streets? A time of settled manners, respect for age and law, of well-ordered morals? A time too free of troubles to give men cause for despair?

Hardly. The time between embraced the Jazz Age, the years of frenzy, the birth of the Red Menace and the Yellow Peril; the crash of an old order, the great depression, the rise of fascism, and the fusing of the scientific explosion soon to ignite the Armageddon that was Hiroshima. If you remember the flapper how can you be startled by the mini-skirt? Is it really forty years since that avant-garde magazine, *Civilization*, trumpeted that "the younger generation is in revolt against right-thinkers and forward-lookers . . . It dislikes almost to the point of hatred and certainly to the point of contempt, the type of people who dominate our present civilization, the people who actually 'run things.' . . ."? Is there not something familiar in seeing Greenwich Village described as a "noxious warren where males wore their hair long, females theirs short" and where both sexes were "of doubtful manners and morals"?

Some people may even remember Lewis Mumford—alas, so long ago —lamenting that the bourgeois "lives in an environment which the jerry-builder, the real estate speculator and the industrialist have created." Or Deems Taylor complaining of composers who wrote music "that we cannot produce." So many movies have so romanticized the gangster era that it's a shock to be reminded how much violence, lawlessness, and bloodshed filled the streets. And not all the murder was so purposeful; Leopold and Loeb killed retail rather than wholesale, but their slaughter of the innocent was as wanton and paranoiac as yesterday's headline.

As for scandals in Washington, the postwar purveyors of mink coats and food freezers were rather gauche amateurs compared with the masters of another day. Teapot Dome was but the icing on the cake. And how long has it been since we had a President who fathered illegitimate children? So much for the mores. Romanticism has also laid its hand on the great depression. In the little magazines those who were never there have begun to write about it with nostalgia, noting that it was a period of firm national spirit, of reform, of a flowering in literature and the arts.

Lest we forget, it was also a period of misery for millions. If they rallied, it was as people besieged and because they had courage. If there was reform, there was also makeshift and blundering. If there was flowering of literature and the arts, it was because creative people kept their faith in man.

There were, indeed, moments of despair. Robert E. Sherwood, writing in the early thirties, saw ahead only "black doubt, punctured by brief flashes of ominous light . . . Behind, nothing but the ghastly wreckage of burned bridges." But neither he nor the others who gave birth to the flowering were whimperers. If there was a difference, it lies there.

There was excuse for despair elsewhere, too. Today's disappointment with the United Nations was matched by yesterday's with the League of Nations or with the Kellogg Peace Treaty, which, so said the dreamers, banished war forever. Meanwhile, the clouds abroad were even more ominous than those at home. If those were your days you will hardly need reminding that before Pearl Harbor every man could feel the oppressive weight that marked the coming of the storm. If they were not your days, reading about them will give you a glimpse of how quiet, peaceful, staid, and unruffled were the days of your fathers. On the beaches of Iwo Jima those dead are as dead as the dead in a Vietnamese jungle.

The moral, or perhaps reminder is a better word in these times, is inescapable. If ours are the worst of times, so were they all. The question is not whether black doubt lies ahead, but how men at different times meet their different doubts, whether with courage and ironic laughter or with whimpering. The despairing Robert Sherwood would not have understood the whimpering Arthur Miller or Edward Albee.

There is another reminder in such tales retold, at least for those who were there. Men were broken on the wheel of depression; others died in wholesale slaughter; still others merely succumbed to the frenzy and wasted their lives. Yet there are rewards for the survivors; they were exciting times, and we would not have missed them for the world. It will probably be so hereafter. Whatever the outcome of that dirty, messy war in Vietnam the day will come when those who were there, like those at Agincourt, will pity those who were not. And old men someday will sit in nostalgia of these times, frowning at young men trumpeting their revolt and despairing of a world they never made.

When that day comes there need be pity only for those who surrender to self-pity, wailing of such toil, trouble, and despair as the world has never known. From them will come no flowering of the arts, no new dreams; for that matter, no new woes.

But, of course, that is an old man speaking. You have to survive before you can fully savor the storm, or appreciate the exhortation, *Olim haec meminisse juvabit*. In the midst of it you find it hard to believe that someday you may remember even these trials with pleasure. All the same, when you look about at the world around you there's a queer comfort in knowing that time moves around in full circles. The prophet offered not despair but solace when he taught that if the sun goeth down it also ariseth, and that if the wind whirleth continually it also returneth according to its circuits. It's the troubled world that abideth forever.

August 15, 1966

QUESTIONS

1. An editorial is organized around a dominant idea. What is the dominant or controlling idea of Royster's "The Wind Returneth"? Prepare a sentence outline of the arguments you advanced to support your understanding.

2. Royster, for over thirty years an editorial writer for *The Wall Street Journal,* makes wide use of reference materials for ideas, supporting detail, and clarity of expression. Who are the following: Mark Sullivan, Frederick Lewis Allen, Jonathan Daniels, Lewis Mumford, Deems Taylor, Leopold and Loeb, Robert E. Sherwood, Arthur Miller, Edward Albee? Write an editorial based on a controlling idea; support this idea by making a wide use of your experiences, references, and relevant supporting detail.

3. In the second paragraph of the editorial Royster uses sentence fragments to convey a host of related ideas. What particular effects are gained through the use of this device? What is the tone of the paragraph? How do you determine "tone"?

4. Write an editorial in which you attempt to refute Royster's view of contemporary "whimperers." Organize your refutation around a precisely stated central idea.

5. Most editorials devoted to current issues offer strong conclusions. Royster's is no exception. How did you find the meaning of the exhortation *Olim haec meminisse juvabit?* How did you find the source of the allusion to the prophet who "offered not despair but solace"? In a brief editorial experiment with the use of allusion as a means of making your meanings clearer.

VIII

Informal Speech

An informal speech may be little more than a hundred word statement to a small group concerning a particular subject, a story through which you make a point or establish an idea, or a fifteen to thirty minute statement in which you establish a number of ideas you hold concerning a particular concept, belief, experience. In each instance you are a speaker, you give a speech, you give it to an audience, and you anticipate and expect some kind of response from this audience.

As a speaker, you deliver a speech at a particular time in a particular place to an audience for which you prepared the speech. As a speaker you may have stated, implied, or hidden reasons for giving the specific speech. For example, Antony in his famous "Friends, Romans, countrymen" speech had a stated purpose of praising Caesar, an implied purpose of testing the immediate temper of the Roman citizenry, and a hidden purpose of arousing the citizenry against Brutus so that he might lose political power. Each speaker must analyze his personal and public motives in view of the human behavior he encounters and attempts to influence through a speech.

The speech with a stated purpose usually involves the speaker in an attempt to describe, to inform, to persuade, to move, to motivate to action, or to affirm. We speak of moving speeches, persuasive speeches, informative speeches. Normally the speech contains within itself a core idea, attitude, and tone, all of which contribute toward the purpose. Thus a eulogy, a speech praising the life and accomplishments of an individual, contains an emphasis on the character of the deceased—his strength of will, his moral influence over others, his dedication to purpose—whereas an informative speech is addressed to transmitting information, informing an audience of matters they have not previously known or considered; many political speeches appear in the guise of information, whereas in truth they are persuasive speeches, representing the speaker's efforts to solicit support on a political issue. As a writer of speeches you must determine your purposes early in the preparation of a speech.

The subject of a speech may be anything—the advantages of an education in a particular discipline, the need for political activism, the desirability of a planned reading program—the what, why, how, when, which, and how many questions of everyday life. Listen to a child's questions and you have the subjects of more speeches than you can prepare and deliver in a lifetime: what did Leonardo da Vinci do? why is the sky blue? how do you decide what, when, how, which, and how many? Effective speeches emerge from personal conviction, sincerity, sound information, and courtesy, all bound together within a rational framework. Discriminating audiences quickly detect false from genuine emotions, accurate or inaccurate information, the insincere from the sincere, the courteous from the discourteous. And more significantly, they analyze what they hear, and sift out carefully supported rational thought from oversimplifications, hasty generalizations, false assumptions, biases, prejudices, propaganda, the whole host of logical fallacies that ineffectual speech-makers utilize. A speech is another form of man reasoning with man; its success must be determined ultimately within this context.

When we view the whole of informal speeches—such as forms of argument, exposition, description, and narration—we recognize that any list of characteristics represents a potpourri rather than the characteristics of a single speech; the following characteristics emerge in different and varying juxtapositions among such speeches: an informal speech usually involves 1) an informal style, which includes an informal or colloquial vocabulary, a personal point of view, a loose organization, and some use of popular rhetoric; 2) occasional digressions; 3) much use of personality; 4) some humor on occasion; 5) the use of anecdotes for illustrative purposes; 6) the idiom of the audience as a vehicle for better understanding, such as the celebrated "quarterbacks of life" figure used at businessmen luncheons; 7) simple sentence structure, present tense, parallel structure of ideas, and memorable statements.

One word of caution. A sermon may be a speech but a speech is not a sermon; you should devote your major attention to what you wish to say to what audience for what purpose. Therein lies your speech.

HALLMARKS OF AN EDUCATED MAN

Thomas Vernor Smith

The New York Library Association, which has been in existence more than a half hundred years, has been holding its annual meeting in Syracuse this week end. At one session this was the topic proposed: "What Are the Hallmarks of an Educated Man?" Now that is a query which interests me profoundly. Hardly more to honor the presence of the librarians among us than to amuse myself, especially at this season when so many colleges graduate so many men and women, I want to try my hand at that question, spreading in my own manner "the mantle of imagination" over the general subject of education.

But first let me express my appreciation of the fact that these book custodians of New York State do not beg the question of their own role. Librarians naturally think well of books. Otherwise they would hardly be spending their lives in libraries. They remind us, however, by the very form of the question, that it is not wise for any professionals to assume that they are the people and that wisdom will die with them and their doings.

As a matter of fact, books are not indispensable, though they are most helpful, in getting an education. Only bookworms can live on books alone, and they but leanly. Books are so important, however, for both use and pleasure, that I propose to celebrate on this program how books give us *information*, how they furnish us *inspiration*, and how they even provide us with *sublimation*.

For the present occasion, however, and in the mood set by the librarians' modesty, I welcome the leeway they offer to have my say about the essentials of education, forgetting its superficials. Knowing that to be even book-wise a man must not be bookish, I agree with these sage lines from Wordsworth:

> . . . convinced at heart
> How little those formalities, to which
> With overweening trust alone we give
> The name of Education, have to do
> With real feeling and just sense . . . .

Since, that is to say, we cannot encourage high school or even college graduates to wear their class colors to work or expect them to carry their diplomas in their hands, we might make a mistake and treat as plumb educated those who aren't at all. As a disappointed Kentucky mountaineer complained to the president of Berea College, "I sent my daughters here to be educated, but after graduation they came home and married—just like any common gals!" The only reassurance we can give, to either men or women students, is this: *Education is as education thinks and does.* By their fruits you shall know them, for better or for worse.

And what are these fruits? Prefacing my analysis with a wise lesson my poetic colleague, A. E. Johnson, gave me more than twenty years ago, that "education is the creation of finer human hungers," I mention six hallmarks, but I'll settle for less. Whoever has one is good, all is perfect, half is better than is wise to hope. My six hallmarks are these: *Curiosity, Imagination, Efficiency, Piety, Humor, Self-sufficiency.*

Curiosity is necessary, because without it man is not man but clodhopper. To prick up one's ears at every sound, to smack one's lips once at least over every new taste, to lift an eager relish to the wealth of the world about us, this is to be educable—and indeed is to have education-in-process. "I won't taste the spinach," said the recalcitrant child; "for if I tasted it, I might like it—and I tell you I hate the green stuff!"

Imagination must be added at once. Curiosity is odious without taste.

Imagination, you see, is curiosity grown up. We all know people, some-times college people, I fear, who poke their noses into everything, asking indelicate questions about the most delicate matters. Thomas Carlyle said of Mrs. John Stuart Mill—I know not how justly—that "She was a woman full of unwise intellect, always asking questions about all sorts of puzzles—why, how, what for, what makes the exact difference. . . ." Woodrow Wil-son told a story which illustrates the proper punishment for such undisci-plined questioning. "How did you lose your leg?" asked a frontier newcomer of a man in a caravan in which he was to ride for three days. "I'll tell you," replied he of the one leg, "provided you ask no further question about my missing leg: it was *bitten off!*" *Bitten off?* And three full days to go! No; curiosity, while indispensable, is not sufficient for education. Imagination is both necessary and in itself sufficient. For imagination is curiosity under control, self-rewarding in its own radiance.

Efficiency is important, on another but an honorable level. Not even the most educated can merely be; he too must do. And if one must act in order to live well, indeed in order to live at all, then he should act well. The man who is good, but good for nothing, is not genuinely educated, though he may wear a Phi Beta Kappa key. To do something, to do some-thing well, to do something better than anybody else can do it, in short, to be efficient is indispensable for outer use or inner happiness, and so is an-other hallmark of the educated man.

Piety is also a high virtue, though today of low repute. It really has nothing to do with religiosity or sanctimoniousness. Piety, in the good old Latin sense—*pietas*—means reverence, for the individuality of the part and for the integrity of the whole.

There is no part of nature or of human society which is not won-drously joined to the whole. Even the evils of life are not to be despised, though they must be diminished. Abraham Lincoln, who never saw a col-lege, or held any elementary certificate either, was educated. He had piety. So he could say, "What I deal with is too vast for malice." So he could say, even of the worst evil of his time, "Wrong as we think slavery is, we can yet afford to let it alone where it is, because that much is due to the necessity arising from its actual presence in the nation." Piety marks, rau-cousness disgraces, the man who would pass as educated.

Humor is the emotional accompaniment of the intellectual quality called imagination. It relieves the heart as imagination extends the mind. To laugh at the errors of our enemies is easy—and useful; for it may pre-vent our murdering them. To chuckle at our own *faux pas* is less easy—but not less valuable; it may prevent gastric ulcers, or save us the wear and tear —and, wow, the expense!—of psychoanalysis. To smile, however wistfully, at the conflicts good men have with good men *because* both are good, and even to squeeze a wry smile at the ambivalence of the highest ideals them-selves, this is very, very hard but very, very necessary if we are to save faith from the foolishness of fanaticism. As Paul Laurence Dunbar writes:

There is a heaven, forever, day by day,
The upward yearning of my soul doth tell me so.
There is a hell, I'm quite as sure; for pray,
If there were not, where would my neighbors go?

Self-sufficiency is the final mark of education. It climaxes humor; for "Only he who tickles himself may laugh as he likes." Whoever calls upon himself and finds somebody at home, is an educated man. If he finds nobody at home to him, then let him become a "joiner" and seek for his soul in the place where, alas, only deformed souls grow, in the hubbub of the crowds. Souls grow in solitude. The educated man must know where to find what he wants. There is no substitute for a soul, nor any satisfaction which compares with its self-sufficiency.

Alone I hail the contented hour
    With but myself and me;
For nought is sad, nought is dour
    When we're the company.

All silent thoughts get spoken
    When three as one agree;
And inner light remains unbroken—
    Once myself and I meet me.

Show me one of these six hallmarks, just one of either curiosity, imagination, efficiency, piety, humor, or best of all self-sufficiency; and I'll salute you as a comrade on the quest. Dazzle me with all these qualities, and I'll revere you as a hero. Exhibit three of them, any three; and I'll love you like an educated man, and take you to my bosom as a friend. I'll not ask how many books you've written, nor care how many or how few you've read. Nor will I look for your hood, or quiz you about your diploma: whence or whether. Only this I'll ask of you, if you be a self-made man: that you do not daily adore your "maker"—or ever disdain those of us who were quickened in college and yet love to visit libraries to revive ourselves on the pabulum of print.

QUESTIONS

1. In the opening paragraph Smith states his pupose: "to try my hand at that question ['What Are the Hallmarks of an Educated Man?'], spreading in my own manner 'the mantle of imagination' over the general subject of education." What are the advantages of posing a question as the central purpose of an informal speech? State your purpose, for a forthcoming speech, in question form and prepare a sentence outline of the main supporting points you wish to present and develop.

2. Sincerity, belief, conviction are essential to effective informal speeches. Smith expresses this idea when he observes, "Whoever calls

upon himself and finds somebody at home, is an educated man." The degree or intensity of your conviction will permeate every part of your speech, bringing vitality and force and significance to ideas and experiences you include in your remarks. Prepare a first draft of the outline developed above, paying special attention to the way in which you say what you wish to say. For example, Smith draws from his broad cultural background his references to Wordsworth, Carlyle, Lincoln, Dunbar, and from his wide range of experiences, which include the story told by the president of Berea College, the comment made by A. E. Johnson, the story of the recalcitrant child, Woodrow Wilson's story about the undisciplined questioner.

3. Smith could have provided commonplace definitions of the six hallmarks he wished to suggest to his audience; instead he chose to illustrate many of his thoughts and feelings through examples, reminiscences, and quotations. Prepare a second draft of your informal speech in which you attempt to "humanize" your subject, to make it relevant to the everyday life of the members of the audience. What effects result from "humanizing" the subject?

4. What specific details of Smith's talk support the view that he adopted an informal tone toward his audience? Make a list of some of these details. What is the "tone" of your second draft? Rewrite this second draft; attempt to project a "tone" to your audience.

5. Does Smith's informal speech itself support the view that he himself has the "hallmarks" of an educated man? Prepare a brief speech in which you address yourself to this question.

REMARKS TO THE PEACE PANEL

Lyndon B. Johnson

I am delighted to have a chance to meet briefly with you gentlemen and to thank you for undertaking to serve as members of a panel of private citizens to work with us in the quest for peace. You gentlemen symbolize a tradition which goes back for a quarter of a century—the tradition of nonpartisan service on matters of war and peace. I see Democrats who have served in Republican Administrations, Republicans who have served with Democratic Administrations, and a number of men who have held office under both parties. And these party affiliations really don't matter very much compared to the common concern and the great operating principles

Reprinted by permission of Lyndon B. Johnson, from *The President Speaks to The People*.

of our American foreign policy. There are four of these principles, and you gentlemen have worked for all four of them.

The *first* is that the United States must be strong in her arms and strong in her will. When I look at General Bradley and Dr. Kistiakowsky and Mr. Dulles, when I think of Mr. Lovett, who can't be with us today, I am looking at men who played a great role in building the strength we now have. We have kept on in this same tradition in the last four years, and we believe the balanced strength of the United States has never been greater than it is today.

But there is always work to be done to keep our defenses strong and up to date, and we look forward to the advice and counsel which you gentlemen will bring in coming discussions of defense planning for the future.

Second, the United States yields to no one in her loyalty to friends and allies. With us today we have Mr. Acheson, Mr. McCloy, and Mr. Hoffman, architects of the recovery of Europe and the Atlantic Alliance. Western Europe has never been more secure, and the future of Atlantic freedom never more bright than it is today. The leaders of that continent rightly seek a growing role in the common cause of freedom. The differences and difficulties which lie ahead of us are the product of success, not failure. As we go on in this great work, our friends in Europe will be encouraged in the knowledge that we shall have advice like yours to guide us.

I am particularly glad to have the help of such men as Mr. Acheson and Mr. McCloy as our minds turn to the future of central Europe, and as we renew our determination to work for the freedom and reunion of the people of divided Germany. One of the great achievements of the last generation is that we have built mutual trust between democratic Germany and the United States, while never forgetting the proper interests of other allies or even the legitimate concerns of adversaries. In that tradition we shall continue, with your help.

And we shall show equal good faith to other friends and allies in other continents as well. Today this determination finds its hardest test in the difficult and demanding task of helping a young nation to grow and defend itself against Communist terror and domestic disorder—the Republic of Vietnam.

We are not discouraged by difficulty, nor will we let ourselves be deflected by partisan critics. In Vietnam today, the best of Americans, from private to Ambassador, are making their sacrifice in this hard cause on the spot. They too will be encouraged to know that the Government in Washington can call on men like you for help and counsel as this ten-year-long commitment of three administrations is continued.

Third, the United States has been not merely the strongest of all nations, and the most reliable of allies, but the leader in proving that we accept the responsibilities of the rich and strong. In the Marshall Plan, which Mr. Hoffman ran, and the World Bank, where Mr. Black and Mr.

McCloy achieved so much, and later still in the Alliance for Progress, where Mr. Moscoso will always be remembered, we have been willing and ready to help free men to help themselves.

And I agree with what General Eisenhower used to say year after year —that these programs are a great bargain for our own national security. Year after year, as the Democratic Majority Leader, I worked to support the Republican President in defending these programs, which have no constituency of their own. The freedom of Europe, the great hopes of India and Pakistan, the new glow of confidence in South America, are the product of this national, bipartisan effort.

Fourth, and finally, the policy of the United States is not simply peace through strength, but peace through positive, persistent, active effort.

For twenty years, in five administrations we have been first in our support for the United Nations—and many of you like Mr. Cowles, Mr. Leibman, Mr. Larson and Mr. Wadsworth, have been among its most determined friends.

For twenty years, in the age of the atom, we have been first in the search for effective disarmament. Mr. Acheson, Mr. Dean and Mr. McCloy have played great roles in that continuing effort.

For twenty years, in crisis after crisis, we have sought the way of reason and restraint. No great power in all history has a better record of respect for the rights of others.

So we are strong in our defenses, loyal in our alliances, responsive to the needs of others, and passionate in the positive search for peace. This is the kind of people we are—this is the kind of service you have given. This is the foreign policy which will continue, with your help, in the years ahead.

QUESTIONS

1. Many individuals are especially self-conscious when they use the "I" point of view; yet an informal speech implies, whether stated or unstated, the point of view of the speaker. In "Remarks to the Peace Panel," President Johnson begins by expressing personal appreciation to the individuals who will serve on the Peace Panel. And throughout his speech he makes clear that he is speaking personally and on behalf of the citizens of the United States. Prepare a draft of a sentence outline of an informal speech in which you speak from the "I" point of view. The emphasis throughout this first draft is on what you think, believe, and understand.

2. President Johnson uses the colloquial vocabulary, the words and phrases of conversation: "party affiliations really don't matter very much," "Mr. Lovett, who can't be with us today," and such. A close examination of the opening paragraph will show that all of the dic-

tional choices with perhaps the exceptions of "nonpartisan" and "affiliations," are words used in daily conversation. Prepare a second draft of your outline, in which you attempt to use the language of daily conversation, your daily conversation.

3. In his "remarks" the President presents four basic principles of American foreign policy. These principles or ideas are given equal weight; they represent a parallel structure of ideas. In your sentence outline you may wish to use an enumeration organization, going from the most important idea to the least, or you may wish to use the parallel structure described above. Prepare a third draft of your outline in which you select a specific organization for specific reasons.

4. An informal speech is addressed to a particular audience. The President acknowledges the presence of General Bradley, Dr. Kistiakowsky, Mr. Dulles, and the absence of Mr. Lovett. He knows the members of his audience. Prepare a fourth draft of your outline in which you include specific detail indicative of your knowledge of the members of your audience, which may be composed of your classmates, members of a club, or a social group.

5. Write an informal speech, based on the previously prepared outlines and drafts. Test the significance of your speech in terms of its suitability to the audience.

CONTROVERSIAL SPEAKERS ON CAMPUS?

Alexander Heard

The role of universities in their communities is a topic of great current concern everywhere in the world. I returned ten days ago from a meeting of the International Association of Universities in Tokyo. This is an organization formed in 1950 that meets every five years and to which this year went delegates of some three hundred universities from all over the world. Most of the principal institutions in the United States were represented, and there were a fair number from behind the Iron Curtain. The importance attached to the meeting by the host country, Japan, was symbolized by the opening session, which was addressed by the Crown Prince, the Prime Minister, and the Minister of Education, and by the unusual gesture of a reception given for the delegates in the Imperial Palace by the Emperor and Empress.

Japan has the fastest growing economy of any major nation, and it knows the significance to its economy and to its general development of

Reprinted by permission of Alexander Heard, from the *Vanderbilt Alumnus,* Vol. 51, No. 2 (September–October 1965).

education, education that culminates in university education. Speaker after speaker, from emerging nation and advanced nation, reflected the view held in his country that the university is the mother, father, sister and brother (as one speaker said) of his country's hopes.

This urgency regarding higher education was reflected in the three topics discussed at the Conference—an agenda arranged by an executive council of persons from all continents.

I think you will be interested in these three topics.

One concerned "access to higher education"—that is, the need of nations to make available to young people of college age the appropriate types of higher education to meet their personal aspirations and to meet the needs of the nation. "How to get into college" is the way the matt r often shapes up in our country. Many nations are faced with deciding what kinds of colleges and universities to build, what courses of study to introduce so that students will be fitted when they finish for the careers that will be open to them.

The second topic dealt with the role of higher education in the social, economic, and cultural development of societies. All around the world it is known that universities are critically significant not only in increasing the gross national product, but also in increasing the richness of individual living, in helping individuals to retain their individuality, and in helping them to grow within themselves to fuller and more meaningful personal lives.

The two topics I have mentioned are intimately related to each other —access to higher education and the role of higher education in national development—and the third topic of the conference is related to them both. This third topic concerned the "autonomy" of universities. Universities have an importance nowadays they have not had before. They require large monies to accomplish their tasks. In the face of these new conditions, can they maintain the independence they need in order to perform fully and well their functions as universities? The comments on this topic by delegates from the Communist countries were, as you can imagine, interesting. They blandly claimed that in their countries universities have no problems of autonomy. These assertions contrasted with uninhibited statements from some other places that acknowledged various kinds of challenges to university autonomy by state, or church, or powerful economic and political interests.

After the discussion of these topics, the Conference adopted a concluding statement that said, in part ". . . situations are continuously changing and . . . the real value and guarantee of university autonomy is to be found not in written statements or in administrative arrangements, but in a public opinion convinced that universities can best serve the community if given the freedom to make their own decisions."

In the United States we in higher education—and here I would like to include trustees, faculty, students, alumni—are steadily concerned that there be sympathetic understanding of why universities conduct their affairs as they do. Universities need the confidence of the communities they serve (which are usually also the communities that in significant part support them). For this reason I wish to say something about visitors to American campuses, particularly the Vanderbilt campus, and about the freedom of speech accorded to them.

I know from my mail box that with a few persons, at least, this is a matter of deep worry.

Two years ago, with the help of friends of Vanderbilt, we obtained an acceptance by the President of the United States of an invitation to speak on our campus. We were proud of this achievement, which you can be sure was envied by other institutions across the country. The President does not visit many campuses during a year. But not everyone was pleased. Came a letter from a Vanderbilt alumnus of 1945:

> "I heartily disapprove of commemorating this anniversary of Vanderbilt's founding with a blatant political maneuver. Mr. Kennedy has no interest in Vanderbilt, and I am extremely disappointed that you would allow him to use this anniversary of ours as an opportunity to try to gain approval of the present administration in Washington."

I may say that after the President's appearance I received communications from persons of all political persuasions applauding the day and the address delivered by the President.

My correspondence about campus speakers comes from many points of the political compass. Last year, after it was announced that former President Eisenhower had accepted an invitation to appear on the campus as one of several speakers on the student-conducted program called "Impact"—a commitment I regret he was later required to cancel—I received a letter from an alumnus of 1925, again obviously sincere, protesting the appearance of partisans on the campus:

> "I am quite surprised at the speakers listed . . . it would be difficult to find more biased Republican partisans than Mr. Eisenhower and Senator [Thurston] Morton . . . I think if this study is to be more than mere propaganda for certain philosophies the panel should include men of national reputation for unbiased opinions . . ."

With respect to another speaker on the "Impact" program—a program representing many points of view and a carefully selected schedule of speakers—I had a protest from an alumnus who holds two degrees from Vanderbilt, the first awarded in 1932:

> "I have decided that I cannot make a contribution this year [to the Living Endowment], on the basis of my disagreeing with the fact that Governor George Wallace has been invited to appear as a speaker. I

can ascribe to the fact that students must hear every side of an issue, but in the case of Governor Wallace, on any campus, it must only make him feel that he has an audience to which he can stir up hate and intolerance."

We had other protests about speakers during the year. One of these, Carl Braden, brought several letters.

As I read the history of American higher education, it was ever thus, and certainly I know from my colleagues in other leading universities that they receive queries and complaints about speakers as a regular part of the year's business.

If you look back across the history of Vanderbilt you find the indications that this is nothing new. Professor Edwin Mims reported in his *History of Vanderbilt* an episode which I fully appreciate, because some of my people lived in Georgia on the line marched by General William Tecumseh Sherman from Atlanta to the sea. Chancellor Garland, Vanderbilt's first Chancellor, created a turmoil when he announced that John Sherman, brother of General William Sherman, would address Vanderbilt students in chapel one afternoon. This was close to The War, and daring indeed. Law students held a meeting of protest and others joined and trooped single file out of the building with student John Bell Keeble in the lead and two future members of the Board of Trust close behind, all playing "Dixie" on their mouth organs.

The anxieties that are felt by public-spirited individuals loyal to their alma mater seem to me to stem from three main sources.

One is the feeling that when a college or university allows a visitor to speak on its campus it is putting its arm around him, dignifying him, and endorsing what he has to say.

Second is the dislike of giving a partisan speaker—usually nowadays, but not always, an advocate of a political viewpoint—a forum in which he can propagandize and spread his doctrine.

Thirdly, anxieties often stem, I suspect, from a lack of understanding of how universities must go about their business if they are to perform their classical functions of discovering, transmitting, and applying knowledge.

Let us look at the first of these three causes of concern. When a university acts formally through its chief executive officer to invite a commencement speaker, or baccalaureate preacher, or visitor on some similar ceremonial occasion, it naturally seeks to select someone whose message it will consider appropriate in style and substance to the occasion. Such occasions often *do* "honor" the invited person, and the institution may in the public mind be credited with some responsibility for what he says, even though in actuality it cannot influence what he says.

There is no ambiguity, however, about the relationship of the institution to other speakers on its campus. It is the business of a university to maintain an open forum. In an open forum, if it is an effective one, conflicting points of view will inevitably be expressed. The institution does not endorse the statements of those who speak in its forum. What they say can in no sense be construed as the views of "the university" simply because they were expressed in a university forum. The forum is official, not the views expressed in it, just as on our campus *The Hustler* may be the official student newspaper, while the views of its editors are not the official campus opinion.

Last year 384 public appearances were made by visiting speakers to the Vanderbilt campus. Many obviously contradicted others and no single person in the University, including the Chancellor, could possibly agree with all of them, even if he knew what they all said.

Think of the campus platform in the same terms as the library. No one to my knowledge has claimed that Vanderbilt dignifies and endorses the views expressed in the books it works so hard to acquire. We have books by every conceivable social protagonist, well written books and poorly written books, some impeccably sound and presumably some less perfect in their composition. We have books by Machiavelli and Thomas Aquinas, by Adam Smith and Karl Marx, by Winston Churchill and Adolf Hitler. These books are the materials with which faculty and students in a university work in studying the society of which they are a part, in teaching about that society, and applying knowledge for the benefit of society. And, so likewise, speakers who come to the campus are part of the University's traditional resources for study and evaluation.

The fear that misinformation, and ideas that a person considers undesirable, may be spread by visiting speakers is surely an understandable one. These are hazards of the educational process wherever it may be found, and especially these are hazards in an educational process dedicated to producing persons who will think independently and creatively. Partisan advocates do have a chance to spread their message. (I might point out that there are many more partisan advocates of particular scholarly doctrines of little interest to the general public, but of great interest and controversy within a university, than there are political partisans who attract outside attention). Some speakers are invited, in fact, so that their message can be heard. But, as someone has said, there is no use trying to make ideas safe for students; you have to make the students safe for ideas. You have to develop within them their own powers of criticism and evaluation.

Young people, and especially young people in college, cannot be shielded from the winds of opinion in our world. There are books in every university library that carry views as daring as any visitor is likely to utter on our campus. As some of you know, Vanderbilt has received an award from the Freedoms Foundation at Valley Forge "for outstanding achievement in bringing about a better understanding of the American way of life." The award recognizes the effective work done by Vanderbilt's summer Institute on the Nature of Communism and Constitutional Democracy, a program that brings to the campus high school teachers from all over the country to learn about the nature of American democracy and Communism, the way they work, and how to guide high school students in their study. The students in this institute are required to read not only books that interpret the American system and examine Communism critically, and that oppose Communist doctrine, but they are required also to read certain writings by Communist authors as part of the educational program.

You may have noticed what the press reported last spring when a visitor was prohibited from speaking on the Ohio State University campus. He was the Director of the American Institute for Marxist Studies in New York. He did not speak, but he appeared silently on the stage while students read aloud from his books which they had checked out of the university library.

Last spring, one of the speakers at Vanderbilt that attracted off-campus attention was a person named Weissman, who had participated in the disturbances at the University of California at Berkeley earlier in the year. Despite considerable advance publicity, few students turned out to hear him. Those who did not go, however, have had ample opportunity to learn his ideas from the extensive coverage given by the press then and since to Mr. Weissman's appearance at Vanderbilt and elsewhere. Students eventually graduate and then they cannot be protected by their university from partisan debate. The university's obligation is not to protect students from ideas, but rather to expose them to ideas, and to help make them capable of handling, and hopefully having, ideas.

This leads me to the third matter, the nature of a university, and of a university education.

The university—meaning universities as a type of social institution in the United States—is the principal instrument through which our society examines itself. It is the business of universities to provide the setting and the means by which man studies himself and his environment. This is the search for truth. Inevitably, in such a process, tentative conclusions and firm conclusions will be reached by scholars and students that criticize our society, as well as applaud it. The universities are one of the great sources of innovation in our society—social innovation as well as scientific and technological innovation. It is inescapable that controversial opinions as well as opinions that are broadly acceptable will emerge from this environment.

In the principles that we follow in these matters, we are following, insofar as I can determine, the basic policies that Vanderbilt has always followed. We are also guided by the same principles that guide the great universities of our nation—some of us who are responsible for these universities keep in rather steady touch with each other on these matters, I may say.

I was interested in seeing the other day a statement by John S. Dickey, the President of Dartmouth College, speaking against legislation proposed in New Hampshire that would have restricted freedom of speech on the campuses of state-supported institutions in that state. It seemed to me that Mr. Dickey at one point spoke to the natural question that arises in the minds of all of us: Why can't you let almost everybody speak, but eliminate the obviously offensive fringe speakers who have no really constructive purpose? President Dickey said, and I would say with him:

". . . Undoubtedly a few speakers come or are brought to our campuses primarily as a form of defiance or to raise trouble rather than for enlightenment, but whether this be annoying or just amusing immaturity, it is still infinitely better than to permit these elements on the campus to poison the climate for everybody by giving them a freedom of speech grievance. I personally don't care for the reasons some people are brought to speak, but I should dislike a lot more the reasons behind a policy of prohibition. And as for the consequences of the two courses, on any count the prohibition policy is all but certain to be both more painful and more harmful. . . . The campus has ways of working its own cures for this kind of trouble if it is not distracted by what looks like an over-riding challenge to its fundamental principles."

QUESTIONS

1. In his speech given to the Nashville Area Junior Chamber of Commerce, Chancellor Heard of Vanderbilt University introduces his subject for the occasion through his observations concerning three issues facing those who are guiding the institutions of higher learning throughout the world: "access to higher education," "the role of higher education in national development," and the "autonomy" of the university. Chancellor Heard asks that communities understand that one part of the university's "autonomy" lies in the "open forum" held continuously on the campus. Summarize the principal arguments Heard offers in support of the concept of a university as an "open forum."

2. Clarity of thought and relationships between and among ideas depend in part upon a clear organization. Outline Heard's speech.

3. John Henry Newman, Victorian Roman Catholic cardinal, writer, and lecturer, defines a university as "a place where universal knowledge is taught." Are visiting speakers and lecturers, both controversial and noncontroversial, public and private, professional and unprofessional, a necessary part of a university? Write an informal speech, for delivery to the leaders of the student government organization or to

the faculty of your university, in which you answer the question posed.
4.   What value lies in the technique of quoting directly rather than paraphrasing? Heard quotes from alumni letters protesting the fact that invitations were extended to President Eisenhower, President Kennedy, and Governor Wallace. Are the quotations effective? Why?
5.   Prepare a speech on an issue involving student participation in university government in which you attempt to persuade the faculty, administration, alumni, and the public of the greater need for self-determination. Anticipate objections and counterarguments by considering them in your speech.

IX

Formal Speech

A formal speech, broadly defined, involves a serious subject treated in a serious way and delivered to a concerned or interested audience. The essential differences between informal and formal speeches appear in the degree of difference of treatment, rather than in strict forms. A commencement address, for example, though it may touch on light subjects, is usually a serious statement concerning the contemporary state of local, national, and world affairs; professional addresses before professional audiences, on such subjects as heart transplants, psychedelic drugs, the significance of a life in public service, an examination of particular contemporary political and social problems, the implications of decisions concerning civil disobedience, the functions of the judicial system in American government, or the importance of a campus newspaper as a molder of student opinion—these and like subjects appear repeatedly in formal speeches.

Moreover, since a formal speech is more influential and is given more widespread public distribution, the speech is devoted oftentimes to timeless as well as timely subjects. At its core the formal speech is a reasoned statement, based on thought and experience, a statement addressed to the intellectual capacities of the local and general audience.

Its characteristics include the following: 1) the thought is more complex, better documented, more analytical than that of the informal speech; 2) the structure of the speech is more complicated and more tightly organized; 3) the speech involves the assumption that the audience is capable of grappling with the subject on an intellectual and experiential basis; thus emotional appeals and rhetorical dissimulations are reduced to a minimum; 4) contrasting ideas are frequently juxtaposed; 5) the point of view is generally personal, but the impersonal point of view is also widespread in the treatment of public subjects. Other characteristics include few or no personal references or illustrations or allusions, little or no humor, few emotionally loaded dictional choices, few if any digressions, more complicated sentence structure, and tense structure based on the present tense. One other characteristic involves the use of memorable phrases and statements; a glance at prominent names in American history will ordinarily invoke memorable statements: Patrick Henry's "Give me liberty or give me death," Abraham Lincoln's "Government of the people, by the people, for the people," Franklin Roosevelt's "All we have to fear is fear itself," John F.

Kennedy's "Ask not what your country can do for you but what you can do for your country."

Herbert Read, in *English Prose Style*, commented: "Those who would persuade us of the truth of a statement must rely, not on an air of conviction or a show of reason, but on the compelling force of an emotional attitude." In the formal speech this attitude, your attitude, must be sincere. From this sincerity your thought and your speech emerge.

IT'S THE IDEA OF THE THING:
THE SEARCH FOR TRUTH

Louis William Norris

One hundred and ninety years ago the Declaration of Independence was enunciated and Phi Beta Kappa was founded. While the nation was proclaiming the inborn rights to life, liberty, and the pursuit of happiness, Phi Beta Kappa was proclaiming, as it were, that these rights must be accompanied and safeguarded by scholarly thought. Subjects discussed at the earliest meetings of the Society at William and Mary reflect this conviction.

In 1837, one hundred twenty-nine years ago, Emerson declared in his Phi Beta Kappa address at Harvard, among other things, the independence of the American Scholar from European thought. We in America had, he announced, "listened too long to the courtly muses of Europe." To some degree the venture Emerson proclaimed remains still to be fully shared.

Let me in 1966 call for a declaration of independence from the commonwealth of new dogmas seeking sovereignty since World War II. First, there is the dogma that the explosion of knowledge baptizes specialized learning with an ultimate holiness. A second dogma is the belief that American democracy can only be guided by appeal to the drives, habits, and conditioned reflexes of its people—by art and not by logic. Third, it is a dogma today that only knowledge of present existence is reliable, and honesty requires disillusionment with every other age. Fourth, there remains with renewed vigor the dogma that scientific fact contains the full ingredients of Utopia, the materials of Walden II, III, or IV.

II

A dogma is a hasty, insupportable opinion. It's chief enemy is reflective thought, the crucial ingredient of which is ideas. If we are able to gain independence of dogma, ideas must be our liberators.

Reprinted by permission of *Vital Speeches of the Day*, Volume 33, Number 15.

Socrates saved civilization from Protagoras' belief that "man is the measure of all things," i.e. the belief that each man's judgment is as good as another's, by an appeal to ideas. This task must be performed in every generation, if dogma and resulting confusion are not to rule over us. When Antisthenes objected to Plato that he could "see a horse but not horse-ness," i.e. the idea "horse," Plato replied, "That is because you have eyes but no intelligence." [1] This generation has traveled more and used its eyes to see more than any before it. Its need is to use its intelligence for a rigorous pursuit of ideas. "The future will not be lost or won by arms . . . but by ideas." [2]

Thought proceeds to order the welter of human experience by its use of terms, units of perception, concepts of given flakes of awareness, or, in other words, by the forming power of ideas. Much of man's irrationality is due to his failure to realize reason's powers. These powers rest in the tools of thought, namely ideas.

Ideas are, at the least, forms, patterns, classes, purviews of consciousness for dealing with some other phase of man's experience of himself or his environment. They arise as man departs from the animal level and develops the power for abstraction, for illustration of a type, for comparison and distinction among features of his environment. They express the capacity to generalize from past experience, and to predict meanings in future experience.

Sounds come to represent the same experiences as words come to represent ideas. An old and familiar sound may come to assume new references. The term "cosmos" first represented a woman's headdress, then trappings of a horse's harness, the decorative cover of animals, the order or class of all in the army who had that decorative cover, and eventually the order of the world. "Ersatz," a relatively new word in occidental usage, came from a verb "to place before" something. The idea of "substitution," "equivalence," "compensation" grew as what was "placed before" an object was broadened to include new illustrations of kinship. This cultural growth of ideas involves growth of the mental pattern the idea embodies, as well as growth in the linguistic form for its overt expression.

An idea is in some sense also an ideal, for it is taken in thought as the "best" identification of its referent that can be found. It is the scheme of articulation that arises as consciousness tries to deal with its environment. If the idea falters as an adequate means for the operation at hand, it is revised or rejected. It carries its own claim to adequacy of identification and expression. This is the truth in Plato's assertion that an idea ultimately is a "perfect" form in which particulars "participate," however partially.[3]

Ideas vary in degree of generality. Some possess "high generality," e.g.

---

[1] Parmenides, 131.

[2] C. Scott Fletcher, "The Great Awakening." Fund for Adult Education, Bulletin, 1958, p. 19.

[3] Timaeus, 30 E; Phaedo, 100A.

"life," "good," "universe," "God," and others "secondary generality," e.g. "carbon," "captain," "slave." Ideas of limited generality have implications for those of high generality, and vice versa. To ignore these mutual implications brings intellectual and behavioral problems, even disaster. In the Mediterranean world people of such different outlooks as Pericles and Cleon, Plato and Alexander, Marius and Sulla, assumed that a civilized society could not function *without* slaves. Today world history is taking shape as the assumption that a civilized society can not operate *with* slaves gains recognition.[4] The involvement of "slave," an idea of "secondary generality," is changing in its "participation" in the "good," an idea of "high generality."

Culture in a given period may influence and even control ideas. On the contrary, ideas may shape an epoch, for "ideas have consequences," as Weaver has emphasized.[5] Democracy assumes that the free search for ideas has an alliance with truth, for ideas are held evidently to have the intrinsic claim of the best grasp of things we can get, as noted above. This "adventure of ideas" Whitehead held to be the clue to history.

Facility in the knowledge and use of ideas conceived in these terms will provide "weapons" [6] for dealing with dogmas that threaten.

III

The dogma that the explosion of knowledge means that true learning can only be highly specialized, and that it soon becomes outdated, has come to be widely held. Recently the McGraw-Hill Company sent a tear sheet carrying one of its advertisements, appearing in *Time, Harper's, Saturday Review,* and *Business Week,* to college administrators. "Knowledge can no longer be wrapped up and delivered," it said. "The only way to avoid obsolescence is to keep your thinking cap on . . . To decide on a life-long program of education . . . The moment that diploma is in your hands your education begins to lose its value under the impact of technological change." The obvious remedy indicated is to keep on buying McGraw-Hill books the rest of your life!

Other evidence for the explosion of knowledge is commonly offered. Some say the knowledge available at the time of Christ doubled by 1900, again by 1950, once more in 1960, and perhaps a fourth time by today. There are 100,000 journals now being printed by scientists alone. Ninety percent of all the scientists in history are still alive. An acquaintance work-

---

[4] A. N. Whitehead, *Adventures of Ideas.* New York: The Macmillan Company, 1933, pp. 13–14.
[5] Richard M. Weaver, *Ideas Have Consequences.* Chicago: The University of Chicago Press, 1948.
[6] cf. Max Lerner's use of the term "weapon" in a slightly different sense. *Ideas as Weapons.* New York: The Viking Press, 1939.

ing for a doctor's degree at Munich, concerning the Latin prefixes of German words, is just well-started as he has covered 64,000 words. His degree may be awarded posthumously! Recently a candidate interviewed for a position at Albion in psychology announced himself as an experimentalist. He, therefore, declined to answer questions put to him about Pavlov, James, Koehler, Rogers, Lewin. These supposed psychologists are in his opinion out-of-date, or in a field so remote from his that a valid judgment could not be expected from him.

This multiplication of "knowledge" so-called overwhelms the scholar only if knowledge is limited to fact. And this generation worships facts, as shown by the popularity of quiz programs, such as "College Bowl." The phrase, "It is a fact that . . ." is often equated with "It is true that . . ." "The facts speak for themselves" has supposedly settled many an argument. Computer research has become a part of every respectable business, and most Ph.D. dissertation programs. Such appeal to fact only ends when an awe-inspiring correlation, positive or negative, is found, or exhaustion proves that reasonable effort at an answer has been put forth.

Here emerges a throwback to the extreme nominalism of Roscellinus in the eleventh century. According to him only particular things are real. But classes, groupings, properties, relations are tools for ordering the mass of facts modern research unearths. If these ideas cannot enable significance of facts to arise, samples of facts to represent similar facts, predictions from some facts to be made about others, rationality collapses and science itself is a hoax. Unrelated details are trivial. But when they are related to others and participate in some *kind* of something, they gain importance. This importance comes from the role of ideas in the mind's grasp of fact.

"Vertical" learning must be added in this generation to "horizontal" learning, to use a distinction emphasized by Margaret Mead.[7] Horizontal learning consists of the factual information that goes out of date, and creates a market for McGraw-Hill. But vertical learning magnetizes the fragments resulting from the explosion of knowledge about a manageable number of ideas. These ideas refer, let it be noted, to the same universe thought has always confronted. The particles have multiplied, but have the ideas they embody increased?

Specialized knowledge has its uses, to be sure. But even these depend for their import on the ideas they express. The meaningful collaboration of specialists requires a bridge of ideas relating their specialties. Armed with articulate ideas, the scholar may confront the world of exploding knowledge expecting clarification, not confusion, and discovery of new ideas for grappling with fact, where old ideas prove dim, narrow, or irrelevant.

Another dogma, namely the belief that American democracy can only

---

[7] "A Redefinition of Education." In C. Scott Fletcher, *Education for Public Responsibility*. New York: W. W. Norton & Company, 1961, pp. 52, 57.

be led by irrational and emotional appeals that dig into conditioned reflexes, ignores also the deserved role of ideas. This anti-intellectualism, capitalized on so often by advertisers, politicians, churchmen, artists, and parents, holds that ideas are weak and secondary to appetites, passions, prejudices and habits.[8] Darwin was the root of this persuasion. Though he recognized that man with a mind was favored in survival, it was not his intellectual powers that enabled him to survive. Freud has impressed upon us
that a large proportion of human actions are due to an automatic response
to unconscious needs. Recent behaviorism, led by B. F. Skinner, holds that
conditioning is the essence of learning and can result in an ideal society.

When the attraction of civil disobedience is considered, the popularity
of "Gunsmoke" and "Bonanza" is reviewed, and the relative ease with
which a movie star can be elected a governor, the formidable character of
this dogma can be appreciated. Lerner may be right in saying that "the rational right-thinking man has as surely ceased to be regarded the center of
our intellectual system as the earth has ceased to be regarded as the center
of our planetary system." [9]

This naturalistic view of ideas, namely the belief that they "take on
meaning" only as the pattern of a struggle for an intuited end, confuses
the use with meaning of ideas. The use or value of an idea can be understood, and the idea leading to an end can be chosen, only if an idea serves
as the matrix or form of thought. It is the tool with which thought grasps
the problem of action. Man has subliminal, irrational, habit-shaped interests, as Plato and any adequate scholar has always recognized. But the control of these sub-rational elements in experience has been the task of learning from man's arrival on earth. His cultural progress has come more from
rational creation than emotional fluttering. It was the threat to civilization
which the Nazi mystique represented which led to its own destruction.

Ideas can arouse emotions, as does the idea "flag" to a soldier, "truth"
to a research agent, or "home at Christmas" to nearly anyone. But emotions are not understood by reference to other emotions. They are understood by reference to their intensity and the ends they seek. They gain import through the ideas they contain, however definitely they may be con-
cealed. They remain transient, unstructured, contradictory, unless they are
brought into the form of ideas. Schopenhauer's master work, *The World
as Will and Idea*, serves as a paradigm that meaning arises only as the will
is objectified in ideas (Vorstellungen).

Can the anti-intellectual and irrational man escape the demand that
he give reasons for his life of unreason? If his only reason consists in the
fact that it is difficult to be rational and he feels lonely in the task, has he

---

[8] Crane Brinton, *Ideas and Men*. Englewood Cliffs, N. J.: Prentice-Hall, Inc., 1960,
pp. 513–525.
[9] Brinton, p. 5.

a right to be followed? Detractors of man's powers to use ideas must have stronger weapons than fatigue and loneliness. They only report the difficulty, not the impossibility, of man's becoming human.

A third dogma on the agenda, viz. that only knowledge of present existence is reliable, ignores the history of ideas, from which vicarious learning comes, and the metaphoric nature of ideas that derive meaning from sources beyond immediate experience.

Despair in the presence of history marks those who hold this point of view. Fascism, communism, liberal democracy have not brought peace and progress, despite the affluence of the most advanced nations. Knowledge of myth-formation undermines the formerly-held authenticity of the Bible, and for many God is as good as dead. Science makes traditional theology vain, but it cannot itself explain man's lot or deliver him from cruelty and unreason.

In such an alien, rootless world nothing remains sure except one's own existence and the power to make one's own destiny. Wisdom requires disillusionment about others, God, and human history. Self-reliance offers the only deliverance from oblivion. "Existence precedes essence," for Sartre. For Heidegger, the father of recent existentialism, facing "nothingness in anticipation of . . . extinction" with fortitude is the mark of each man's grandeur.

With this flavor in the air, the youth slogan "No one beyond thirty can be trusted" can be accounted for. Decline in the average age of marriage reflects a new premium on satisfactions of present existence. Much literature shows man alien to nature and preoccupied with the fragments or his own experience. James Joyce's *Ulysses* spins out the ramifications of images in his own stream of consciousness, because nothing else promises anything of importance to him. Abstract art has obtained vogue because traditional approaches to art have no meaning presumably. *The Stranger* of Camus becomes duplicated in the killers reported by Capote's *In Cold Blood*.

These existentialists [10] play fast and loose with the metaphoric nature of ideas in thinking.[11] Subjects thought of are "of a sort," a member of a class, an illustration of an idea. To rate present existence above other circumstances of history presumes a reliable comparison, a classification of successes and failures of states, families, and individuals including oneself. These signs of past times are taken as reliable in the act of comparison. But if one's despair derives from experiences *like* those of Kennedy in Dallas, Wilson at Versailles, Hamlet at the play, or Job in his diseases, what of

---

[10] Some other existentialists, like Tillich of course, believe that reason can help man finding meaning in being.

[11] "Thinking is radically metaphoric," says I. A. Richards. *Interpretation in Teaching.* London: George Routledge & Sons, Ltd., 1938. p. 48.

experiences of Kennedy in Berlin, Wilson at Princeton, Hamlet before his father died, or Job's "Though he slay me, yet will I trust him"? These comparisons are valid, too.

The vaunted fortitude of the existentialist, who extols self-reliance, turns out to be timidity in trusting the ideas which he cannot avoid in understanding his present existence. These relate to experiences he has not had, but which help explain those he has. There is a vicariousness to ideas which none can deny. Even "anxiety" and "firsthand" experience, as personal identity is sought, are not utterly private. They could not bear this significance if they did not bring with them references to experiences of others, both like and unlike them. The meaning of any experience is in some sense borrowed from others. Ideas possess this property of bringing reference from one specific instance to another. It is arbitrary to exclude the momentum of past experience as instruction for present existence.

Furthermore, ideas recur in history, i.e. they gain a new acceptance in a later age they had lost in an earlier one. Despair follows every major war for the defeated, and for some of the victors. The primacy of self-existence was held by Augustine, Descartes, Berkeley, Kant, Fichte, to name but a few. Emerson's essay on "Self-Reliance" made indelible the proposition: "Trust thyself. Every heart vibrates to that iron string."

The fourth dogma slated for discussion is the belief that science and its methods will bring Utopia. It is argued that the only "cumulative" knowledge is that found by observation and scientific testing. If Archimedes, so the argument goes, were brought to General Motors for a visit he would have to catch up on developments since 212 B.C., but much knowledge since would build on and be added reliably to his conception of specific gravity. Much other so-called knowledge, it is held, is "non-cumulative." Knowledge about "justice," "beauty," "love" remains much the same today as it was in the time of Socrates and Plato. If one of these were brought to Detroit to discuss "justice" with a civil rights worker, he could begin without a fill-in on developments since his time, for there have been none!

Knowledge about values remains secondary and relative because values cannot be observed and measured under controlled, or at least accurately specified conditions. To say that "God is just" would be a meaningless proposition for it refers to an unobservable and hence unverifiable supposed object. So prestigious has this point of view become that the influence of the church has been declining. Creeds are taken to be symbolic and hence adjustable. Ethics are "situational," the right and good being dependent upon the circumstances. It is noteworthy that Sputnik led to the revitalizing of education, not the failure of two World Wars, the social passion of the church, or the new philosophy of educators.

Once more, ideas are the elements which make science possible. They are forms, themes, concepts about whose properties knowledge is cumulative. The history of knowledge would be better construed as discovery of new twigs on old trees, with occasional location of a new seedling, than as addition of new bricks to a wall. "Justice" has certainly found new expressions under differing circumstances, and perhaps in more complex ways than the "specific gravity" of Archimedes. The generalizations of science, whether descriptive or experimental, are abstractions from particular phenomena possible only through the medium of ideas.

Observe, further, that the quantifications crucial in science remain impossible apart from qualifications, which are said to be unverifiable. Forms, relations, values are ideas, and the measurements of science are always about some kind of something. Belief that one measurement is better than others, that the statistics sought have consequences for solution of a problem in science, stems from the valuing, the idea-forming capacity of consciousness. Eagerness for results from science results in neglect of this prior thrust toward pattern, or idea, which orders the phenomena investigated by the scientist.

Present prestige of science over ideas and values traces more to exercise in its methods for the sake of take-home pay, than from its transcendent value and prior validity in method. Comparable exercise in the analysis and verification of ideas and values would transform our culture. A college graduate may study mathematics sixteen years, but logic, ethics, religion not at all. No wonder Arthur Miller reports that the literary men of today are demoralized by this prestige of science to the point where they are afraid to say that life has values worth striving for.[12] This fear of writing about values arises from their inexperience of them or else from their failure to see that values have their own methods of study not outmoded by science.

IV

Today's dogmas, as perhaps those of every age, involve a disrespect for ideas. Recent stress on semantics by Korzybski, Richards, Chase, Wittgenstein and others has called attention to the use of terms and ideas in thinking. This emphasis has left many philosophers talking to themselves about semantics, however. The non-professional philosopher and the lay scholar have not been helped much to see the true role of ideas in scholarship.

Use of ideas across lines of specialized scholarship, with proper attention to new contexts, can facilitate communication and collaboration. The scholar carries with him the duty to be understood, and this duty extends beyond the narrow circle of the initiated in his chosen field. This means that contact with neighboring subjects, perspective on previous scholars,

---

[12] "The Writer as Independent Spirit." *Saturday Review.* XLIX:23 (June 4, 1966), 16.

and suggestions to the wayfaring man are responsibilities of the scholar. Ideas, the common theme of particular cases, the form of relations, the pattern of qualities, the grasp of values, are his most precise and precious tools.

Historical knowledge in Western thought has been organized about one hundred basic ideas in the monumental *Syntopicon* by Mortimer Adler. Whether one adopt this precise list of ideas doesn't matter. It does contain ideas, nevertheless, which provide a structure for understanding the most significant thoughts of Western man. Nor is it necessary to erect this list into a scheme of ideas after some metaphysics according to Plato, Aquinas, Hegel, or Whitehead, to derive great value from it. Whether ideas have an ontological status of their own is a story all by itself. The fact remains that significant thinking cannot proceed without them.

An educational program for higher education can be devised with basic ideas as its themes. Fear of orthodoxy, or of commitments to metaphysics, and the stress on "What do you think?" in student discussions, threaten to obscure the role of ideas in learning. If there is such a thing as "truth," and every program of education assumes there is in some sense, the forms of thought necessary to apprehension of that truth should be definable. However vague these thoughts at their best may be, and however they may change from occasion to occasion, the possibility of finding truth is proportionate to the care with which the mind gropes after and grasps ideas.

QUESTIONS

1.   Norris' speech, delivered in 1966 before the Detroit Association of Phi Beta Kappa, is clearly organized into four divisions. Outline these four divisions.

2.   A formal speech normally contains a more complex treatment of thought. Examine the second division of Norris' speech for the concept of an "idea." Norris offers the characteristics of an "idea." Write a brief speech in which you present an abstraction, an "idea," through an enumeration of characteristics and examples.

3.   Norris explains that ideas are "weapons" whereby dogmas may be examined. What relationships, according to Norris, exist between "facts" and "ideas"? Norris makes copious use of examples. In a brief speech defend "specialized learning" against Norris' attack.

4.   In the contemporary world, according to Norris, anti-intellectualism is "capitalized on so often by advertisers, politicians, churchmen, artists, and parents. . . ." Gather data from advertisements, political speeches, sermons, statements on art, or from your own observations of parents, and then prepare a brief speech in which you support or attack Norris' statement on contemporary anti-intellectualism.

5. Prepare a carefully illustrated speech in which you support or argue against the following statement: "No one beyond thirty can be trusted." Remember your argument will be based on "ideas."

A TRIBUTE TO HIS BROTHER
Edward M. Kennedy

Your eminences, your excellencies, Mr. President. In behalf of Mrs. Kennedy, her children, the parents and sisters of Robert Kennedy, I want to express what we feel to those who mourn with us today in this cathedral and around the world.

We loved him as a brother and as a father and as a son. From his parents and from his older brothers and sisters, Joe and Kathleen and Jack, he received an inspiration which he passed on to all of us.

He gave us strength in time of trouble, wisdom in time of uncertainty and sharing in time of happiness. He will always be by our side.

Love is not an easy feeling to put into words. Nor is loyalty or trust or joy. But he was all of these. He loved life completely and he lived it intensely.

A few years back Robert Kennedy wrote some words about his own father which expresses the way we in his family felt about him. He said of what his father meant to him, and I quote:

"What it really all adds up to is love. Not love as it is described with such facility in popular magazines, but the kind of love that is affection and respect, order and encouragement and support.

"Our awareness of this was an incalculable source of strength. And because real love is something unselfish and involves sacrifice and giving, we could not help but profit from it."

And he continued:

"Beneath it all he has tried to engender a social conscience. There were wrongs which needed attention, there were people who were poor and needed help, and we have a responsibility to them and this country.

"Through no virtues and accomplishments of our own, we have been fortunate enough to be born in the United States under the most comfortable condition. We therefore have a responsibility to others who are less well off."

That is what Robert Kennedy was given.

What he leaves to us is what he said, what he did and what he stood for.

A speech he made for the young people of South Africa on their day

---

Reprinted by permission of *Vital Speeches of the Day*, Volume 34, Number 18.

of affirmation in 1966 sums it up the best, and I would like to read it now.

"There is discrimination in this world and slavery and slaughter and starvation. Governments repress their people. Millions are trapped in poverty, while the nation grows rich and wealth is lavished on armaments everywhere.

"These are differing evils, but they are the common works of man. They reflect the imperfection of human justice, the inadequacy of human compassion, our lack of sensibility towards the suffering of our fellows.

"But we can perhaps remember, even if only for a time, that those who live with us are our brothers, that they share with us the same short moment of life, that they seek as we do nothing but the chance to live out their lives in purpose and happiness, winning what satisfaction and fulfillment they can.

"Surely this bond of common faith, this bond of common goals, can begin to teach us something. Surely we can learn at least to look at those around us as fellow men. And surely we can begin to work a little harder to bind up the wounds among us and to become in our own hearts brothers and countrymen once again.

"The answer is to rely on youth, not a time of life but a state of mind, a temper of the will, a quality of imagination, a predominance of courage over timidity, of the appetite for adventure over the love of ease. The cruelties and obstacles of this swiftly changing planet will not yield to the obsolete dogmas and outworn slogans; they cannot be moved by those who cling to a present that is already dying, who prefer the illusion of security to the excitement and danger that come with even the most peaceful progress.

"It is a revolutionary world which we live in, and this generation at home and around the world has had thrust upon it a greater burden of responsibility than any generation that has ever lived. Some believe there is nothing one man or one woman can do against the enormous array of the world's ills. Yet many of the world's great movements of thought and action have flowed from the work of a single man.

"A young monk began the Protestant Reformation. A young general extended an empire from Macedonia to the borders of the earth. A young woman reclaimed the territory of France, and it was a young Italian explorer who discovered the New World, and the 32-year-old Thomas Jefferson who explained that all men are created equal.

"These men moved the world, and so can we all. Few will have the greatness to bend history itself, but each of us can work to change a small portion of events and in the total of all those acts will be written the history of this generation.

"Each time a man stands for an ideal, or acts to improve the lot of others, or strikes out against injustice, he sends forth a tiny ripple of hope.

"And crossing each other from a million different centers of energy and daring, those ripples build a current that can sweep down the mightiest walls of oppression and resistance. Few are willing to brave the disapproval of their fellows, the censure of their colleagues, the wrath of their society. Moral courage is a rarer commodity than bravery in battle or great intelligence. Yet it is the one essential vital quality for those who seek to change a world that yields most painfully to change.

"And I believe that in this generation those with the courage to enter the moral conflict will find themselves with companions in every corner of the globe.

"For the fortunate among us there is the temptation to follow the easy and familiar paths of personal ambition and financial success so grandly spread before those who enjoy the privilege of education. But that is not the road history has marked out for us.

"Like it or not, we live in times of danger and uncertainty. But they are also more open to the creative energy of men than any other time in history. All of us will ultimately be judged and as the years pass, we will surely judge ourselves, on the effort we have contributed to building a new world society and the extent to which our ideals and goals have shaped that event.

"Our future may lie beyond our vision, but it is not completely beyond our control. It is the shaping impulse of America that neither faith nor nature nor the irresistible tides of history but the work of our own hands matched to reason and principle will determine our destiny."

There is pride in that, even arrogance, but there is also experience and truth, and in any event it is the only way we can live. That is the way he lived. That is what he leaves us.

My brother need not be idealized or enlarged in death beyond what he was in life. He should be remembered simply as a good and decent man who saw wrong and tried to right it, saw suffering and tried to heal it, saw war and tried to stop it.

Those of us who loved him and who take him to his rest today pray that what he was to us, and what he wished for others, will some day come to pass for all the world.

As he said many times, in many parts of this nation, to those he touched and who sought to touch him:

"Some men see things as they are and say why. I dream things that never were and say, why not."

QUESTIONS

1. Edward Kennedy's "tribute" is organized around three basic ideas: first, what Robert Kennedy was given; second, what he leaves to mankind—"what he said, what he did and what he stood for"; and third, what his life means to the future of mankind. Write a brief speech in

which you present the meanings of someone's life to you, your family, and your community.

2.   "Differing evils," Robert Kennedy said in his speech to the young people of South Africa, "are the common works of man." Among these evils he mentions discrimination, slavery, slaughter, starvation, governmental repression, and poverty. In a brief speech present your proposal on how such a problem as poverty or discrimination should be approached.

3.   Robert Kennedy described "youth" as "a state of mind, a temper of the will, a quality of imagination, a predominance of courage over timidity, of the appetite for adventure over the love of ease." In a speech prepared for a high school commencement explain your conception of "youth."

4.   What are the specific advantages of quoting Robert Kennedy's speech to the young people of South Africa? Is the speech a stronger and more moving speech through the inclusion of Robert Kennedy's beliefs? Why? In what way is he demonstrating by his life his ideas of "moral courage"? In a short speech illustrate your ideas of moral courage by examples you have selected from your own life and experiences.

5.   "Some men see things as they are and say why. I dream things that never were and say, why not." Build a formal speech around the meanings of this or a similar statement made by someone you admire.

X

Informal Essay

The informal essay is so dominated by the personality and character of the essayist that it is frequently difficult to determine whether or not you are reading autobiography or an informal essay. Whereas the subject of autobiography is the writer himself, the writer of an informal essay is dealing with a subject other than himself, although he may use personal examples to illustrate the subject. But the most often used descriptive words assigned to the informal essay are "lively," "charming," "intimate," and such, all related to the personality of the writer and to the emotional tone and appeal he creates. Your purpose is to express a personal opinion, to provide enjoyment and entertainment for your reader.

Aldous Huxley in a well-known essay entitled "The Essay" stated: "The essay is a literary device for saying almost everything about anything." In many ways such a starting point represents the basic philosophy of the informal or familiar essayist: he may write an informal essay entitled "How to Write and Be Read," as Jacques Barzun did; or "What College Did to Me," by Robert Benchley; or "About Talking Dogs" by James Thurber; or "Togetherness? No!" by Charles Frankel. It is clear, from such titles as these, that the informal essay may be humorous or didactic, whimsical or serious, charming or bitter, in short, reflective of any tone or mood an essayist may project. The treatment of the subject is casual and informal, in part based on personal experience; whether the tone be contemplative, reflective, or critical, the vocabulary and style are conversational, idiomatic, and anecdotal, with loose, sometimes rambling, digressions, relaxed organization, and ephemeral subjects. And, too, the informal essay is usually a short prose piece, of approximately five hundred to a thousand words. Two of the best informal essayists of recent years who illustrate the above characteristics are E. B. White, the editor of *The New Yorker* magazine, and James Thurber, one of the best-known humorists of recent years.

As an informal essayist your purpose is to provide enjoyment, to stimulate man's mind and imagination. Moreover, your purpose is to express your personal ideas and opinions in an original and creative way. Obviously the informal essay is one of the most enjoyable types of literature.

YOU, TOO, CAN WRITE
THE CASUAL STYLE

William H. Whyte, Jr.

A revolution has taken place in American prose. No longer the short huffs and puffs, the unqualified word, the crude gusto of the declarative sentence. Today the fashion is to write casually.

The Casual Style is not exactly new. Originated in the early Twenties, it has been refined and improved and refined again by a relatively small band of writers, principally for the *New Yorker*, until now their mannerisms have become standards of sophistication. Everybody is trying to join the club. Newspaper columnists have forsaken the beloved metaphors of the sports page for the Casual Style, and one of the quickest ways for an ad man to snag an award from other ad men is to give his copy the low-key, casual pitch; the copy shouldn't sing these days—it should whisper. Even Dr. Rudolf Flesch, who has been doing so much to teach people how to write like other people, is counseling his followers to use the Casual Style. Everywhere the ideal seems the same: be casual.

But how? There is very little down-to-earth advice. We hear about the rapier-like handling of the bromide, the keen eye for sham and pretension, the exquisite sense of nuance, the unerring ear for the vulgate. But not much about actual technique. The layman, as a consequence, is apt to look on the Casual Style as a mandarin dialect which he fears he could never master.

Nonsense. The Casual Style is within everyone's grasp. It has now become so perfected by constant polishing that its devices may readily be identified, and they change so little that their use need be no more difficult for the novice than for the expert. (That's not quite all there is to it, of course. Some apparently casual writers, Thurber and E. B. White, among others, rarely use the devices.)

The subject matter, in the first place, is not to be ignored. Generally speaking, the more uneventful it is, or the more pallid the writer's reaction to it, the better do form and content marry. Take, for example, the cocktail party at which the writer can show how bored everyone is with everyone else, and how utterly fatuous they all are anyhow. Since a non-casual statement—*e.g.*, "The party was a bore"—would destroy the reason for writing about it at all, the Casual Style here is not only desirable but mandatory.

Whatever the subject, however, twelve devices are the rock on which all else is built. I will present them one by one, illustrating them with examples from such leading casual stylists as Wolcott Gibbs, John Crosby, John McCarten, and (on occasion) this magazine's "Mr. Harper." If the reader will digest what follows, he should be able to dash off a paragraph indistinguishable from the best casual writing being done today.

(1) *Heightened Understatement.* Where the old-style writer would say, "I don't like it," "It is not good," or something equally banal, the casual writer says it is *"something less than* good." He avoids direct statement and strong words—except, as we will note, where he is setting them up to have something to knock down. In any event, he qualifies. "Somewhat" and "rather," the bread-and-butter words of the casual writer, should become habitual with you; similarly with such phrases as "I suppose," "it seems to me," "I guess," or "I'm afraid." "Elusive" or "elude" are good, too, and if you see the word "charm" in a casual sentence you can be pretty sure that "eludes me," or "I find elusive," will not be far behind.

(2) *The Multiple Hedge.* Set up an ostensibly strong statement, and then, with your qualifiers, shoot a series of alternately negative and positive charges into the sentence until finally you neutralize the whole thing. Let's take, for example, the clause, "certain names have a guaranteed nostalgic magic." Challenge enough here; the names not only have magic, they have guaranteed magic. A double hedge reverses the charge. "Names which have, *I suppose* [hedge 1], a guaranteed nostalgic magic, *though there are times that I doubt it* [hedge 2] . . . ."

We didn't have to say they were guaranteed in the first place, of course, but without such straw phrases we wouldn't have anything to construct a hedge on and, frequently, nothing to write at all. The virtue of the hedge is that by its very negating effect it makes any sentence infinitely expansible. Even if you have so torn down your original statement with one or two hedges that you seem to have come to the end of the line, you have only to slip in an anti-hedge, a strengthening word (*e.g.,* "definitely," "unqualified," etc.), and begin the process all over again. Witness the following quadruple hedge: "I found Mr. Home entertaining *from time to time* [hedge 1] on the ground, *I guess* [hedge 2], that the singular idiom and unearthly detachment of the British upper classes have *always* [anti-hedge] seemed *reasonably* [hedge 3] droll to me, *at least in moderation* [hedge 4]." The art of plain talk, as has been pointed out, does not entail undue brevity.

If you've pulled hedge on hedge and the effect still remains too vigorous, simply wipe the slate clean with a cancellation clause at the end. "It was all exactly as foolish as it sounds," says Wolcott Gibbs, winding up some 570 casual words on a subject, "and I wouldn't give it another thought."

(3) *Narcissizing Your Prose.* The casual style is nothing if not per-

sonal; indeed, you will usually find in it as many references to the writer as to what he's supposed to be talking about. For you do not talk about the subject; you talk about its impact on you. With the reader peering over your shoulder, you look into the mirror and observe your own responses as you run the entire range of the casual writer's emotions. You may reveal yourself as, in turn, listless ("the audience seemed not to share my boredom"); insouciant ("I was really quite happy with it"); irritated ("The whole thing left me tired and cross"); comparatively gracious ("Being in a comparatively gracious mood, I won't go into the details I didn't like"); or hesitant ("I wish I could say that I could accept his hypothesis").

(4) *Preparation for the Witticism.* When the casual writer hits upon a clever turn of phrase or a nice conceit, he uses this device to insure that his conceit will not pass unnoticed. Suppose, for example, you have thought of something to say that is pretty damn good if you say so yourself. The device, in effect, is to say so yourself. If you want to devastate a certain work as "a study of vulgarity in high places," don't say this flat out. Earlier in the sentence prepare the reader for the drollery ahead with something like "what I am tempted to call" or "what could best be described as" or "If it had to be defined in a sentence, it might well be called. . . ."

Every writer his own claque.

(5) *Deciphered Notes Device; or Cute-Things-I-Have-Said.* In this one you are your own stooge as well. You feed yourself lines. By means of the slender fiction that you have written something on the back of an envelope or the margin of a program, you catch yourself good-humoredly trying to decipher these shrewd, if cryptic, little jottings. *Viz.*: "Their diagnoses are not nearly as crisp as those I find in my notes"; ". . . sounds like an inadequate description, but it's all I have on my notes, and it may conceivably be a very high compliment."

(6) *The Kicker.* An echo effect. "My reactions [included] an irritable feeling that eleven o'clock was past Miss Keim's bedtime,"—and now the Kicker—"*not to mention my own.*" This type of thing practically writes itself. "She returns home. She should never have left home in the first place. __ ___ ___ _." [1]

(7) *Wit of Omission.* By calling attention to the fact that you are not going to say it, you suggest that there is something very funny you could say if only you wanted to. "A thought occurred to me at this point," you may say, when otherwise stymied, "but I think we had better not go into *that.*"

(8) *The Planned Colloquialism.* The casual writer savors colloquialisms. This is not ordinary colloquial talk—nobody is more quickly provoked than the casual writer by ordinary usage. It is, rather, a playful descent into the vulgate. Phrases like "darn," "awfully," "as all getout,"

---

[1] "And neither should I."

"mighty," and other folksy idioms are ideal. The less you would be likely to use the word normally yourself the more pointed the effect. Contrast is what you are after, for it is the facetious interplay of language levels—a blending, as it were, of the East Fifties and the Sticks—that gives the Casual Style its off-hand charm.

(9) *Feigned Forgetfulness.* Conversation gropes; it is full of "what I really meant was" and "maybe I should have added," backings and fillings and second thoughts of one kind or another. Writing is different; theoretically, ironing out second thoughts beforehand is one of the things writers are paid to do. In the Casual Style, however, it is exactly this exposure of the writer composing in public that makes it so casual. For the professional touch, then, ramble, rebuke yourself in print ("what I really meant, I guess"), and if you have something you feel you should have said earlier, don't say it earlier, but say later that you guess you should have said it earlier.

(10) *The Subject-Apologizer, or Pardon-Me-for-Living.* The Casual Stylist must always allow for the possibility that his subject is just as boring to the reader as it is to him. He may forestall this by seeming to have stumbled on it by accident, or by using phrases like: "If this is as much news to you as it is to me," or "This, in case you've been living in a cave lately, is. . . ."

(11) *The Omitted Word.* This all began modestly enough the day a *New Yorker* writer dropped the articles "the" and "a" from the initial sentence of an anecdote (*e.g.*, "Man we know told us"; "Fellow name of Brown"). Now even such resolutely lowbrow writers as Robert Ruark affect it, and they are applying it to any part of speech anywhere in the sentence. You can drop a pronoun ("Says they're shaped like pyramids"); verb ("You been away from soap opera the last couple of weeks?"); or preposition ("Far as glamour goes . . .").

(12) *The Right Word.* In the lexicon of the casual writer there are a dozen or so adjectives which in any context have, to borrow a phrase, a guaranteed charm. Attrition is high—"brittle," "febrile," "confected," for example, are at the end of the run. Ten, however, defy obsolescence: *antic, arch, blurred, chaste, chill, crisp, churlish, disheveled, dim, disembodied.*

They are good singly, but they are even better when used in tandem; *c.f.*, "In an arch, antic sort of way"; "In an arch, blurred sort of way"; "In an arch, crisp sort of way." And so on.

Finally, the most multi-purpose word of them all: "altogether." Frequently it is the companion of "charming" and "delightful," and in this coupling is indispensable to any kind of drama criticism. It can also modify the writer himself (*e.g.*, "Altogether, I think . . ."). Used best, however, it just floats, unbeholden to any other part of the sentence.

Once you have mastered these twelve devices, you too should be able to write as casually as all getout. At least it seems to me, though I may be wrong, that they convey an elusive archness which the crisp literary crafts-man, in his own dim sort of way, should altogether cultivate these days. Come to think of it, the charm of the Casual Style is something less than clear to me, but we needn't go into *that*. Fellow I know from another mag-azine says this point of view best described as churlish. Not, of course, that it matters.

QUESTIONS

1. In your own words, state the central idea of Whyte's essay. Remember, since a writer's purpose may be stated or implied, the problem in part involves the relationship you find existing between Whyte's tone and what he says in the essay.
2. To achieve clarity of meaning, Whyte illustrates each of the twelve devices of the Casual Style. Write a paragraph in which you il-lustrate a device or technique you have found helpful in expressing your thought.
3. Whyte is critical of manneristic writing, in this instance the Cas-ual Style. Write a paragraph in which you use one of the devices or techniques mentioned, such as the "Planned Colloquialism." Did you find the device an aid to clear expression? If so, why? If not, why?
4. You make dictional choices, word choices, on the basis of their ap-propriateness to your subject, your audience, and yourself. Examine the second paragraph of Whyte's essay for word choices and defend or attack the appropriateness of his choices.
5. Write an informal essay in which you are critical of a contempo-rary viewpoint, institution, group, or standard. Illustrate and support your critical comments. Re-examine your essay for clarity of thought.

COURTSHIP THROUGH THE AGES

James Thurber

Surely nothing in the astonishing scheme of life can have nonplussed Nature so much as the fact that none of the females of any of the species she created really cared very much for the male, as such. For the past ten million years Nature has been busily inventing ways to make the male at-tractive to the female, but the whole business of courtship, from the ma-rine annelids up to man, still lumbers heavily along, like a complicated mu-sical comedy. I have been reading the sad and absorbing story in Volume 6

(Cole to Dama) of the Encyclopædia Britannica. In this volume you can learn all about cricket, cotton, costume designing, crocodiles, crown jewels, and Coleridge, but none of these subjects is so interesting as the Courtship of Animals, which recounts the sorrowful lengths to which all males must go to arouse the interest of a lady.

We all know, I think, that Nature gave man whiskers and a mustache with the quaint idea in mind that these would prove attractive to the female. We all know that, far from attracting her, whiskers and mustaches only made her nervous and gloomy, so that man had to go in for somersaults, tilting with lances, and performing feats of parlor magic to win her attention; he also had to bring her candy, flowers, and the furs of animals. It is common knowledge that in spite of all these "love displays" the male is constantly being turned down, insulted, or thrown out of the house. It is rather comforting, then, to discover that the peacock, for all his gorgeous plumage, does not have a particularly easy time in courtship; none of the males in the world do. The first peahen, it turned out, was only faintly stirred by her suitor's beautiful train. She would often go quietly to sleep while he was whisking it around. The Britannica tells us that the peacock actually had to learn a certain little trick to wake her up and revive her interest: he had to learn to vibrate his quills so as to make a rustling sound. In ancient times man himself, observing the ways of the peacock, probably tried vibrating his whiskers to make a rustling sound; if so, it didn't get him anywhere. He had to go in for something else; so, among other things, he went in for gifts. It is not unlikely that he got this idea from certain flies and birds who were making no headway at all with rustling sounds.

One of the flies of the family Empidae, who had tried everything, finally hit on something pretty special. He contrived to make a glistening transparent balloon which was even larger than himself. Into this he would put sweetmeats and tidbits and he would carry the whole elaborate envelope through the air to the lady of his choice. This amused her for a time, but she finally got bored with it. She demanded silly little colorful presents, something that you couldn't eat but that would look nice around the house. So the male Empis had to go around gathering flower petals and pieces of bright paper to put into his balloon. On a courtship flight a male Empis cuts quite a figure now, but he can hardly be said to be happy. He never knows how soon the female will demand heavier presents, such as Roman coins and gold collar buttons. It seems probable that one day the courtship of the Empidae will fall down, as man's occasionally does, of its own weight.

The bowerbird is another creature that spends so much time courting the female that he never gets any work done. If all the male bowerbirds became nervous wrecks within the next ten or fifteen years, it would not surprise me. The female bowerbird insists that a playground be built for her with a specially constructed bower at the entrance. This bower is much more elaborate than an ordinary nest and is harder to build; it costs a lot more, too. The female will not come to the playground until the male has filled it up with a great many gifts; silvery leaves, red leaves, rose petals, shells, beads, berries, bones, dice, buttons, cigar bands, Christmas seals, and the Lord knows what else. When the female finally condescends to visit the playground, she is in a coy and silly mood and has to be chased in and out of the bower and up and down the playground before she will quit giggling and stand still long enough even to shake hands. The male bird is, of course, pretty well done in before the chase starts, because he has worn himself out hunting for eyeglass lenses and begonia blossoms. I imagine that many a bowerbird, after chasing a female for two or three hours, says the hell with it and goes home to bed. Next day, of course, he telephones someone else and the same trying ritual is gone through with again. A male bowerbird is as exhausted as a night-club habitué before he is out of his twenties.

The male fiddler crab has a somewhat easier time, but it can hardly be said that he is sitting pretty. He has one enormously large and powerful claw, usually brilliantly colored, and you might suppose that all he had to do was reach out and grab some passing cutie. The very earliest fiddler crabs may have tried this, but, if so, they got slapped for their pains. A female fiddler crab will not tolerate any cave-man stuff; she never has and she doesn't intend to start now. To attract a female, a fiddler crab has to stand on tiptoe and brandish his claw in the air. If any female in the neighborhood is interested—and you'd be surprised how many are not—she comes over and engages him in light badinage, for which he is not in the mood. As many as a hundred females may pass the time of day with him and go on about their business. By nightfall of an average courting day, a fiddler crab who has been standing on tiptoe for eight or ten hours waving a heavy claw in the air is in pretty sad shape. As in the case of the males of all species, however, he gets out of bed next morning, dashes some water on his face, and tries again.

The next time you encounter a male web-spinning spider, stop and reflect that he is too busy worrying about his love life to have any desire to bite you. Male web-spinning spiders have a tougher life than any other males in the animal kingdom. This is because the female web-spinning spiders have very poor eyesight. If a male lands on a female's web, she kills him before he has time to lay down his cane and gloves, mistaking him for a fly or a bumblebee who has stumbled into her trap. Before the species figured out what to do about this, millions of males were murdered by ladies they called on. It is the nature of spiders to perform a little dance in front of the female, but before a male spinner could get near enough for the female to see who he was and what he was up to, she would lash out at him with a flatiron or a pair of garden shears. One night, nobody knows when, a very bright male spinner lay awake worrying about calling on a lady who had been killing suitors right and left. It came to him that this business of dancing as a love display wasn't getting anybody anywhere except the grave. He decided to go in for web-twitching, or strand-vibrating. The next day he tried it on one of the nearsighted girls. Instead of dropping in on her suddenly, he stayed outside the web and began monkeying with one of its strands. He twitched it up and down and in and out with such a lilting rhythm that the female was charmed. The serenade worked beautifully; the female let him live. The Britannica's spider-watchers, however, report that this system is not always successful. Once in a while, even now, a female will fire three bullets into a suitor or run him through with a kitchen knife. She keeps threatening him from the moment he strikes the first low notes on the outside strings, but usually by the time he has got up to the high notes played around the center of the web, he is going to town and she spares his life.

Even the butterfly, as handsome a fellow as he is, can't always win a mate merely by fluttering around and showing off. Many butterflies have to have scent scales on their wings. Hepialus carries a powder puff in a perfumed pouch. He throws perfume at the ladies when they pass. The male tree cricket, Oecanthus, goes Hepialus one better by carrying a tiny bottle of wine with him and giving drinks to such doxies as he has designs on. One of the male snails throws darts to entertain the girls. So it goes, through the long list of animals, from the bristle worm and his rudimentary dance steps to man and his gift of diamonds and sapphires. The golden-eye drake raises a jet of water with his feet as he flies over a lake; Hepialus has his powder puff, Oecanthus his wine bottle, man his etchings. It is a bright and melancholy story, the age-old desire of the male for the female, the age-old desire of the female to be amused and entertained. Of all the creatures on earth, the only males who could be figured as putting any irony into their courtship are the grebes and certain other diving birds. Every now and then a courting grebe slips quietly down to the bottom of a lake and then, with a mighty "Whoosh!," pops out suddenly a few feet from his girl friend, splashing water all over her. She seems to be persuaded that this is a purely loving display, but I like to think that the grebe always has a faint hope of drowning her or scaring her to death.

I will close this investigation into the mournful burdens of the male with the Britannica's story about a certain Argus pheasant. It appears that the Argus displays himself in front of a female who stands perfectly still without moving a feather. (If you saw "June Moon" some years ago and remember the scene in which the songwriter sang "Montana Moon" to his grim and motionless wife, you have some idea what the female Argus probably thinks of her mate's display.) The male Argus the Britannica tells about was confined in a cage with a female of another species, a female who kept moving around, emptying ashtrays and fussing with lampshades all the time the male was showing off his talents. Finally, in disgust he stalked away and began displaying in front of his water trough. He reminds me of a certain male (Homo sapiens) of my acquaintance who one night after dinner asked his wife to put down her detective magazine so that he could read her a poem of which he was very fond. She sat quietly enough until he was well into the middle of the thing, intoning with great ardor and intensity. Then suddenly there came a sharp, disconcerting *slap!* It turned out that all during the male's display, the female had been intent on a circling mosquito and had finally trapped it between the palms of her hands. The male in this case did not stalk away and display in front of a water trough; he went over to Tim's and had a flock of drinks and recited the poem to the fellas. I am sure they all told bitter stories of their own about how their displays had been interrupted by females. I am also sure that they all ended up singing "Honey, Honey, Bless Your Heart."

QUESTIONS

1. The informal essayist, in expressing his personality and personal opinions, provides both intellectual and emotional enjoyment and challenge. Thurber's joy in life, sense of humor, and delight in bon mots are evident throughout the essay. Find examples of each of these characteristics. Write a paragraph, on a subject of your own choosing, in which you attempt to infuse your personality into what you write. Then write a second paragraph explaining the devices you used.

2. What is Thurber's basic opinion concerning courtship? How did you determine your answer? Write a brief informal essay in which you treat human eccentricities, idiosyncrasies, or peculiarities. For example, what is the place of superstition or of astrology in your experiences?

3. Thurber illustrates his thesis with a host of examples from the natural world. Are the examples, as he presents them, both illustrative and intrinsically interesting? Compare his remarks on the bowerbirds and the grebes. Write an informal essay in which you project your personality through a series of examples you have selected to develop your theme.

4. Thurber's mastery of speech and idiom is an organic part of "Courtship Through the Ages." For example, he uses such phrases as "turned down," "thrown out of the house," "cuts quite a figure," "the Lord knows what else," "pretty well done," "the hell with it," "sitting pretty," "passing cutie," "in pretty sad shape," and so on. Write an informal essay in which you attempt to catch the idiom of one of your fellow students, your grandmother, your teachers, or yourself.

5. In this essay Thurber uses extended comparison infusing his comparisons of human life with his observations about the natural world. The bowerbirds, for example, do not "shake hands" or say "to hell with it." Examine carefully Thurber's use of comparisons. Prepare an informal essay in which you use a single figure of speech or image as a device for achieving unity.

XI

Formal Essay

Whereas the informal essay is dominated by the character and personality of the essayists, the formal essay is governed generally by the subject matter being discussed. An informal essay may be devoted to nostalgic reminiscences of the Model T Ford, such as E. B. White and Richard Lee Strout presented in an informal essay entitled "Farewell, My Lovely!" but the formal essayist will not indulge himself in nostalgia and will more likely examine the significance of the automobile industry or mass production in their meanings to American life. The suggestion made here is not that the informal essay may not be serious, which it frequently is, but that the formal essay is usually a serious examination of a subject. W. Somerset Maugham's *The Summing Up* may be viewed as a kind of autobiography or a collection of informal essays; on the other hand, a periodical such as *Dædalus* contains serious essays devoted to such contemporary issues as "The Contemporary University: U.S.A.," "Toward the Year 2000: Work in Progress," "Philosophers and Kings: Studies in Leadership," or "Historical Population Studies." A formal essay represents a more learned, more studied, more serious, more carefully-wrought expression of opinion than the informal essay. Limitations, definitions, and illustrations are organic characteristics. Moreover, the subjects dealt with are those of civilization—social, political, and cultural ideas, problems, actions, people.

The viewpoint of the formal essayist is intellectual, the appeal of his essay is to the mind of man. The essay is usually tightly organized around a specific purpose, systematic, logical, coherent, and more extended than in the informal essay. The essayist adopts an impersonal tone, though not always, observes standard conventions of English usage in syntax, vocabulary, and grammar, and provides few or no digressions.

As a formal essayist you may, at first, find a formal manner contrary to what you consider your normal disposition, habit patterns, and thought, but you will be on safe ground the moment you wish to express honest opinions you hold concerning a specific subject.

THE REVOLUTION
IN WESTERN THOUGHT

Huston Smith

Quietly, irrevocably, something enormous has happened to Western man. His outlook on life and the world has changed so radically that in the perspective of history the twentieth century is likely to rank—with the fourth century, which witnessed the triumph of Christianity, and the seventeenth, which signaled the dawn of modern science—as one of the very few that have instigated genuinely new epochs in human thought. In this change, which is still in process, we of the current generation are playing a crucial but as yet not widely recognized part.

The dominant assumptions of an age color the thoughts, beliefs, expectations and imaginings of the men and women who live within it. Being always with us, these assumptions usually pass unnoticed—like the pair of glasses which, because they are so often on the wearer's nose, simply stop being observed. But this doesn't mean they have no effect. Ultimately the assumptions which underlie our outlooks on life refract the world in ways that condition our art and our institutions: the kinds of homes we live in, our sense of right and wrong, our criteria of success, what we conceive our duty to be, what we think it means to be a man, how we worship our God or whether, indeed, we have a God to worship.

Thus far the odyssey of Western man has carried him through three great configurations of such basic assumptions. The first constituted the Graeco-Roman, or Classical, outlook, which flourished up to the fourth century A.D. With the triumph of Christianity in the Roman Empire, this Graeco-Roman outlook was replaced by the Christian world view which proceeded to dominate Europe until the seventeenth century. The rise of modern science inaugurated a third important way of looking at things, a way that has come to be capsuled in the phrase "the modern mind."

It now appears that this modern outlook, too, has run its course and is being replaced by what Dirk Jellema of Case Institute and others have begun to speak of as the Post-Modern Mind. What follows is an attempt to describe this most recent sea change in Western thought. I shall begin by bringing the Christian and modern outlooks into focus; for only so can we see how and to what extent our emerging thought patterns differ from those that have directly preceded them.

From the fourth-century triumph of Christianity in the Roman Empire through the Middle Ages and the Reformation, the Western mind was above all else theistic. "God, God, God; nothing but God"—in the twentieth century one can assume such an exclamation to have come, as it did, from a theologian. In the Middle Ages it could have come from anyone. Virtually without question all life and nature were assumed to be under the surveillance of a personal God whose intentions toward man were perfect and whose power to implement these intentions was unlimited.

In such a world, life was transparently meaningful. But although men understood the purpose of their lives, it does not follow that they understood, or even presumed to be capable of understanding, the dynamics of the natural world. The Bible never expands the doctrine of creation into a cosmogony for the excellent reason that it asserts the universe to be at every point the direct product of a will whose ways are not man's ways. God says, "Let there be"—and there is. That is all. Serene in a blaze of lasting light, God comprehends nature's ways, but man sees only its surface.

Christian man lived in the world as a child lives in his father's house, accepting its construction and economics unprobed. "Can anyone understand the thunderings of God's pavilion?" Elihu asks Job. "Do you know the ordinances of the heavens, how the clouds are balanced or the lightning shines? Have you comprehended the expanse of the earth, or on what its bases were sunk when the morning stars sang together and all the sons of God shouted for joy?" To such rhetorical questions the answer seemed obvious. The leviathan of nature was not to be drawn from the great sea of mystery by the fishhook of man's paltry mind.

Not until the high Middle Ages was a Christian cosmology attempted, and then through Greek rather than Biblical inspiration, following the rediscovery of Aristotle's *Physics* and *Metaphysics*. Meanwhile nature's obscurity posed no major problem; for as the cosmos was in good hands, it could be counted on to furnish a reliable context in which man might work out his salvation. The way to this salvation lay not through ordering nature to man's purposes but through aligning man's purposes to God's. And for this objective, information was at hand. As surely as God had kept the secrets of nature to Himself, He had, through His Divine Word and the teachings of His church, made man's duty clear. Those who hearkened to this duty would reap an eternal reward, but those who refused to do so would perish.

We can summarize the chief assumptions underlying the Christian outlook by saying they held that reality focuses in a person, that the mechanics of the physical world exceed our comprehension, and that the way to our salvation lies not in conquering nature but in following the commandments which God has revealed to us.

It was the second of these three assumptions—that the dynamics of nature exceed man's comprehension—which the sixteenth and seventeeth centuries began to question, thereby heralding the transition from the Christian to the modern outlook. The Renaissance interest in the early Greeks revived the Hellenic interest in nature. For the first time in nearly 2000 years Western man began to look intently at his environment instead of beyond it. Leonardo da Vinci is symbolic. His anatomical studies and drawings in general disclose a direction of interest that has turned eye into camera, in his case an extraordinary camera that "could stop the hawk in flight and fix the rearing horse." Once again man was attending to nature's details as a potential messenger of meaning. The rage to know God's handiwork was rivaling the rage to know God Himself.

The consequence, as we know, was modern science. Under scrutiny, nature's blur was found to be more apparent than final. With patience the structure of the universe could be brought into marvelous focus. Newton's exclamation caught the excitement perfectly: "O God, I think thy thoughts after thee!" Although nature's marvels were infinitely greater than had been supposed, man's mind was equal to them. The universe was a coherent, law-abiding system. It was intelligible!

It was not long before this discovery began to reap practical rewards. Drudgery could be relieved, health improved, goods multiplied and leisure extended. As these benefits are considerable, working with intelligible nature began to overshadow obedience to God's will as a means to human fulfillment. God was not entirely eclipsed—that would have entailed a break with the past more violent than history usually allows. Rather, God was eased toward thought's periphery. Not atheism but deism, the notion that God created the world but left it to run according to its own inbuilt laws, was the modern mind's distinctive religious stance. God stood behind nature as its creator, but it was through nature that His ways and will were to be known.

Like the Christian outlook, the modern outlook can be summarized by identifying its three controlling presuppositions. First, that reality may be personal is less certain and less important than that it is ordered. Second, man's reason is capable of discerning this order as it manifests itself in the laws of nature. Third, the path to human fulfillment consists primarily in discovering these laws, utilizing them where this is possible and complying with them where it is not.

The reason for suspecting that this modern outlook has had its day and is yielding to a third great mutation in Western thought is that reflective men are no longer confident of any of these three postulates. The first two are the ones that concern us here. Frontier thinkers are no longer sure that reality is ordered and orderly. If it is, they are not sure that man's mind is capable of grasping its order. Combining the two doubts, we can define the Post-Modern Mind as one which, having lost the conviction that reality is personal, has come to question whether it is ordered in a way that man's reason can lay bare.

It was science which induced our forefathers to think of reality as primarily ordered rather than personal. But contemporary science has crashed through the cosmology which the seventeenth-to-nineteenth-century scientists constructed as if through a sound barrier, leaving us without replacement. It is tempting to attribute this lack to the fact that evidence is pouring in faster than we can throw it into perspective, but although this is part of the problem, another part runs deeper. Basically the absence of a new cosmology is due to the fact that physics has cut away so radically from our capacity to imagine the way things are that we do not see how the two can get back together.

If modern physics showed us a world at odds with our senses, postmodern physics is showing us one which is at odds with our imagination, where imagination is taken as imagery. We have made peace with the first of these oddities. That the table which appears motionless is in fact incredibly "alive" with electrons circling their nuclei a million billion times per second; that the chair which feels so secure beneath us is actually a near vacuum—such facts, while certainly very strange, posed no permanent problem for man's sense of order. To accommodate them, all that was necessary was to replace the earlier picture of a gross and ponderous world with a subtle world in which all was sprightly dance and airy whirl.

But the problems the new physics poses for man's sense of order cannot be resolved by refinements in scale. Instead they appear to point to a radical disjunction between the way things behave and every possible way in which we might try to visualize them. How, for example, are we to picture an electron traveling two or more different routes through space concurrently or passing from orbit to orbit without traversing the space between them at all? What kind of model can we construct of a space that is finite yet unbounded, or of light which is both wave and particle? It is such enigmas which are causing physicists like P. W. Bridgman of Harvard to suggest that "the structure of nature may eventually be such that our processes of thought do not correspond to it sufficiently to permit us to think about it at all. . . . The world fades out and eludes us. . . . We are confronted with something truly ineffable. We have reached the limit of the vision of the great pioneers of science, the vision, namely, that we live in a sympathetic world in that it is comprehensible by our minds."

This subdued and problematic stance of science toward reality is paralleled in philosophy. No one who works in philosophy today can fail to realize that the sense of the cosmos has been shaken by an encyclopedic skepticism. The clearest evidence of this is the collapse of what historically has been philosophy's central discipline: objective metaphysics, the attempt to discover what reality consists of and the most general principles which describe the way its parts are related. In this respect the late Alfred North Whitehead marked the end of an era. His *Process and Reality: An Essay in Cosmology* is the last important attempt to construct a logical, coherent scheme of ideas that would blueprint the universe. The trend throughout the twentieth century has been away from faith in the feasibility of such undertakings. As a tendency throughout philosophy as a whole, this is a revolutionary development. For 2500 years philosophers have argued over which metaphysical system is true. For them to agree that none is, is a new departure.

The agreement represents the confluence of several philosophical streams. On one hand it has come from the positivists who, convinced that truth comes only from science, have challenged the meta-physician's claim to extrascientific sources of insight. Their successors are the linguistic analysts, who have dominated British philosophy for the last several decades and who regard all philosophical perplexities as generated by slovenly use of language. For the analysts, "reality" and "being in general" are notions too thin and vapid to reward analysis. As a leading American proponent of this position, Professor Morton White of Harvard recently stated, "It took philosophers a long time to realize that the number of interesting things that one can say about all things in one fell swoop is very limited. Through the effort to become supremely general, you lapse into emptiness."

Equal but quite different objections to metaphysics have come from the existentialists who have dominated twentieth-century European philosophy. Heirs of Kierkegaard, Nietzsche and Dostoevski, these philosophers have been concerned to remind their colleagues of what it means to be a human being. When we are thus reminded, they say, we see that to be human precludes in principle the kind of objective and impartial overview of things—the view of things as they are in themselves, apart from our differing perspectives—that metaphysics has always sought. To be human is to be finite, conditioned and unique. No two persons have had their lives shaped by the same concatenation of genetic, cultural, historical and interpersonal forces. Either these variables are inconsequential—but if we say this we are forgetting again what it means to be human, for our humanity is in fact overwhelmingly shaped by them—or the hope of rising to a God's-eye view of reality is misguided in principle.

The traditional philosopher might protest that in seeking such an overview he never expected perfection, but we ought to try to make our perspectives as objective as possible. Such a response would only lead the existentialist to press his point deeper; for his contention is not just that objectivity is impossible but that it runs so counter to our nature—to what it means to be human—that every step in its direction is a step away from our humanity. (We are speaking here of objectivity as it pertains to our lives as wholes, not to restricted spheres of endeavor within them such as science. In these latter areas objectivity can be an unqualified virtue.) If the journey held hope that in ceasing to be human we might become gods, there could be no objection. But as this is impossible, ceasing to be human can only mean becoming less than human—inhuman in the usual sense of the word. It means forfeiting through inattention the birthright that is ours: the opportunity to plumb the depths and implications of what it means to have an outlook on life which in important respects is unique and will never be duplicated.

Despite the existentialist's sharp rebuke to metaphysics and traditional philosophy in general, there is at least one important point at which he respects their aims. He agrees that it is important to transcend what is accidental and ephemeral in our outlooks and in his own way joins his colleagues of the past in attempting to do so. But the existentialist's way toward this goal does not consist in trying to climb out of his skin in order to rise to Olympian heights from which things can be seen with complete objectivity and detachment. Rather it consists in centering down on his own inwardness until he finds within it what he is compelled to accept and can never get away from. It this way he, too, arrives at what he judges to be necessary and eternal. But necessary and eternal *for him*. What is necessary and eternal for everyone is so impossible for a man to know that he wastes time making the attempt.

With this last insistence the existentialist establishes contact with the metaphysical skepticism of his analytic colleagues across the English Channel. Existentialism and analytic philosophy are the two dominant movements in twentieth-century philosophy. In temperament, interest and method they stand at opposite poles of the philosophical spectrum. They are, in fact, opposites in every sense but one. Both are creatures of the Post-Modern Mind, the mind which doubts that reality has an absolute order which man's understanding can comprehend.

Turning from philosophy to theology, we recall that the modern mind did not rule out the possibility of God; it merely referred the question to its highest court of appeal—namely, reality's pattern as disclosed by reason. If the world order entails the notions of providence and a creator, God exists; otherwise not. This approach made the attempt to prove God's existence through reason and nature the major theological thrust of the modern period. "Let us," wrote Bishop Joseph Butler in his famous *The Analogy of Religion*, "compare the known constitution and course of things . . . with what religion teaches us to believe and expect; and see whether they are not analogous and of a piece. . . . It will, I think, be found that they are very much so." An enterprising Franciscan named Ramón Lull went even further. He invented a kind of primitive computer which, with the turning of cranks, pulling of levers and revolving of wheels, would sort the theological subjects and predicates fed into it in such a way as to demonstrate the truths of the Trinity and the Incarnation by force of sheer logic working on self-evident propositions. Rationalism had entered theology as early as the Middle Ages, but as long as the Christian outlook prevailed, final confidence was reserved for the direct pronouncements of God Himself as given in Scripture. In the modern period,

God's existence came to stand or fall on whether reason, surveying the order of nature, endorsed it. It was as if Christendom and God himself awaited the verdict of science and the philosophers.

This hardly describes the current theological situation. Scientists and philosophers have ceased to issue pronouncements of any sort about ultimates. Post-modern theology builds on its own foundations. Instead of attempting to justify faith by appeals to the objective world, it points out that as such appeals indicate nothing about reality one way or the other, the way is wide open for free decision—or what Kierkegaard called the leap of faith. One hears little these days of the proofs for the existence of God which seemed so important to the modern world. Instead one hears repeated insistence that however admirably reason is fitted to deal with life's practical problems, it can only end with a confession of ignorance when confronted with questions of ultimate concern. In the famous dictum of Karl Barth, who has influenced twentieth-century theology more than anyone else, there is no straight line from the mind of man to God. "What we say breaks apart constantly . . . producing paradoxes which are held together in seeming unity only by agile and arduous running to and fro on our part." From our own shores Reinhold Niebuhr echoes this conviction. "Life is full of contradictions and incongruities. We live our lives in various realms of meaning which do not cohere rationally."

Instead of "These are the compelling reasons, grounded in the nature of things, why you should believe in God," the approach of the church to the world today tends to be, "This community of faith invites you to share in its venture of trust and commitment." The stance is most evident in Protestant and Orthodox Christianity and Judaism, but even Roman Catholic thought, notwithstanding the powerful rationalism it took over from the Greeks, has not remained untouched by the post-modern perspective. It has become more attentive to the extent to which personal and subjective factors provide the disposition to faith without which theological arguments prove nothing.

It is difficult to assess the mood which accompanies this theological revolution. On one hand there seems to be a heightened sense of faith's precariousness: as Jesus walked on the water, so must the contemporary man of faith walk on the sea of nothingness, confident even in the absence of rational supports.

But vigor is present too. Having labored in the shadow of rationalism during the modern period, contemporary theology is capitalizing on its restored autonomy. Compensating for loss of rational proofs for God's existence have come two gains. One is new realization of the validity of Pascal's "reasons of the heart" as distinct from those of the mind. The other is a recovery of the awe without which religion, as distinct from ethical philosophy piously expressed, is probably impossible. By including God within a closed system of rational explanation, modernism lost sight of the endless qualitative distinction between God and man. Post-modern theology has reinstated this distinction with great force. If God exists, the fact that our minds cannot begin to comprehend his nature makes it necessary for us to acknowledge that he is Wholly Other.

These revolutions in science, philosophy and theology have not left the arts unaffected. The worlds of the major twentieth-century artists are many and varied, but none resembles the eighteenth-century world where mysteries seemed to be clearing by the hour. The twentieth-century worlds defy lucid and coherent exegesis. Paradoxical, devoid of sense, they are worlds into which protagonists are thrown without trace as to why—the world which the late French novelist Albert Camus proclaimed "absurd," which for his compatriot Jean-Paul Sartre is "too much," and for the Irish dramatist and short-story writer, Samuel Beckett, is a "void" in which men wait out their lives for a what-they-know-not that never comes. Heroes driven by a veritable obsession to find out where they are and what their responsibility is seldom succeed. Most of Franz Kafka is ambiguous, but his parable, "Before the Law," closes with as clear a countermand to the modern vision of an ordered reality as can be imagined. "The world-order is based on a lie."

Objective morality has gone the way of cosmic order. Even where it has not been moralistic, most Western art of the past has been created against the backdrop of a frame of objective values which the artist shared. As our century has progressed, it has become increasingly difficult to find such a framework standing back of the arts.

A single example will illustrate the point. One searches in vain for an artistic frame of reference prior to the twentieth century in which matricide might be regarded as a moral act. Yet in Sartre's play *The Flies*, it is the first authentic deed the protagonist Orestes performs. Whereas his previous actions have been detached, unthinking or in conformity with the habit patterns that surround him, this one is freely chosen in the light of full self-consciousness and acceptance of its consequences. As such, it is the first act which is genuinely his. "I have done my deed, Electra," he exults, adding, "and that deed was good." Being his, the deed supplies his life with the identity which until then it had lacked. From that moment forward, Orestes ceases to be a free-floating form; his acquisition of a past he can never escape roots his life into reality. Note the extent to which this analysis relativizes the moral standard. No act is right or wrong in itself. Everything depends on its relation to the agent, whether it is chosen freely and with full acceptance of its consequences or is done abstractedly, in imitation of the acts of others, or in self-deception.

We move beyond morality into art proper when we note that the traditional distinction between the sublime and the banal, too, has blurred. As long as reality was conceived as a great chain of being—a hierarchy of worth descending from God as its crown through angels, men, animals and plants to inanimate objects at the base—it could be reasonably argued that great art should attend to great subjects: scenes from the Gospels, major battles or distinguished lords and ladies. With cubism and surrealism, the distinction between trivial and important disappears. Alarm clocks, driftwood, pieces of broken glass become appropriate subjects for the most monumental paintings. In Samuel Beckett and the contemporary French anti-novelists the most mundane items—miscellaneous contents of a pocket, a wastebasket, the random excursions of a runaway dog—are treated with the same care as love, duty or the question of human destiny.

One is tempted to push the question a final step and ask whether the dissolution of cosmic order, moral order and the hierarchic order of subject matter is reflected in the very forms of contemporary art. Critic Russel Nye thinks that at least as far as the twentieth-century novel is concerned, the answer is yes. "If there is a discernible trend in the form of the modern novel," he writes, "it is toward the concept of the novel as a series of moments, rather than as a planned progression of events or incidents, moving toward a defined terminal end. Recent novelists tend to explore rather than arrange or synthesize their materials; often their arrangement is random rather than sequential. In the older tradition, a novel was a formal structure composed of actions and reactions which were finished by the end of the story, which did have an end. The modern novel often has no such finality." Aaron Copland characterizes the music of our young composers as a "disrelation of unrelated tones. Notes are strewn about like *membra disjecta*; there is an end to continuity in the old sense and an end of thematic relationships."

When Nietzsche's eyesight became too poor to read books, he began at last to read himself. The act was prophetic of the century that has followed. As reality has blurred, the gaze of post-modern man has turned increasingly upon himself.

Anthropological philosophy has replaced metaphysics. In the wake of Kierkegaard and Nietzsche, attention has turned from objective reality to the individual human personality struggling for self-realization. "Being" remains interesting only as it relates to man. As its order, if it has one, is unknown to us, being cannot be described as it is in itself; but if it is believed to be mysteriously wonderful, as some existentialists think, we should remain open to it. If it is the blind, meaningless enemy, as others suspect, we should maintain our freedom against it.

Even theology, for all its renewed theocentrism, keeps one eye steadily on man, as when the German theologian Rudolph Bultmann relates faith to the achievement of authentic selfhood. It is in art, however, that the shift from outer to inner has been most evident. If the twentieth century began by abolishing the distinction between sublime and banal subject matter, it has gone on to dispense with subject matter altogether. Although the tide may have begun to turn, the purest art is still widely felt to be entirely abstract and free of pictorial representation. It is as if the art-ist had taken the scientist seriously and responded, "If what I see as nature doesn't represent the way things really are, why should I credit this appear-ance with its former importance? Better to turn to what I am sure of: my own intuitions and the purely formal values inherent in the relations of colors, shapes and masses."

I have argued that the distinctive feature of the contemporary mind as evidenced by frontier thinking in science, philosophy, theology and the arts is its acceptance of reality as unordered in any objective way that man's mind can discern. This acceptance separates the Post-Modern Mind from both the modern mind, which assumed that reality is objectively ordered, and the Christian mind, which assumed it to be regulated by an inscruta-ble but beneficent will.

It remains only to add my personal suspicion that the change from the vision of reality as ordered to unordered has brought Western man to as sharp a fork in history as he has faced. Either it is possible for man to live indefinitely with his world out of focus, or it is not. I suspect that it is not, that a will-to-order and orientation is rather fundamental in the human make-up. If so, the post-modern period, like all the intellectual epochs that preceded it, will turn out to be a transition to a still different perspective.

But if reality does get reordered for the Western mind, this order is certain to be very different from that which the modern mind envisioned. What it will be like cannot at this juncture be surmised. The most that can be ventured is the abstract prediction that it will be more complicated than the modern mind suspected and that its order will be recognized as partially imposed by man's mind and not just passively mirrored within it. The order will not describe reality as its exists by itself apart from us. In-stead it will describe an ellipse in which man in his entirety—his purposes and feelings as well as his intellect—stands as one focus in balance and ten-sion with its complementing focus: the cosmos in which his life is set and against which his destiny must be enacted.

Questions

1.   Smith, in his effort to describe the "most recent sea change in Western thought," presents three historic periods as antecedents to what he calls the "Post-Modern Mind." Outline the assumptions Smith gives as underlying these three historic periods: the Graeco-Ro-man, the Christian, the period of Modern Science.

2.   What are Smith's views concerning the basic assumptions of the "Post-Modern Mind"? List these assumptions in outline form.

3.   In the second paragraph of the essay, Smith explains the import-ance of contemporary "assumptions": they "underlie our outlooks on life." Write a brief essay in which you explain your reasons for sup-

porting or rejecting a specific, contemporary "assumption," in art, philosophy, science, literature, architecture, engineering, or history.

4.   In this essay Smith provides some insight into his wide study of the subject through his references to such writers as Aristotle, Newton, Whitehead, Kierkegaard, Nietzsche, Dostoevski, Butler, Barth, Reinhold Niebuhr, Pascal, Camus, Sartre, Kafka, Beckett, Copland, and Bultmann. Based on your own reading and experiences write a short essay on the problems you have encountered in "struggling for self-realization."

5.   The vocabulary of Smith's essay raises many questions. Look up the dictionary meanings of the following words: Reformation, leviathan, cosmology, salvation, deism, imagination, skepticism, positivist, metaphysics, existentialist, rationalism, and surrealism. Then re-read the essay for new understanding. Write a 500-word essay explaining the meanings and illustrating one of these concepts.

SCIENTIFIC CONCEPTS
AND CULTURAL CHANGE

Harvey Brooks

There are many difficulties of communication between the sub-groups within our culture—for example, between the natural sciences, social sciences, and humanities. But there are also ways in which they are becoming increasingly united, and most of this essay will be an effort to trace a few common themes and viewpoints derived from science which I see as increasingly pervading our culture as a whole.

Perhaps one of the most important is the common allegiance of scholarship to the ideal of objective research, to the possibility of arriving by successive approximations at an objective description of reality. Whether it be concerned with the structure of a distant galaxy or the sources of the art of the nineteenth century poet, there exists a common respect for evidence and a willingness to follow evidence wherever it leads regardless of the preconceptions or desires of the scholar. This is, of course, only an ideal; but failure to conform to this ideal, if detected, damns a scholar whether he be a scientist or a humanist. In a sense the whole apparatus of academic scholarship is an attempt to bring scientific method into the pursuit of knowledge through progressive refinements in the uncovering and use of evidence.

A characteristic of scholarship, as of science, is that it prefers to tackle

Reprinted by permission from *Daedalus*, Journal of the American Academy of Arts and Sciences, Boston, Massachusetts, Vol. 94, No. 1.

well-defined, finite problems that appear to be soluble with the methods and evidence available. This often means eschewing the more fundamental, the more "metaphysical" issues, in the belief that the cumulative result of solving many smaller and more manageable problems will ultimately throw more light on the larger issues than would a frontal attack. One of the paradoxes of modern sciences has been that the greater its success in a pragmatic sense, the more modest its aims have tended to become in an intellectual sense. The goals and claims of modern quantum theory are far more modest than those of Laplace, who believed that he could predict the entire course of the universe, in principle, given its initial conditions. The aim of science has changed from the "explanation" of reality to the "description" of reality—description with the greatest logical and aesthetic economy. The claims to universality of nineteenth century physics have been replaced by a greater awareness of what still remains to be discovered about the world, even "in principle." The day of global theories of the social structure or of individual psychology seems to have passed. Experience has taught us that real insight has often been achieved only after we were prepared to renounce our claim that our theories were universal. The whole trend of modern scholarship has been towards greater conservatism in deciding what can be legitimately inferred from given evidence; we are more hesitant to extrapolate beyond the immediate circumstances to which the evidence applies. We are quicker to recognize the possibility of unrevealed complexities or unidentified variables and parameters. Even in artistic criticism we tend to recognize greater diversity in the influences playing on an artist, greater ambiguity in his motives or artistic intentions. Art, scholarship, and science are united in looking further behind the face of common-sense reality, in finding subtleties and nuances. It is, of course, this search for subtlety which has made communication between disciplines more difficult, because to the casual observer each discipline appears to be working in an area beyond common sense.

The admission of finite aims in scholarship has been connected with an increasingly sophisticated view of the scope and limitations of evidence in all fields. But the emphasis on finite and limited aims in scholarly inquiry has also been paralleled by the extension of scientific and scholarly attitudes to practical affairs. One sees a close analogy between the preoccupation of science with manageable problems and the decline of ideology and growth of professional expertise in politics and business. One of the most striking developments of the post-war world has been the increasing irrelevance of political ideology, even in the Soviet Union, to actual political decisions. One sees the influence of the new mood in the increasing bureaucratization and professionalization of government and industry and in the growth of "scientific" approaches to management and administration. The day of the intuitive entrepreneur or the charismatic statesman, seems to be waning. In a recent volume of *Dædalus* on "A New Europe?"

the recurring theme is the increasing relegation of questions which used to be matters of political debate to professional cadres of technicians and experts which function almost independently of the democratic political process. In most of the western world the first instinct of statesmanship is to turn intransigent problems over to "experts" or to "study groups." There appears to be an almost naive faith that if big problems can be broken down sufficiently and be dealt with by experts and technicians, the big problems will tend to disappear or at least lose much of their urgency. Although the continuing discourse of experts seems wasteful, "Parkinsonian," the fact remains that it has worked surprisingly well in government, just as it has in science and scholarship. The progress which is achieved, while slower, seems more solid, more irreversible, more capable of enlisting a wide consensus. Much of the history of social progress in the twentieth century can be described in terms of the transfer of wider and wider areas of public policy from politics to expertise. I do not believe it is too fanciful to draw a parallel between this and the scientific spirit of tackling soluble problems.

The trend towards the acceptance of expertise has been especially striking in Europe where both ideology and the apolitical professional bureaucracy have been stronger than in the United States. But even in this country there has been increasing public acceptance of expert analysis and guidance in such areas of government as fiscal policy and economic growth. In the realm of affairs, as in the realm of knowledge, the search for global solutions or global generalizations has been replaced by the search for manageable apolitical reformulations of problems. The general has been replaced by the specific. Concern with the theoretical goals and principles of action has been replaced by attempts at objectively predicting and analyzing the specific consequences of specific alternative actions or policies. Often the problems of political choice have become buried in debates among experts over highly technical alternatives.

It remains to be seen to what degree this new reign of the bureaucrat and the expert reflects the influence of science and scientific modes of thinking and to what degree it represents a temporary cyclic phenomenon resulting from unprecedented economic growth and the absence of major social crises. However, the modes of thought which are characteristic of science have penetrated much deeper into scholarship and practical affairs than the hand-wringing of some scientists would tend to suggest, and the general adoption of these modes of thought does not appear to have relegated genuine human values to the scrap heap to the degree which some of the humanists would have us believe. Indeed it has brought us closer to a realization of many of the human values which we regard as desirable.

On the other hand, it must be recognized, that some of this reliance on expertise has moved us in directions in which we would not have gone had we been more aware of the unspoken and unrecognized assumptions underlying some of our "technical" solutions. For example, economic growth and technology have come to be accepted as valuable in themselves. The assembly line has brought more and more goods to more and more people, but it has also introduced monotony into work and a sometimes depressing standardization into our products. The technology of production tends to accept as its goals values which technology alone is well adapted to achieving without balanced consideration of other, equally important goals.[1] The very definition of gross national product connotes measurement of economic progress in purely quantitative terms without reference to changes in the quality of the social and physical environment or improvement and deterioration in the quality and variety of the products available. The inclination to tackle the soluble problems first often extrapolates to the view that the more intractable problems are less important.

In the preceding paragraphs I have argued that both scholarship and practical affairs have increasingly adopted the spirit and mode of thought of the natural sciences. An interesting question is to what extent the actual concepts and ideas of science have entered into other disciplines and into our culture generally. There are, of course, some very obvious ways in which this has occurred. Scarcely any other scientific theory, for example, has influenced literature and art so much as Freud's psychoanalytical theory. Though some of Freud's ideas might be said to contain dogmatic elements which are essentially non-scientific or even anti-scientific in spirit, nevertheless, psychoanalysis is based on largely empirical observation and professes to test itself against objective evidence. It is clearly a scientific theory which, though extensively elaborated and modified, is still basically valid in its description of the irrational and subconscious elements in human motivation and behavior. It has completely altered our view of human nature, and this changed viewpoint is reflected almost universally, though in varying degrees, in modern literature and art, as well as in the interpretation of history and political behavior. The orderly Lockean world embodied in the American Constitution, in which each man acts rationally in his own self-interest, can no longer be accepted in quite the undiluted way that the Founding Fathers believed in it. There is ample evidence of neurotic and irrational behavior on the part of whole communities and social systems, often in opposition to their own self-interest. Even organized religion has largely accepted and adapted many of the principles of psychoanalysis, while rejecting some of the world views which have been extrapolated from it.

A more problematic example is the parallel between the increasingly abstract and insubstantial picture of the physical universe which modern physics has given us and the popularity of abstract and non-representational forms of art and poetry. In each case the representation of reality is increasingly removed from the picture which is immediately presented to us by our senses. As the appreciation of modern physics requires more and more prior education, so the appreciation of modern art and music requires a more educated—some would say a more thoroughly conditioned—aesthetic taste. In physics the sharp distinction which used to be made between the object and its relations to other objects has been replaced by the idea that the object (or elementary particle) is nothing* but the nexus of the various relations in which it participates. In physics, as in art and literature, form has tended to achieve a status higher than substance.

It is difficult to tell how much psychological reality there is to this parallel. It is not sufficient to reply that a physical picture is still a definite model which can be related by a series of clear and logical steps to the world which we see and that no such close correspondence exists between abstract art and the sensible world. For physical models depend to a larger degree on taste than is generally appreciated. While correspondence with the real world exists, this probably is not sufficient by itself to constitute a unique determinant of a model. Yet the successful model is one that has evolved through so many small steps that it would take a bold imagination indeed to construct another one which would fit the same accumulation of interconnected facts or observations. What is regarded as acceptable evidence for a model of reality, even in physics, is strongly dependent on the scientific environment of the time. Evidence which favors theories already generally accepted is much less critically scrutinized than evidence that appears to run counter to them. One always makes every effort to fit new evidence to existing concepts before accepting radical modifications; if a theory is well established the contradictory evidence is usually questioned long before the theory, and usually rightly so. Established theories depend on many more bits of accumulated evidence than is often appreciated, even by the scientist himself. Once a principle becomes generally accepted the scientific community generally forgets much of the detailed evidence that led to it, and it takes a real jolt to lead people to reconsider the evidence. In fact, scientific theories are seldom fully displaced; rather they are fitted into the framework of a more comprehensive theory, as Newtonian mechanics was fitted into the formulations of relativity and quantum mechanics. This, in itself, suggests that there are many theories or models which will fit given facts.

All of this points to the fact that a scientific theory is the product of a long evolutionary process which is not strictly logical or even retraceable. The mode of presentation of science, especially to the non-scientist, usually suppresses or conceals the process by which the results were originally arrived at, just as the artist does not reveal the elements which went into his creation. Thus it seems possible that there is some common or universal element in the modern mentality which makes quantum theory acceptable to the physicist, abstract art to the artist, metaphysical poetry to the poet, atonal music to the musician, or abstract spaces to the mathematician. The attack on these aspects of modern culture by totalitarians of both the right and the left perhaps lends further credence to these common threads. It is interesting to observe that children with previously untrained tastes have little trouble in appreciating and enjoying modern art or music and that the younger generation of physicists has no trouble in absorbing the ideas of quantum mechanics quite intuitively with none of the sense of paradox which still troubles some of the older generation. It is probable that the main elements of taste, whether it be scientific or aesthetic, are formed quite early in our experience and are strongly conditioned by the cultural climate. Science, as one of the most dynamic of contemporary intellectual trends, is undoubtedly a strong factor in creating this cultural climate, but it would be rash to ascribe causal connections. It would be interesting to know whether some psychologist, by studying current tastes in art or poetry, could predict what *kinds* of theories were likely to be acceptable in elementary particle physics, or perhaps vice versa!

Another obvious but superficial way in which scientific ideas enter our culture is through some of the dominant "themes" of science. One such theme, for example, is evolution and natural selection, and the derived philosophical concept of progress. Today we take the idea of evolution so much for granted that we are inclined to forget that until the nineteenth century it was generally believed that the present state of society and man was the result of degeneration from some antecedent golden age or hypothetical ideal "state of nature." The Puritan Revolution in England and the French Revolution had ideologies which appealed to a hypothetical prehistoric past for their model of an ideal society. Only with Marx did revolution present itself as a forward movement into a more "advanced," previously non-existent state of human society.

In the nineteenth century the idea of evolution and particularly the concepts of natural selection, competition between species, and the "survival of the fittest" were seized upon as an explanation of and justification for the contemporary laissez-faire capitalist society. State intervention in the competitive economic process was regarded as an almost immoral interference with the "balance of nature" in human society. In the United States and Britain the first science of sociology was built upon an interpretation of the ideas of natural selection. A whole generation of future American businessmen was educated in the ideas of men like Sumner. This sociology stressed the dangers of permitting organized society to tamper with the inexorable laws of social evolution.

In the early part of the twentieth century Darwin's ideas lost some of their original influence, but now, in the second half, they have regained much of their influence in biology and have tended to be reinforced by recent discoveries in biochemical genetics. However, it is interesting to note that a subtle change of emphasis has crept into the interpretation of natural selection. The modern evolutionary biologist tends to stress the concept of the "ecological niche" and the fact that natural selection, when looked at more carefully, leads to a kind of cooperation among species, a cooperation which results from finer and finer differentiation of function and of adaptation to the environment.[2] Indeed, biologists stress the fact that natural selection generally leads not to the complete domination of one species, but rather to a finer and finer branching of species, a sort of division of labor which tends ultimately to minimize competition. Is it too much to suggest a parallel here between the changing scientific interpretations of biological evolution and changing attitudes towards cooperative action in human societies? Is there any connection between the modern view of ecology and the progressive division of labor and specialization of function which are characteristic of modern economic organization? Certainly the analogies with biological evolution have been extremely suggestive in the development of modern cultural anthropology.

Another theme which is involved here is that of dynamic equilibrium or balance, also fruitful in the study of chemical equilibrium. When dynamic equilibrium exists, a complex system can be apparently static from the macroscopic viewpoint even though rapid changes are taking place in its elementary components. All that is necessary is that the rates of changes in opposite directions balance. This is the kind of equilibrium that is envisioned as occurring in an ecological system or in a social or economic system. It would, perhaps, be wrong to suggest any causal or genetic relation between the growth of such ideas of chemical theory and their application to social or biological systems. The fact is, however, that the concepts arose at similar periods in scientific development and helped to establish a kind of climate of taste in scientific theories which undoubtedly facilitated intuitive transfer from one discipline to another. One finds the images and vocabulary of chemical equilibrium theory constantly recurring in descriptions of social and economic phenomena.

Two of the germinal ideas of twentieth-century physics have been "relativity" and "uncertainty." Philosophers generally recognize that both of these themes have had an important influence on their attitudes, but the physical scientist finds it more difficult to connect the philosophical view with its role in physics. At least the connection is not so self-evident as it is in the case of evolution or of psychoanalysis. Indeed, both relativity and uncertainty are words which have rather precise operational meanings in physics, but which have been given all sorts of wishful or anthropomophic interpretations in philosophy. Indeed, scientific popularizers have themselves been especially guilty of this type of questionable semantic extrapolation.[3] The situation has been aggravated by the tendency of physicists to use words from everyday discourse to denote very subtle and precise technical concepts. The popularizer and the layman then use the technical and the everyday term interchangeably to draw conclusions bearing little relation to the original concept.

Let us consider relativity first. The basic idea of relativity is that all the laws of mechanics and electromagnetism are the same, independent of the state of uniform motion in which the observer happens to be moving. Relativity is "relative" in the sense that there is no "absolute" motion, no fixed reference point in the universe that has greater claim to validity than any other. On the other hand, the elimination of absolute motion is achieved only at the price of introducing an absolute velocity which is the same in all reference systems, namely, the velocity of light. Thus it may be legitimately questioned whether "relativity" or "absolutism" is the correct name for the theory. Nevertheless, the first terminology was the one that caught the popular and speculative imagination and provided the basis of a revolution in viewpoint which affected many areas of knowledge. Not long after relativity was absorbed into physics, the anthropologists were stressing the extraordinary diversity of human customs and ethical norms and were arguing that moral standards had to be viewed not in an absolute sense but relative to the particular culture in which they were found. The judgments of history became less moralistic; the actions of individuals tended to be viewed in the context of the ethical norms of their time. The realistic novel or drama in which human behavior was depicted without moral judgment became fashionable. Yet if these things have little to do with "relativity" in the sense that Einstein intended, the very fact that the word caught fire so easily suggests there does exist a kind of common taste in such matters and that this taste forms part of the intellectual climate of the time.

The other key idea of physics is "uncertainty," as embodied in the Heisenberg Uncertainty Principle. The philosophical interpretation of this principle has been the subject of interminable debate by both scientists and laymen. On one extreme, people have viewed the uncertainty principle as repealing the laws of causality and reintroducing "free will" into the physical as well as the mental universe. Most working physicists tend to take a somewhat more pedestrian view of the principle. They interpret it as being the result of an attempt to describe the state of the universe in terms of an inappropriate and outmoded concept, namely that of the point mass or "particle," a concept derived by analogy with macroscopic, i.e. common-sense, physics. Nevertheless, regardless of the exact interpretation, the uncertainty principle does imply that the idealized classical determinism of Laplace is impossible. The laws of quantum theory are deterministic or "causal" in the sense that the state of the universe at any time is determined by its "state" at some previous time. The lack of determinism in the Laplacian sense comes from the impossibility of specifying the "state" at any time in terms of any set of operations which will not themselves change its state and thus spoil the assumptions. What is wrong in the old determinism is the idea that the universe can be uniquely and unequivocally distinguished from the observing system, which is a part of it. In this sense the uncertainty principle can be seen as merely a further extension of the concept of relativity.[4] Interpreted in this light, we find the same idea cropping up in many fields of knowledge. The social scientist is increasingly conscious that the measurements that he can make on any social system affect the future behavior of the system. A good example is public opinion polls, which, if made public, affect the attitude of the public on the very matters the polls are supposed to measure "objectively." Another example is educational tests, which not only measure human ability, but tend to change the cultural and educational norms which are accepted and sought. This aspect of the uncertainty principle in the social sciences is, in quantitative terms, a matter of some debate, but it is an important factor in social measurement, which has to be dealt with just as in physics. In many social situations the mere fact that the subjects know they are being observed or tested affects their behavior in ways which are difficult to discount in advance. Even in a subject like history a sort of analog of the uncertainty principle is found. It lies basically in the fact that the historian knows what happened afterwards and therefore can never really describe the "initial conditions" of his system in a way which is independent of his own perspective. In seeking to discern the underlying causes of events he inevitably tends to stress those factors which demonstrably influenced events in the way they actually came out, minimizing factors or tendencies which did not develop even though the relative strengths of the two tendencies may have been very evenly balanced at that time. The modern historian, of course, tends to be very aware of this uncertainty principle and to allow for it as much as possible. Again, while there is probably little intellectual connection between these various attitudes in the different disciplines, there is a general intellectual climate which stresses the interaction between the observer and the system being observed, whether it be in history, physics, or politics.

There are a number of themes in science having a somewhat more direct and traceable intellectual connection between different disciplines. Here I should like to mention three, namely, energy, feedback, and information. Each of these is a highly technical concept in physics or engineering; however, each also has broad and increasing ramifications in other disciplines. Of these, the oldest and most loosely used is probably energy. This concept is closely associated with that of "transformation." That is, the reason energy is a useful concept is that it has many different forms or manifestations which may be transformed into each other. In physics it is probably the most general and unifying concept we have. All physical entities or phenomena, including "matter" or "mass," are forms or manifestations of energy. Though it may be transformed, its quantity is "invariant," and this is what makes it important. The concept of energy has, of course, been important in biology almost as long as in physics. Living matter functions by transforming energy, and much of the early science of physiology was concerned with studying the transformations of energy in living systems. But the term "energy" has also found its way into many other fields of knowledge, where it is used often more metaphorically than with precise significance. Nevertheless, even in its metaphorical use it tends to partake of some of the characteristic properties of physical energy; namely, it is subject to transformation into different forms, and in the process of transformation the total energy is in some sense preserved. One speaks of psychic energies, historical energies, social energies. In these senses energy is not really measurable, nor is it directly related to physical energy. Nevertheless, like physical energy it can be released in the form of enormous physical, mental, or social activity; and, when it is, we tend to think of it as somehow "potential" in the pre-existing situation. The term "tension" denotes a state of high potential energy, like a coiled spring; and a high state of tension, whether social or psychological, is usually followed by a "release" or conversion into kinetic energy or activity of some variety. Thus the language of energy derived from physics has proved a very useful metaphor in dealing with all sorts of social and psychological phenomena. Here the intellectual connection is more clear than in the case of relativity or uncertainty, but it is more metaphorical than logical.

The concept of feedback is one of the most fundamental ideas of modern engineering. It underlies the whole technology of automatic control and automation. The original concept was quite restricted in application. It arose in connection with the design of electronic amplifiers in which a part of the output was fed back into the input in order to control the faithfulness with which the amplifier would reproduce in the output the form of the input signal.[5] An amplifier with what is called negative feedback reproduces the time behavior of the input more faithfully than the same amplifier without feedback, the more so the greater the feedback.

The concepts and methods of analysis originally developed for amplifiers were rapidly applied to control systems, where they had a far more fundamental influence. In recent years the feedback concept has been extended still further to embrace the idea of "information feedback," which is important in biological and social phenomena as well as in the engineering of physical systems. The idea has been stated by Forrester [6] in the following way:

"An information feedback system exists whenever the environment leads to a decision that results in action which affects the environment and thereby influences future decisions."

At first this may seem unrelated to amplifiers and control systems, but if we identify "environment" with "input" and "decision" with "output" we can readily see how the more general definition includes amplifiers and control systems as a special case. In the case of the amplifier the decision is completely and uniquely determined by the environment, but the concept of information feedback applies equally well when the decision is a discrete rather than a continuous function and when it is related to the environment only in a probabilistic sense.

In this more general use of the words environment and decision we can see many examples of the information feedback concept in biology and the social sciences. For example, the process of natural selection in evolution is itself a type of feedback. The selection process—the particular population which survives in each generation—is the decision, and this is fed back into the genetic constitution of the next generation; in this way the characteristics of the population adjust to the environment over successive generations.

The muscular activities of animals also illustrate information feedback. In this case, the environment, which must be considered as including both the external environment and the relation of the body to it, influences the decision through perception. The work of the muscles is the analog of the amplifier or controller, and the perception of the organism provides the feedback loop. The process of learning may be readily regarded as an information feedback system. Indeed the theory behind the teaching machine is essentially designed to establish a tighter feedback, through the process of "reinforcement," which helps the student to decide whether he has learned correctly. Much of the concern with the techniques of teaching is related to improvement of the feedback loop in the learning process.

The consideration of such processes as learning or cultural evolution as feedback systems would be merely a convenient metaphor, like energy, were it not for the fact that information feedback systems have certain general properties which tend to be independent of their particular embodiment. The two most important properties are those of stability and response. There exists a whole theory of the stability of feedback systems, which depends on the amplification or "gain" of the system and the time delays which occur throughout the whole decision-environment-decision loop. High gain and large time lags tend to produce instability which will cause the system as a whole to "hunt," that is, the state of the system oscillates in a more or less uncontrolled way about the position of adjustment to the environment. The term "response" relates to the closeness and rapidity with which the system in question will adjust to a changing environment; this is analogous to the closeness with which the time behavior of the output of a feedback amplifier will reproduce the time behavior of the input.

The mathematics of the stability of linear amplifiers and control systems—that is, physical systems in which the output or "decision" is directly proportional to input or "environment"—is highly elaborated and well understood. Real feedback systems, however, are often non-linear, probabilistic in nature, and discrete rather than continuous. The mathematics for dealing with such systems is not very well developed, and for this reason it has not, until recently, proved very profitable to look at biological or social systems from the standpoint of information feedback. However, the advent of the high speed digital computer has speeded up the processes of ordinary arithmetical calculation by a factor of more than a million and has brought much more complicated and pathological (from the mathematical standpoint) systems within the purview of calculation. The usefulness of the computer lies in the fact that the behavior of feedback systems depends on only certain of their abstract properties; these properties, in turn, can be readily modeled or "simulated" on a computer. Thus we are enabled to study the dynamics of the model in great detail and, if necessary, at a speed much greater than that of the real life situation.

It is now being recognized that many types of unstable behavior that occur in biological and social systems are, in fact, examples of unstable feedback systems, the instability usually arising from unacceptable time lags in the transmission of information through the system. A case which is by now fairly well documented is that of inventory policy in a business.[7] In times of high demand a business may tend to build up inventory in anticipation of future demand, and this further increases demand; but there is a lag between orders and production as well as between the measurement of demand and the decision to increase inventory. This can have the effect of introducing a highly fluctuating factory output in a situation in which the external demand is actually rather steady. Forrester [8] has given an analysis which suggests strongly that exactly this model may account for the notorious instability of production and employment in the textile industry.

It seems highly likely that the business cycle in the economy as a whole represents a form of feedback instability to which many individual elements of decision making contribute through their time lags. In fact all forms of social decision making tend to contain an inherent time lag arising from the fact that anticipations of the future are simply linear extrapolations of past trends. Thus one can even discern a similar tendency in history for political and social attitudes towards public issues to be those appropriate to the experience of the recent or distant past rather than to the actual situation which is faced. For example, the philosophies of laissez-faire economics were conditioned by the mercantile and pre-industrial era in which the principal problem was the inhibiting effects of state interference in the economy. Or, to take a more recent example, early post-war American economic policy was based on the fear of a major depression similar to what followed the first war, while much of present public thinking is based on the fear of inflation of the type which followed World War II. Such lags in social attitudes probably contribute to many of the cyclic phenomena which are often attributed to history. Of course, the examples given above are somewhat crude oversimplifications, but the basic idea is one which may have quantitative as well as suggestive or metaphorical value.

Another possible example is the cycle in moral attitudes. Attitudes towards moral values, because of the long time they take to diffuse throughout society, tend to lag behind the actual social conditions for which they were most appropriate. Thus, for example, Victorian attitudes towards sex arose partly as a reaction to the extreme laxity which existed in previous times, and conversely modern liberal attitudes towards sex are to some extent a response to the social and psychological effects of Victorian repression. Such attitudes tend to go in cycles because their inherent time lag produces unstable feedback in the social system. Such lags are especially important in the dynamic or "high gain" cultures characteristic of the West.

The problem of stability in feedback theory is relevant to situations in which the environment without considering feedback is more or less constant. When an unstable feedback situation exists, the system "hunts" about the stable situation of adjustment to the environment. The other important concept, however, is that of the response of the system to environmental changes imposed from without, or, in amplifier terminology, the faithfulness and speed with which the output follows the input. This introduces the idea of "optimization" in control systems. An optimized system is one which responds to its environment in the best way as defined by some quantitative criterion. Of course, the optimal configuration of the control system will be dependent on the properties of the environment to which it is expected to respond or adapt. We can imagine an environment which is subject to short-term and long-term changes and a feedback system which is optimized for the short-term changes occurring during a certain period. If the nature of the short-term changes also varies slowly in time, then the feedback system will not remain optimum. We could then imagine a feedback system whose properties change with time in such a way as to keep the response optimal as the short-term changes in the environment occur. The continuing optimization can itself be described as a form of information feedback. For example, we can imagine a man learning a game requiring great physical skill. When he has learned it, his muscular and nervous system may be thought of as a feedback system which has been optimized for that particular game. If he then engages in a new game, his muscles and nerves will have to be optimized all over again for the new game, and the process of learning is itself a form of information feedback. In this way we arrive at the concept of a whole hierarchy of feedback systems—of systems within systems, each operating on a different time scale and each higher system in the hierarchy constituting the learning process for the next lower system in the hierarchy. In the technical literature these hierarchies are referred to as adaptive control. Adaptive control systems appear to "learn" by experience and thus come one step closer to simulating the behavior of living systems. In fact we may imagine that biological and social systems are information feedback systems with many more superimposed hierarchies than we are accustomed to dealing with in physical control systems.

The other key idea from engineering which has had an important impact on social and biological theory is that of information, and the closely associated concept of noise. The idea that information was a concept that could be defined in precise mathematical terms was recognized by Leo Szilard in 1929.[9] Szilard was the first to point out the connection between the quantity of information we have about the physical world and the physical concept of the entropy of a system. However, Szilard's ideas lay fallow until twenty years later when they were rediscovered by Shannon [10] and precisely formulated in their modern form—the form which has revolutionized modern communications. There is a very close relation between information and probability. In fact, the amount of information in an image or a message is closely connected with its deviations from a purely random pattern. The concept of information is basic to the quantitative study of language and has provided one of the cornerstones of a new science known as mathematical linguistics. It is also generally recognized that the transmission of genetic properties from generation to generation is essentially a communication of information. This has led to the idea of the "genetic code" which contains all the information necessary to reproduce the individual. So far the attention of biologists has mostly been focused on the elementary code, that is, on the relationship between the structure of the DNA molecule and the genetic information which it carries. The possibility of precise definition of the quantity of information in a system, however, opens up the possibility of considering evolution from the standpoint of a system of information transmission.[11]—a type of study which is still in its infancy. A remarkable consequence of information concepts is the realization that the information embodied in the biological constitution of the human race is essentially contained in the total quantity of DNA in the human germ cells—at most a few grams in the whole world. One suspects that it may be possible to apply information concepts similarly to the study of cultural evolution and to the transmission of culture from generation to generation.

One cannot talk about information without considering noise, which is the random background on which all information must ultimately be recognized. By its very nature noise is the absence of information. When an attempt is made to transmit a definite piece of information in the presence of noise, the noise destroys a definite amount of the information in the transmission process. No transmission system is completely faithful. Noise is, in the first instance, a physical concept; but, as in the case of information and feedback, the concept may be extended in a somewhat vague way to social and biological systems. For example, in evolutionary theory the "noise" is the random variations in the genetic constitution produced by cosmic radiation and other external influences on the genetic material. In the transmission of cultural information, the "information" communicated by a piece of literature or a work of art depends not only upon the intrinsic information content of the work but also on the experience and education of the recipient. Unless the artist and the recipient have had the same experience, the communication is always less than faithful.

In the foregoing I have tried to suggest how a number of important themes from the physical and biological sciences have found their way into our general culture, or have the potential for doing so. In the case of the concepts of feedback and information, the ideas appear to have an essentially quantitative and operational significance for social and cultural dynamics, although their application is still in its infancy. The most frequent case is that in which a scientific concept has served as a metaphor for the description of social and political behavior. This has occurred, for example, in the case of the concepts of relativity, uncertainty, and energy. In other cases, such as evolution and psychoanalysis, the concept has entered even more deeply into our cultural attitudes.

References

1. Lewis Mumford, "Authoritarian and Democratic Technics," *Technology and Culture*, 5 (1964), 1.
2. Ernst Mayr, *Animal Species and Evolution* (Cambridge: Harvard Belknap Press, 1963).
3. L. S. Stebbing, *Philosophy and the Physicists* (New York: Dover Publications, Inc., 1958).
4. P. W. Bridgman, *The Logic of Modern Physics* (first edition, New York: Macmillan, 1927). Although written as a philosophical interpretation of relativity before the discovery of quantum mechanics in its modern form, this work is extraordinarily prescient with respect to the philosophical ideas underlying quantum theory.
5. H. S. Black, U. S. Patent No. 2,102,671 (1934); cf. also, H. W. Bode, *Network Analysis and Feedback Amplifier Design* (New York: van Nostrand, 1945).
6. J. W. Forrester, *Industrial Dynamics* (Cambridge and New York: M.I.T. Press and John Wiley, 1961).
7. *Ibid.*
8. *Ibid.*
9. L. Szilard, Z. *Phys.* 53 (1929), 840; cf. also, L. Brillouin, *Science and Information Theory* (New York: Academic Press, 1956).
10. C. E. Shannon and W. Weaver, *The Mathematical Theory of Information* (Urbana: University of Illinois Press, 1949).
11. W. Bossert, private communication.

Questions

1. In a formal essay the writer usually presents a serious examination of a subject of current interest. Brooks, in the opening sentence of his

essay, acknowledges the difficulties among and between "sub-groups within our culture," but he indicates he wishes to examine "ways in which they are becoming increasingly united," particularly as "themes and viewpoints derived from sciences" pervade our culture. Select a subject you wish to examine seriously, investigate, in the library, some recent periodical essays on the subject, and write an opening purpose paragraph.

2. The learned character of Brooks' essay is evident in the ideas, subjects, and examples he provides. Make an outline of the essay.

3. Much of Brooks' essay is devoted to the "themes" of science which have become a part of contemporary culture. Such concepts as evolution and natural selection, dynamic equilibrium, relativity, uncertainty, energy, feedback, and information are among the "themes" discussed. Write a brief formal essay on one of these "themes," an essay devoted to explaining the concept and illustrating its meanings. You may wish to examine a number of articles and textbooks before you write your paper.

4. Study the dictional choices of one of the paragraphs in Brooks' essay. For example, what are the meaning of the following dictional choices, all from the second paragraph—"scholarship," "objective research," "reality," "evidence," "scientist," "humanist," "scientific method"?

5. Look up the words "formal" and "tone" in a good dictionary. In what ways is the tone of Brooks' essay "formal"? Write a brief essay explaining and supporting your findings.

THE ROLE OF THE CREATIVE ARTS IN CONTEMPORARY SOCIETY

Lewis Mumford

Contemporary society has concentrated on the control of nature and forgotten the nature of man or the resources needed to further his own continued development. As a result, the only part of modern man's life that seems real to him is that which is tethered to the machine, either to perform services for it or to receive with due gratitude its abundant products. This subordination of the personal life to impersonal processes has been taking place in the creative arts: the very area where man has hitherto been most self-sufficing. These arts, instead of nourishing and replenishing man, leave him still emptier, for they have become mere auxilia-

Reprinted by permission of Lewis Mumford and *The Virginia Quarterly Review*, from *Virginia Quarterly Review*, Volume 33, Number 4, Autumn, 1957.

ries to mechanical organization. What has caused this perverse development? Under what conditions may it be altered and turned to human account? This is the situation I shall examine: these are the questions I shall seek to answer.

Before discussing the role of the creative arts in contemporary society it would be well for me perhaps to put up a few guideposts and markers, to stake out the field we are going to cover. In some quarters there is a tendency to identify creativity in the arts exclusively with the production of poems, paintings, music, statues; and it goes so far that many people regard the writing of any work of the imagination as a creative act in itself, no matter how poor the product, while they dismiss a good page of expository prose as a dull pedestrian business, a mere manipulation of facts. This is mealy nonsense. From the position I shall take here, creativity is something that may manifest itself in almost any human field. Where it is present, as Emerson perceived, one may give to "pots and trays and pans grace and glimmer of romance." I will go further: in their high moments of creativity, there is no inner difference, even in emotional tension, between a poet, a physicist, a surgeon, or an engineer; for in the creative act itself they are passing beyond the limits of routine behavior into the realm of form and significance. This of course takes issue with the kindergarten notion of creativity, and disposes of the too simple belief that associates it with a conspicuous absence of intellectual content or technical skill.

Yet those who use the term "creative arts" are not altogether on a false scent, when they single out a special group of activities as being committed, with a certain intensity of purpose and singleness of goal, to the creative act as such. For what we mean here by "creative" is that these arts have no other reason for existence than to draw forth from human experience new values and to embody those values in forms to which the artist has given an independent and self-sustaining life, which may long outlast the occasion that brought them into being. This is a special kind of creativity. Though the creative arts have always occupied a secure and even generous place in the human economy, it is only now that we begin to suspect what an important part they play in molding the human personality; and how much that part may be fortified by a certain withdrawal from practical duties and environmental pressures. If we shrink from the social implication of the Ivory Tower or the religious implications of the cloister, let us remember the parallel development in the sciences during the last three centuries. Only in modern times has science cut loose from magic and religions, from practical needs and limited technological interests, to investigate general phenomena like cell-growth or electricity without any thought of an immediate application. As a result, we have accumulated in the sciences an immense reservoir of knowledge that now stands ready to irrigate and fertilize a far larger part of the natural world than man was ever able to cultivate before. Greater practical results have come about through this detached creativity than was possible when the scientist sought some direct, immediate gain. So it may prove with the cultivation of the arts.

We can better understand this detached order of creativity if we contrast it with the more usual kind, that associated with a practical function. Take the case of a bridge whose design is due, in the first place, not to the esthetic impulse of the engineer but to our lowly necessity to cross a river. We rightly demand here that the first concern of the engineer shall be to design his bridge so that it will carry a maximum load and will not, in a windstorm, become a twisted mass of steel. In asking for this, we do not exclude creativity; for we recognize that, if the engineer's talents are sufficient, he may within these practical limitations exhibit such creativity as the Roeblings showed in the Brooklyn Bridge or as the Swiss engineer, Freyssinet, showed in many daring concrete structures. But we properly shrink from encouraging abstract forms in bridge building, no matter how pure and elegant, if they flout human needs in order to express the engineer's own emotional tensions or otherwise hidden fantasies. If he is more concerned with his subjective life than with the needs of traffic, he should confine himself to sculpture or music.

Now just the opposite rule holds in the creative arts. To say of one of those arts that it has a certain practical use—that a novel serves as a bandage for the eyes on a dull railroad journey, or that music may take the place of a sleeping pill before going to bed—is not to say anything in favor of its essential nature. For the only true use of the creative arts is creation itself. Their function is to engender creativity in the observer and participant, releasing him from habit and routine, deepening his feelings and emotions, focusing more sharply his perceptions, clarifying his inner nature, bringing into existence a meaningful unity out of what seemed in the act of living a contradictory or a bafflingly incomplete experience, lacking in value or significance.

The creative arts have no other mission, then, than the affirmation and enhancement of life, first of the artist's own life and then that of those with whom he effectively communicates. Though our present civilization identifies success in life with increased production or increased consumption, neither of these quantitative changes has any ultimate human meaning unless it issues in an increase in creativity. Where creativity is blocked or thwarted, our very capacity to become fully human is endangered: so much so that the affirmation of life may take the form of negative creativity—that is, senseless violence and destruction, as has indeed happened on a large scale in our own day.

Now this special function of the creative arts, their office of revealing human wishes, goals, values, ideals, and directing the human personality to ends that lie far beyond mere animal existence, is an ancient one. From the times of the earliest paleolithic cave paintings, man has always acted as if the symbols and forms of art were in some special way connected with the achievement of a truly human self. As Emerson said of the coming of music to raw pioneer settlements: The more piano the less wolf. By his cosmetics and costumes, his images and symbols, by his words and musical notes, man has fabricated out of the materials given by nature a new self, otherwise unfathomable and inexpressible. In these creative productions man separates himself most completely and definitely from the rest of the animal world. Man shares many happy traits like loyalty or parental affection with other creatures. But there is nothing in the animal world that resembles the creative and self-expressive arts: they are as peculiar to man as the formal burial of the dead. What has given the arts this special place? That is no easy question to answer; and no one can be sure that he has a sound and full explanation of their basic social function. But I suggest that we have a clue to the importance of esthetic symbols in the singular success that psychologists have lately had in using projective techniques like the Rorschach blots or the Murray-Morgan thematic apperception tests, for revealing the character and the development of the human personality in all its dimensions. Every aspect of the personality, from its original nature to its ultimate goals, seems to disclose itself in the presence of these simple images. Obviously, the psychologist's blots and pictures do not pretend to be works of art. But if a mere blot can evoke a response that reveals some of the most secret aspects of the human soul, is it not possible, indeed highly likely, that the more complex and subtle structures of the artist may be even more fully evocative? Even when the arts do not mirror external nature, they hold the mirror up to man's inner nature: indeed, at their best, they penetrate it like an X-ray. Man has constant need for this self-knowledge. Because works of art, unlike the dream, have a stable, public form, so that they may be revisited and re-viewed, even as they are open to inspection by others, they have always been one of man's essential means for both self-discovery and mutual understanding.

Let us agree, then, at least for the purposes of this discussion, that the creative arts are concerned with the expression and affirmation of the human person; and so, by subtle and indirect means, with his further development. Only at second or third remove do these arts produce any changes in the environment. This absorption in man's inner concerns, however, has been foreign to the whole mood of Western culture these last four centuries. In our civilization, particularly during the last fifty years, if I may use Sigfried Giedion's memorable title, Mechanization takes command; and our machines and mechanical collectives, our mass organizations and our mass media, have use for only so much of the human personality as they can profitably exploit. So it follows that the creative arts have been forced into a corner and reduced to performing a minor role. Only a small part of our creativity is concerned with man's inner life, as compared with what goes into science or technics. Our ideal image is not that of the whole man, with all his varied potentialities fully developed. On the contrary, our rewards and opportunities have been bestowed on the detached intelligence, as precise and impersonal as the machine, most adept in projecting its narrowed powers—and incidentally, its limitations—into extra-human contrivances. But we now begin to see that what is mechanization within the proper sphere of the machine is likewise dehumanization within the proper sphere of man.

Yet in spite of the pressure of mechanization, in spite of the depletion and even the depression of the human personality, the creative arts have not altogether disappeared from our society. Astonishingly enough, just the opposite has happened: we have witnessed, quantitatively speaking, an extraordinary increase and spread of the creative arts. This is quite a different outcome from that pictured, a century ago, by the Victorian philosophers of the machine. Since these utilitarians believed that industry, invention, and rational science would satisfy all the needs of man, they expected the creative arts to disappear, as activities that belonged only to the childhood of the race. People would discard these ancient images and symbols, Herbert Spencer thought, as the child, in growing up, discards his dolls and toys.

Doubtless the arts today lack a good deal of their old confidence and energy, as compared with the audacious manifestations of creativity one finds in the sciences. This failure of belief in their own importance and validity has dogged the arts for a long while: did not Henry Adams observe in his autobiography more than a generation ago that if anyone was unreal it was the poet, not the business man? That remains pretty much the feeling of our whole society today. Yet the creative arts have saved themselves, after a fashion, by adapting themselves to the very forces that direct so much of man's attention toward the external environment. They have used the characteristic technical facilities of our age for multiplying their own products and widening their distribution. This has proven easier than one might have suspected, for mass production, which people think of usually in purely utilitarian terms, first began in the arts, in the very ancient processes of molding and stamping, applied to inscriptions and images. This innovation was widened in the fifteenth century through the invention of movable types for printing; and now a great variety of reproductive techniques is available in literature, the graphic arts, drama, and music. By these means, the creative arts, once restricted to a devoted minority, have become diffused in time and space, as they never were capable of being spread before; and the arts, instead of being rare, aristocratic, sacred, reserved for moments of great ritual significance or high emotional tension, have become universally accessible, indeed, cheaply profane.

But observe: the constant presence of a great wealth of esthetic stimuli does not in itself testify to our present-day creativity, for only a limited portion of this art is produced by our own society, and only a small part of this current production is anything but trivial and commonplace. But even if we consider only genuine art, our capacity for reproduction has far outrun our capacity for assimilation. You have only to listen to your neighbor's phonograph, if you live in a sufficiently highbrow neighborhood, to hear sixteenth-century music from Italy, a Gregorian chant that goes back to the Dark Ages, now intoned in a French monastery, the beat of an African drum from the depths of the Congo, or the swoon of a trombone from the even more primeval depths of a fashionable metropolitan night club. No other culture, not even Rome in its imperial decadence, has ever presented such a variety of exotic stimuli in the arts.

Do not mistake the point of these observations. The final effect of this immense widening of cultural choices, with all history and all geography on tap at any moment, may be immensely stimulating and prove in the long run altogether desirable. But the mere fact that this distracting multiplicity of offerings exists, and that it has been produced by modern inventions, does not establish its value: certainly one can no longer take for granted that good results will happen automatically, still less, that whatever happens automatically is good. One of the reasons indeed for discussing the role of the creative arts today is to take the measure of this whole problem, so that we may pass from fatuous complacence and confusion to rational evaluation and selection, directed to a more purposeful human development. If, in this general expansion of the arts, we lose our provincialisms of taste and ideology we may be merely widening the empire of chaos and turning ourselves into docile nonentities; or we may in time, as I hope, be re-establishing the dominance of man over his machines, and laying the foundations for a veritable world culture. But if we see the problem as solved merely in terms of more and more people consuming more and more art at a faster and faster rate through larger and larger mass media, we have made a bad choice, which may undermine our creativity, ultimately, in every department.

Now what is the general problem, of which the multiplication and insistent distribution of works of art is just a part? It is the new problem of quantity; and this problem arises directly out of our unparalleled successes in mass organization and mass production. For long, two weaknesses haunted every civilization: one was the fact that it rested upon compulsory labor, and the other was that, however ruthlessly this labor might be pressed and driven, it never produced a sufficient quantity of food and other goods, except for a small privileged minority. Our civilization is now beginning to be haunted by two other spectres, equally formidable, but just for the opposite reasons. Instead of forced labor, we have the prospect of forced leisure: instead of relentless human activity in production, an equally relentless activity in consumption; and instead of near-starvation and scarcity, surfeit and superabundance. So great are the arrears and so persistent the habits brought over from the past that, for most of us, this new-found wealth is still limited enough to be bearable in the realm of food, clothing, and housing; but even here, the penalties are already becoming plain. Like the Sorcerer's Apprentice, in Goethe's poem or in Disney's motion picture, we are now threatened with a quantitative productivity we can neither direct, once we start it, nor turn off. So in the arts we are swept away by a spring freshet of muddied creativity that overflows its natural banks and covers with rocks and rubbish the precious silt that it might otherwise have deposited upon the waiting fields.

Abstractly speaking, our ability to multiply works of art once a master work is produced is neither good nor bad. The question is how far are we able to direct our energies toward a fuller human development, and this means, at bottom, how are we to get fresh master works created by the artist without imposing extraneous limitations and conformities in the interest of wide and profitable distribution. In this area, the needs of individual creativity and the needs of mass consumption are far from identical. Perhaps the greatest threat to the creative arts in our pecuniary, mass-market culture is not so much absolute neglect of the arts as their being made to serve purposes foreign to their nature and hostile to their best use. We recognize this evil without difficulty in Russia, when we observe with proper indignation the Kremlin's attempt to make the arts subservient to their largely Fascist ideology. But there are too many ways in which our own community degrades the creative arts to permit our sense of self-righteous complacency to linger very long. Here in the United States we frequently see the paintings of van Gogh or Renoir used to supply motifs for department store window displays. We hear the masterpieces of Bach and Beethoven used as a prelude to selling motor cars or home permanents: we sometimes even behold contemporary artists of not altogether inferior talents supplying the esthetic background for whiskey and cigarette advertisements. All this is done by the advertiser on the same psychological principle by which, at other moments, he tries to associate the image of a comely young woman, as nearly naked as possible, with his particular product. As in Pavlov's famous experiment with the conditioned reflex, art is used like a bell, to start the consumer's saliva flowing.

The danger we face, then, does not come from the utter absence of creative art in our civilization: our disabilities spring rather from a certain nauseating familiarity with such art, offered at the wrong time, at the wrong place, for the wrong purpose. This round-the-clock offering of creativity threatens to rob us of what that wise ancient, Bernard Berenson, calls the life-enhancing function of art. Just as there are scores of words that a writer now hesitates to use, because they have appeared so often, for cheap or factitious purposes, in publisher's blurbs and advertising slogans—one of those words, incidentally, is the word "creative"—so there are images that should have remained precious but have now become disgusting, either by association or by endless mechanical repetition. The perception that "In short measures life may perfect be" applies particularly to the intensities and perfections of art. Only one kind of destitution would be worse than the complete absence of art; and that would be the constant nagging presence of works of art, in such abundance and duration that the most powerful stimulus would be as empty and ineffective as the most feeble. With art, as with all other living processes and organic consummations, "too much" is as fatal as "too little." In the face of the consumer's repletion, the artist must flog the dulled appetites with some form of sensationalism. Mechanical novelty will then take the place of true originality; and the sadistic whip will violate the natural impulses of love.

Not the least sinister effect of the misuse and overuse of the arts is the effect upon the artist himself. In order to achieve popularity or to hold it, he resorts to sensationalism and self-advertisement; sometimes in his methods, sometimes in his themes; often in both. An artist may not always go as far as Salvador Dali and jump through the plate glass window of a department store in order to attract attention to his work; but there are many ways of breaking glass without risking one's skin; and no small part of what might, under happier auspices, have been admirable creativity goes into the production of mere shockers and thrillers: esthetic crimes, esthetic mysteries, in which the once living organism of art is represented by an artfully dismembered corpse, dead before the story opens. In all the creative arts today, the shocker has become the fashionable mode of art; anxiety, torture, and nausea are the favored psychological states; and the pathological has become the only province identified with the human personality, in its ultimate moment of freedom. Even if significant work that was free from these qualities came forth in these times, it would almost automatically be dismissed as dull and old-fashioned, and buried with yawns. But the fact is that the surviving taste for what is vital and healthy—fortunately this is no small part of the total demand for art—must be satisfied almost exclusively by historic works of art. Yet apart from this current demand for the sensational, as a substitute for rational meaning and value, we must ask ourselves why so much of the genuine creativity of our time is deeply involved in themes of destruction. I propose at least to touch on this formidable question before our discussion ends.

But first let me look at one more related fact that has placed the creative arts under a handicap in our society: this is the elevation of the envelope or the package above the true work of art. One may describe a genuine work of art by saying that it is a product wrought by mind and hand in such a way that the inner content and the outer form exist in an indissoluble organic unity. Whether it is an abstract image or a building, a motion picture or a symphony, what gives it an independent life is the very fact that form and value and meaning are one; so that if one alters any one of these, even in a small degree, every other part is affected. In that sense, the work of art behaves like a veritable organism. This unity is so deep that the artists of the Renaissance, in their exploration of the nude, felt correctly that they could not render the surface of the human body without a detailed and exact knowledge of the anatomy beneath. So, with a modern constructivist sculptor, like Naum Gabo, working in abstract forms to interpret the new forces, the new tensions, the new potentialities that science and technics have brought in. It is no accident that Gabo approached sculpture through the study of engineering, or that, after fabricating new images as a sculptor, he was the first artist to fathom the possibilities of shell construction in architecture to create floors and roofs of the lightest and strongest kind, on the principle of a clam or scallop shell. Such abstract shapes as Gabo creates—witness his new monument in Rotterdam—are not capricious and whimsical; they are an expression of the internal forces that the artist senses and feels and then re-creates.

Now one may define the art of the package by saying that it rests on just the opposite principle: the complete dissociation between the external form and the inner content. The art of the package is the art of concealing the contents under an arbitrary shape, designed only to hold the eye, as if the package alone were important. As has happened already in the wrapping of Christmas gifts in this country, more time, more effort and ingenuity, go into the process of wrapping than often goes into the selection of the present itself. But whether the container is empty or full actually makes no difference to the designer so long as the lure of the package ensures its sale. This subject is one I find highly depressing to contemplate; for it illustrates the pervasive irrationality of our society, with its deceptive surface slickness and its inner futility and emptiness. Since the criticism of the package holds for both the creative arts and the arts of use, I shall use the latter for illustrations, for each of us can readily supply the needed illustrations. Let us pass quickly over the lowest levels of industrial design, where we find pencil sharpeners and kettles with meaningless aerodynamic shapes, or typewriters and cameras marketed in a nonsensical variety of colors, to conceal the fact that so few technical changes that could be disguised as art were possible. Perhaps the most sick-making example of the package is the current design for American motor cars, with contrasting colors and tones, chosen as if to grace some elegant boudoir for a Texas oil magnate. The result is a miracle of meretricious taste and utilitarian ineptitude, looking as if a woman's powder compact had mated with an airplane and brought forth a hybrid monster—fortunately, let us hope, sterile. What matters about a motor car, of course, is what sort of engine lies under the hood and what relation its horsepower and brakes have to its performance; finally, what sensible compromise has been worked out between safety, speed, economy, and comfort, and how thoroughly all these factors have been integrated in the overall design. These are vital subjects that the package artists and that vast public whose taste has been debauched by package esthetics sedulously ignore.

Under the pressure of conforming to the needs of an industrial society that seeks to promote the exorbitant production of mass-produced goods, all the arts tend to accept the same standards. The measure of their success is the mass audience and the mass market that they reach; and on those terms Grandma Moses is a greater painter than Tintoretto. The logical outcome of this process of seeking the lowest common denominator would be to turn the production of art over to one of our thinking machines; and we already have a cybernetic brain capable, I am told, of composing three hundred popular songs in five minutes. Though on the higher levels of art we must still resort to composition by mechanically inadequate human beings, much of this is now tailored, more and more, to fit the consumer demand.

But it is not merely through the overemphasis on the duties of conforming to mass needs that our mechancial organizations now tend to kill the creative arts, with meretricious patronage. Far more deadly is the capturing for the productive and consumptive processes of energies and interest that should go into esthetic creation, or, on the consumer's side, into the development of his personal tastes and choices, into his own inner being. It would be absurd to say that there is a general lack of creativity in our civilization today, quite as absurd as to suppose, in the face of the rising birthrate, that there is any lack of biological vitality. But the fact is that this creativity is not devoted to the enhancement of the person, to the extension of his facilities for development. Quite the opposite: it is directed away from the person to the machine; and its characteristic end-products are automatic factories, atomic piles, nuclear weapons, mechanical brains, all of which are dedicated with mounting intensity of effort to the deadly purposes of annihilation and extermination. Even in the more peaceful aspects of our existence, our activities have become increasingly negative, for we have become a race of shameless Pyramid builders. Though we call our own characteristic forms of the pyramid by other names—air raid shelters, superhighway construction, mile-high skyscrapers, interplanetary rockets, machines and buildings deliberately planned with built-in weaknesses to ensure obsolescence and early removal—we may identify their real nature by the fact that, in addition to their sheer wastefulness, they are closely tied up with the cult of death, like the more ancient Egyptian monuments of stone; and like them, they absorb the energies and vitalities that should have sustained the living.

In other words, our industrial society turns out in its highest expressions of scientific knowledge and inventive skill to be a sort of super-package in its own right. Its external means and methods are marvelous exhibitions of scientific rationality and order; but its inner contents, its purposes and goals, are often frighteningly innocent of any vital human purpose; indeed, a part of those contents in our own day has become downright irrational, however glibly our leaders may rationalize their almost automatic compulsions and their sleep-walking routines. This irrationality is nowhere better reflected and exposed than in the creative arts; and that accounts, I believe, for their own peculiar negations and nihilisms. For the last generation, all but a handful of our best artists have recorded a succession of surrealist nightmares: their images, now primitive and infantile, now fragmentary and violently dismembered, now harsh, rigid, prisonlike, reveal as nothing else does the inner contents, the final spiritual effect, of this death-oriented civilization. Deliberately denying form and composition, the artist himself, in his surrender to these forces, submits to accident and decomposition. Precisely those artists whom we properly count as among the most original minds of our time, a Kafka, a Picasso, a Joyce, a Thomas Mann, a Henry Moore, have in their works of art disclosed both the inner content of this society and its ultimate destiny, if it continues along its present course. This society, this super-package, is streamlined and chromium plated, like the hood of a car; but if one raises the lid, as the true artist must, to inspect what lies below that glossy canopy one finds that the engine itself is a booby-trap, which at any moment may explode in our face and wreck the car, too. Those who find this kind of art revolting do wrong to hate the artist for exposing this inner content; but their impulse to hate it shows a better understanding of the artist's message than the shallow delight of those who merely praise its originality or its studious unintelligibility, without a faint notion of its actual meaning.

If we dare to face the realities of our time as courageously as the creative artist, we must admit a general miscarriage of human purpose: a constant passage of rational means into irrational ends, of productivity into destruction, of life-preservation into random extermination. And how could all this come about without having a sinister and depressing effect upon creativity in the arts? During the last forty years between thirty and forty million people have met premature death by war and genocide alone, on the battlefield, in bombed cities, in extermination camps and human incinerators; and this is only a small laboratory sample of the horrors of extermination that might be packed into forty days with the atrocious instruments of death that we not only command but have already shown our willingness to use upon the innocent and the helpless. Can anyone imagine that this condition is an incentive to creativity? Most of us try to thrust this lethal prospect out of our consciousness, recoiling naturally from the meaninglessness of a life that points toward such a final destination for man's long historic development. But the artist, because he is an artist, cannot help telling what he sees and expressing what he feels: indeed, the more he tries to bury it, like his reputedly sane neighbors, the more surely will he find images of fear and destruction, of emptiness and irrationality, welling up out of the deepest levels of his being. In so far, then, as the creative artist responds to the realities of his age, he is by that very fact condemned to death: his works will accordingly celebrate all the possible forms of death, the violent, the criminal, the infantile, the irrational, the degraded, the totally annihilated. John Ruskin, with astonishing insight and prescience, pointed this fact out in literature a century ago; and by now it characterizes all the arts.

This is why, though the creative arts address themselves directly to the person, one cannot turn to the arts and hope that they will, through further cultivation and popularization, offset our present preoccupation with the over-mechanized, the savagely dehumanized, the meaningless, the valueless, the deformed and the disrupted. If the arts themselves were so quarantined that they could escape infection from the morbid processes at work in our society, one might be tempted to say simply, Let us have more of them, as many people now say, with equally pathetic naïveté, Let's have more religion. But the case is not so easy as that; for the artist himself needs help in order to achieve his own integration and be ready for the new tasks of creation; and if he had only the forces immediately available in his own generation, he would find this as impossible a task as the proverbial lifting oneself up by one's bootstraps.

Does this bring us to a final counsel of despair? By no means. Fortunately, I have deepened the shadows in this picture by confining my observations to the contemporary scene alone and to the negative forces that are now so compulsively at work. What keeps our state from being quite as black as I have painted are two conditions: the deep and durable nature of man, and the continuity of human experience in history, which brings into the present moment, however desperate, the salvage of the past and the possibility of salvation in the future. Man has, to begin with, remarkable powers for adapting himself to hostile conditions, and can survive under circumstances that would cause even a rat to sicken and die. Moreover, like all living organisms, he has a tendency to re-establish his equilibrium and continue along his curve of growth; to make over the circumstances that threaten him, in order better to ensure his survival, to actualize his potentialities, despite contrary pressures from without. If the youth of Hungary, sedulously brought up to revere their totalitarian slavery as an ideal, could throw off their fetters and blinkers and be ready to die for freedom, then there is hope for the rest of the human race. Our present blindness to our actual state, and the cowed conformity that goes with it, cannot last forever. We, too, have been indoctrinated, indeed have indoctrinated ourselves, with false notions: with the belief that mechanization is more important than humanization, that power can flourish by itself without being guided by love, that our prospects of survival are increased by manufacturing atomic, bacterial, and chemical weapons whose use against an enemy might, in proportion to their immediate success, not merely wreck civilization but destroy the human race.

Only our memory of the past, our hope for the future, will keep this nightmare from having a permanent stranglehold over us. We still have access to religious visions, philosophical ideas, ethical doctrines, and works of art that are capable of restoring our threatened humanity. By concentrating upon these products of health, sanity, and creative insight, we may recover the one thing needful for both the creative arts and our society today; namely, confidence in the function of creation itself, and respect for the human self through whom the creative forces are channeled and expressed. Plainly, the task of renewal in the arts—which is part of the larger task of becoming fully human—is not easy. In order to recover the initiative, we may have daily to practice withdrawal and detachment from our present society, examining every current value and weeding out the false ones, challenging every habit and rejecting those that restrict and diminish life, throwing off every automatism, however innocent it may seem, until we have brought forth a self strong enough and purposeful enough to resume command over our machines and our mechanical collectives. This is such a mission as the Christians had when they retreated from Roman culture in the fourth century to build up a new life; and happily for us, just as the Christians could draw even in the Church upon the great administrative skill and organization of the Roman state, so we can draw energy from the very institutions that now blindly dominate us. Because of our very successes in mass production, we now have enough leisure available to give everyone an opportunity to bring to light and to cultivate his repressed human functions, those necessary to further human integration and self-development; and here the artist, who best knows the uses of leisure, can lead the way. Certainly, this is no light task: the way of creation is just the opposite of the line of least resistance. If we continue to be the docile, other-directed persons we have become, we shall remain the victims of a purely consumptive ritual of conspicuous waste; so that even if we escape wholesale extermination, we shall probably only find ourselves buried more deeply in the inner vaults of one of our new-fangled Pyramids. In that plight, we would have no use for the arts as a means of enhancing and extending our creative powers: they would serve, rather, as they so largely do now, as sedatives and tranquilizers, to keep us from being too cruelly aware of the emptiness of our existence. But if the culture of life finally prevails over the cult of death, the creative arts will possibly turn out to be one of the great instruments of our awakening, and of ensuring our ultimate renewal. The choice is still ours—if we are alive enough to make it.

QUESTIONS

1. The careful essayist limits his subject. In what ways has Mumford limited or defined "creative arts"? Prepare a sentence outline in which you define the concept "creative"; include selected illustrations to support your definition.

2. In the opening paragraph Mumford makes several sweeping gener-

alizations, such as "the only part of man's life that seems real to him is that which is tethered to the machine, either to perform services for it or to receive with due gratitude its abundant product," or the creative arts "have become mere auxiliaries to mechanical organization." Write two argumentative paragraphs, one in support of Mumford's generalizations and one in opposition; then write a third paragraph in which you take sides in the argument.

3. One way essayists make a meaning clearer is through illustrations. What kind of illustrations appear in Mumford's essay? Can you explain the relevancy of each illustration? Rewrite the outline above and prepare a 500-word paper based on the outline; include relevant illustrations of your supporting ideas.

4. Throughout the essay Mumford argues the creative arts are life-giving, awakening, human expressions of human beings; on the other hand, he argues, the mechanization of contemporary life leads to dehumanization, mass organization, mass production, mass-market culture, mass audiences, mass needs, and "other-directed" individuals. Select one contemporary mass force—such as the TV, the newspaper, the film—and argue for both its humanizing and dehumanizing significance. Which do you consider its basic import? Write an essay in which you express and support your fundamental viewpoint.

5. Mumford asserts: "We still have access to religious visions, philosophical ideas, ethical doctrines, and works of art that are capable of restoring our threatened humanity." Select one work of art,—a poem, painting, building, statue, musical composition, play, bridge, or ballet—and show in what ways it has had a humanizing effect upon contemporary life. Remember, it is important that you think, not indulge in sentimental reflections and observations.

XII

Book Review

A book review is a guide to recently published books, or an informative and evaluative brief overview of the qualities of selected books, depending upon the publication policies of the book-review editors of periodicals and newspapers and upon the type of audience and reading public for whom the reviews are prepared. In a periodical such as *The Saturday Review,* for example, a "Checklist of the Week's New Books" lists books published on the following subjects: Crime, Suspense; Current Affairs; Fiction; History, Literary History, Criticism; Miscellany; Personal History; Psychology, Sociology; Religion, Philosophy. In other issues of the same periodical other categories include International Affairs; Poetry, Plays; Political Science; Business, Economics. In each issue of this periodical, book reviews on books in the above mentioned categories serve as guides to the readers of *The Saturday Review.* Likewise, in professional, technical, scholarly, and popular periodicals book reviews serve as guides to future reading for their audiences. As a writer of a book review, therefore, the determination of your audience is one of your first concerns.

In turn you must ask yourself what you should include in a specific book review. A cursory examination of representative reviews—in newspapers, such as the *New York Times* and *The Christian Science Monitor,* and in such varied periodicals as *The Sewanee Review, The Atlantic,* and *Newsweek*—reveals certain common characteristics among most reviews; the reviewer will comment on the book, the author's previous work and thought, other comparable books, and the quality of the book being reviewed.

Observations on the specific book will usually include a restatement of the author's purpose or theme and the methods by which he develops this purpose; the reviewer may include a brief biographical sketch of the intellectual life of the author, linking the present book to the author's previous books and general background; moreover, the reviewer frequently provides, from his own thought and experience, relationships that may exist among the author, the book being reviewed, and similar literature; finally, the reviewer offers an evaluation, based on the previous statements in part, of the value of the book in terms of whether or not the book is original, competent, significant, accurate, and soundly executed. In general this evaluation provides a guide to the readers of the review. However, since the policy of many book-review editors excludes reviews of books of poor quality, most published reviews represent either mixed evaluations or recommendations.

Each reviewer develops his own techniques, depending upon his personal abilities and interests; thus the following list of general characteristics is subject to the practices of each reviewer: 1) common use of one or more special techniques including the abstract (a restatement of the essential content), the critique (a criticism), the summary (a concise restatement in the same order given), and the synopsis (a general view, frequently applied to narrative); 2) the adoption of critical, comparative, and contrastive points of view; 3) the use of illustrative excerpts representative of theme, content, argument, and style; 4) regular use of professional jargon, that is, the commonplace language of the professional in a given field or discipline; 5) some comment on the "flavor" of the book; and 6) occasionally, opinions on the kinds of readers who will enjoy the book.

As a reviewer you have an opportunity to exercise your judgment, to say whether or not you like a book, whether or not you consider it worthwhile or irrelevant. You have an opportunity, in short, to use your best critical judgment for the benefit of a wide audience.

THE ART OF BIOGRAPHY
Granville Hicks

In 1953 Leon Edel, professor of English at New York University, published "Henry James: The Untried Years," the first of three volumes to be devoted to the novelist. His experiences in writing the life of a man of letters interested him in literary biography, and it was to this subject that he devoted the 1956 Alexander Lectures at the University of Toronto. "*Literary Biography*," which was published in Canada and England in 1957, has now been made available in this country (Doubleday-Anchor, paper, 95¢).

"It seemed to me," he says in the preface, "that this branch of biography had never been sufficiently isolated from the general discussion of the biographical art." Yet he quickly goes on to admit: "Obviously all the practices and traditions of biography apply to this particular kind of biographical writing: the differences between it and other categories reside essentially in the nature of the subject and corollary questions of emphasis and shading." The book, then, is a study of biography in general, with special attention to the problems that arise when the subject is a writer.

Edel begins by pointing out that although there was biographical writing in early times, biography, in our sense of the term, has developed in the past two centuries. Boswell's "Johnson" was one of the earliest as well as one of the greatest biographies. Boswell not only had the advantage of knowing Johnson; he found ways, as Edel amusingly shows, of maneuvering his hero into situations that would make good copy.

But if Boswell could be a reporter and stage manager, most biographers are research men. Today great masses—sometimes whole libraries—of documents are available, and tomorrow, as Edel observes, the problem will be worse: "I hesitate to think of what lies ahead: when the biographer will find confronting him radio transcripts, recorded telephone calls, and tape recordings of interviews, as well as film strips and kinescopes preserving television appearances." At the same time the biographer has to be something of a detective. There are still men who try to cover their tracks; Henry James was one of them, and Edel describes some of his own feats of detection. But even when there has been no attempt at concealment, an obscure fact, ingeniously ferreted out, may prove more revealing than stacks of documents.

With the man of letters there is, of course, the special problem of the use that can and should be made of his writings. Today, Edel reminds us, we have a school of critics who rigorously set the writings apart from the writer. For them the text is sacred; it cannot be used as a source of biographical information, and all biographical information is irrelevant to the understanding of it.

This type of criticism is a reaction against the excessive preoccupation with biographical and historical data, and insofar as it has focused attention on the thing created rather than on the circumstances of creation, it has been a healthy influence. But the dogma as a dogma is untenable, from either the critic's point of view or the biographer's. The critic can use all the insight he can get, and the poet may be a clue to the poem. On the other hand—and this is Edel's main point—the observer can surely find the poet in the poetry if he knows how to look. To show what he means, Edel examines certain of T. S. Eliot's poems, finding in them a revealing kind of spiritual autobiography. This sort of evidence the biographer cannot afford to ignore.

Some other kinds of evidence are less dependable. What, Edel asks, of psychoanalysis? Its techniques, he answers, can be helpful, but they have to be used with caution, and, to illustrate, he examines the problem of Willa Cather's "The Professor's House." First he sets forth E. K. Brown's purely literary analysis of the novel, and shows that, although it is sound as far as it goes, it leaves questions unanswered. He then offers a psychoanalytical interpretation, which helps us to understand Professor St. Cloud's dilemma, but only in general terms. Finally he relates St. Cloud's difficulties to Miss Cather's, and by so doing clarifies the novel and helps to explain its weaknesses. "To arrive at this view," he concludes, "the biographer has had to unite the qualities of critic and psychoanalyst." But in point of fact Edel has drawn only a hint or two from the psychoanalytical technique, and I think that hints are all the biographer ought to expect.

In his last chapter Edel defines three types of biography:

> The first and most common is the traditional documentary biography, an integrated work in which the biographer arranges the materials— Boswell did this—so as to allow the voice of the subject to be heard constantly. . . . The second type of biography is the creation, in words, of something akin to the painter's portrait. Here the picture is somewhat more circumscribed; it is carefully sketched in, and a frame is placed around it. The third type, which has been fashioned increasingly in our time is one in which materials are melted down and in which the biographer is present in the work as omniscient narrator.

It is with the third variety that Edel is chiefly concerned, and he discusses the suitability of certain techniques of fiction, especially in the treatment of time.

Edel surprises me by speaking of critical biography as a hybrid and an accident. Critical biography seems to me the most interesting kind of literary biography, a kind that has been written with notable success in recent years. Think, for instance, of Newton Arvin's "Melville," Mark Van Doren's "Hawthorne," F. W. Dupee's "Henry James," and other volumes in the American Men of Letters Series. In critical biography the biographer not only approaches the writer by way of his writings; he treats the writings as the most important part of the life, the great central fact. This means that such a biographer must be a first-rate critic, but I should think that it was almost always a mistake for anyone but a good critic to write the life of a man of letters, and, in view of what Edel says about the fruitful relationship between criticism and biography, I should expect him to agree.

But this is a minor objection to an enlightening, entertaining study. Edel writes with humor and charm, and he is adroit in the use of illustrative material. Fundamentally, of course, he is completely serious. Art, he recognizes, is no substitute for scholarship: the biographer "needs above all to be a serious and painstaking questioner—in a word, an honest scholar." But, he tells us, in the shaping of the results of research art is indispensable.

QUESTIONS

1. In the opening paragraph of this review Hicks establishes Edel's qualifications for writing *Literary Biography*; in the second paragraph the reviewer restates Edel's purpose: "The book, then, is a study of biography in general, with special attention to the problems that arise

when the subject is a writer." Select a biography you wish to review, study it, and prepare a sentence outline of what you consider the purpose of the biography and its particular strengths and weaknesses.

2. In his review Hicks includes Edel's observations on the characteristics of recent biography, the research necessary, the value of certain critical approaches and methods, and types of biography. Based on your interpretations of the problems raised in this review, write a first draft of the paper outlined above.

3. Hicks, disagreeing with Edel, believes critical biography "the most interesting kind of literary biography," and cites examples to support his view. Include, in a second draft of your review, a reaction to one of the views stated by the biographer you studied and support your reaction.

4. In the final paragraph Hicks makes clear his recommendation of Edel's *Literary Biography* as a worthwhile book, one that readers will find "enlightening" and "entertaining." Prepare your review for submission; include a final recommendation to your audience.

5. Select from a newspaper or periodical a review of a book you have read. Then analyze the review for comments on the book, the author's previous work and thought, other comparable books, and the quality of the book being reviewed. Write a brief evaluation of the review.

A PASSION FOR HONESTY,
A GENIUS FOR DECENCY

Hilton Kramer

The Collected Essays, Journalism and Letters of George Orwell. Edited by Sonia Orwell and Ian Angus. Illustrated. Vol. I: An Age Like This, 1920–1940. 574 pp. $8.95. Vol. II: My Country Right or Left, 1940–1943. 477 pp. $8.95. Vol. III: As I Please, 1943–1945. 435 pp. $7.95. Vol. IV: In Front of Your Nose, 1945–1950. 555 pp. $8.95. New York: Harcourt, Brace & World.

There are writers whose importance is confirmed by the vicissitudes of our interior life, by the natural history of our emotions and the conflicts they engender. But there are others whose importance is confirmed by the march of events. Writers of this persuasion have a special affinity for dealing with the tyranny of history over the fate of whole societies. They may be no less concerned about the destiny of the individual than their more introspective counterparts, but they are more alert to the external forces that preside over that destiny. Indeed, at their best, such writers often have an uncanny gift for divining what it is in the individual consciousness of a given historical moment that contributes to and sustains these forces.

Among the English writers of his generation, none was more alert to the external pressures of history than George Orwell, and none succeeded so brilliantly in creating a body of work that in substance was a virtual lexicon of these pressures and in style such an effective antidote to their demoralizing power. Orwell, who died in 1950 at the age of 46, achieved an international renown as the author of "Animal Farm" (1945) and "Nineteen Eighty-Four" (1949), the novels—if "novels" they may be called—that reflected his mature political convictions and the only works that won him a large audience in his lifetime. But for much of his writing life, Orwell was primarily a journalist—a critic, reporter, reviewer and pamphleteer, a prolific and immensely gifted analyst of literature, politics and popular culture—and it looks more and more as if his greatest achievement will be found in this large body of nonfictional prose.

Such, in any event, is the conclusion I am drawn to after reading through these four stout volumes of Orwell's "Collected Essays, Journalism and Letters." Orwell stipulated in his will that no biography of him should be written. In honoring his wishes Sonia Orwell (his widow) and Ian Angus have produced instead a comprehensive documentary record of Orwell's literary career that, in effect, allows Orwell to be his own biographer. The result, conceived on the massive scale of a Victorian life-and-letters monument, is far superior to all but the very greatest of literary biographies.

All the well-known essays are here—the studies of Dickens and Kipling and Gandhi, the essays on language and propaganda, and the pioneering inquiries into a whole range of subintellectual cultural forms. In addition, we are given a voluminous anthology of Orwell's reviews and polemics, a collection of the columns he wrote for the left-wing *Tribune* during the years 1943–1947, his "London Letters" to *Partisan Review* during the same period, and the texts of "The Lion and the Unicorn" and "The English People."

There is a generous selection of personal letters that provide a running commentary on his life and work, and a number of important unpublished diaries and notes, including his "Notes on the Spanish Militias," written in 1939, which form a valuable appendix to his book on the Spanish Civil War, "Homage to Catalonia." No doubt a biography of Orwell will some day be written, but it is difficult to see how it could be more than an extended footnote to the present work.

Politics dominates the collection—above all, the politics of totalitarianism in Germany and the Soviet Union, and the various responses to it, in England and in Europe generally, throughout the thirties and forties. The collection thus forms a fragmentary and highly personal history of these turbulent decades. Orwell writes as a deeply committed but completely disabused Socialist who had a profound, unsentimental sympathy for the working classes, a genuine respect for their style of life, and a positive loathing for political slogans—whatever their source—that did violence to their actual condition.

As a political writer, he was, to be sure, something of an oddity, and certainly a more original and complex figure than is commonly supposed. He came to politics reluctantly and clearly regarded nearly all politicians with extreme distaste. In pure political theory he had almost no interest at all. Yet, convinced that the history of his time left a writer of his particular gifts and loyalties no alternative but to confront the political crisis in which he lived, he was determined to take a view of politics large enough to accommodate everything that interested him—everything, it might be said, that most political writers are only too happy to ignore—from the mundane details of everyday life to the most exalted accomplishments of high culture.

About the ideology and rhetoric of politics, and about the crimes committed in their name, he wrote at length, over and over again. His experience as both a soldier and a reporter in the Spanish Civil War made him into a kind of specialist in dealing with the mendacities of the left, but a specialist of a particular sort—the left-wing anti-Stalinist who wished to save the Socialist movement from the counter revolutionary strategies of Soviet foreign policy. For it was in the left—in the future of Democratic Socialism—that his own hopes and ideals were overwhelmingly invested. Yet even as a committed Socialist, Orwell had a horror of dogma, and it was not, finally, the tenets of Socialism that determined his outlook as a writer so much as it was his abiding concern for a certain quality of life that he felt all the orthodoxies of modern politics were conspiring to destroy.

"What I have most wanted to do throughout the past ten years," he wrote in 1946, "is to make political writing into an art." To this task he brought a sizable fund of experience, an extraordinary passion for honesty and a standard of humane decency that amounted, at times, to a touch of genius. The experience was garnered in a wide variety of settings—as a student at Eton and as a tramp in Paris and London, as an imperial policeman in Burma and as a corporal in the Spanish Civil War, where he received a bullet in the neck—but it was, characteristically, the experience of the odd man out.

Orwell had a distinct talent for immersing himself in the grubby particulars of whatever experience he sought out and yet at the same time remain an outsider. He was, moreover, an acute observer, and the whole ethos of his political outlook and of his literary style is to be found in a scrupulous refusal to allow either ideology or propaganda or political loyalties of any kind to deny the evidence of his own senses. It is this passion for honesty—honesty of feeling as well as of facts—that gives to so much of Orwell's writing, in other respects so plain-spoken and self-deprecating, its eloquence and power. Another aspect of this honesty is Orwell's exceptional gift for empathy. Whether he is writing about Hitler or Churchill or a nameless militiaman glimpsed on the Spanish front, Orwell's references are always to a recognizable human dimension. He is at his best, I think, in reporting his own experience, as we see in "Homage to Catalonia" and "The Road to Wigan Pier," but there are literally hundreds of pages in the present work that testify to his ability to see even his enemies as particular human beings inhabiting a familiar and frightful world. He often detests what that world is coming to and frequently passes harsh judgments on it, but no one is deprived of his essential humanity.

As a moralist, however, Orwell was most troublesome—intentionally troublesome—in dealing with those closest to him politically. More than once he raises painful questions about the role of Socialists like himself under liberal democratic regimes. In 1939 he wrote: "In a prosperous country, above all in an imperialist country, left-wing politics are always partly humbug. There can be no real reconstruction that would not lead to at least a temporary drop in the English standard of life, which is another way of saying that the majority of left-wing politicians and publicists are people who earn their living by demanding something that they don't genuinely want."

Three years later, in his essay on Kipling, he returned to the same point: "All left-wing parties in the highly industrialised countries are at bottom a sham, because they make it their business to fight against something which they do not really wish to destroy. They have internationalist aims, and at the same time they struggle to keep up the standard of life with which those aims are incompatible. We all live by robbing Asiatic coolies, and those of us who are 'enlightened' all maintain that those coolies ought to be set free; but our standard of living, and hence our 'enlightenment,' demands that the robbery shall continue."

Needless to say, such avowals did not endear Orwell to his fellow Socialists. Nor is it likely that some of the more comfortable intellectual patrons of the current New Left will find such assertions any more welcome —or any more answerable. But this is the only one of a great many political questions that are raised in Orwell's essays—questions that the passage of time has only exacerbated.

A good many of the essays in these volumes are devoted to literary criticism, and in this realm, too, Orwell exhibits a remarkable originality. The key to his critical method may be found, I think, in a letter he wrote to the anthropologist Geoffrey Gorer in 1936: "What you say about trying to study our customs from an anthropological point of view opens up a lot of fields of thought, but one thing to notice about ourselves is that people's habits, etc., are formed not only by their upbringing & so forth but also very largely by books. I have often thought it would be very interesting to study the conventions etc. of *books* from an anthropological point of view." Most of Orwell's ambitious critical writing dealt with popular authors whose work could profitably be approached in this manner. This was not a separate enterprise from his political vocation, but a specialized aspect of it.

It was an approach, moreover, that made him especially alert to changes in language, particularly changes of political origin. He became an expert on propaganda, and the result was not only his many superb observations on the subject—the excellent indexes to these four volumes properly list them in detail—but the horrific, dehumanized political jargon in "Nineteen Eighty-Four," probably the only political novel of our time in which language itself is shown to be such a powerful instrument of brutality.

All in all, this new edition of Orwell's writings—wonderfully readable throughout—establishes him, I believe, as the greatest essayist England has produced since Hazlitt, and certainly as Hazlitt's equal. The editors have performed their task with great industry and great tact, and have given us a classic.

Questions

1. The reviewer attempts to inform the reader of the general contents of the book or books being reviewed. Kramer performs this function through his comments on the essays, reviews, columns, personal letters, unpublished diaries, and notes included in the *Collection.* Write a draft of a review, of a non-fictional work, in which you attempt to provide the reader with an overview of the content of the book being reviewed.

2. A second function the reviewer must perform involves the relationship of the book being reviewed to the author's previous work. Kramer provides the reader with a sketch of Orwell's life, his concern with political and social philosophy, the basis of his literary reputation, and similar observations. Rewrite the draft above by relating the contents of the book being reviewed to the life and intellectual concerns of the author.

3. Although Kramer does not, in the review, compare and contrast Orwell's central concerns with those of similar writers, he does comment on ways in which Orwell's political philosophy, his special kind of socialism, differs from those of strict socialism. In a third draft of your review compare and contrast the book being reviewed with other recent, comparable books.

4. A sound review leads to a judgment of the quality of the book being reviewed. Kramer concludes that this *Collection* establishes Orwell "as the greatest essayist England has produced since Hazlitt, and

certainly Hazlitt's equal." This judgment includes all English essayists of the past one hundred and forty years, including such essayists as Arnold, Macaulay, Carlyle, Pater, Stevenson, Churchill, Huxley, and Russell; hence the judgment is high praise indeed. Prepare a fourth draft of your review, one in which you state and support your judgment of the quality of the book you have chosen to review.

5. Prepare a final draft of your review. Devote your attention especially to the problem of coherence.

PART IV

Writing for Under-standing

XIII

Literary Criticism

The literary critic attempts to understand literature: he analyzes, interprets, evaluates, judges, and compares works of literature, literary philosophies, literary methods and techniques, and literary forms and traditions; he examines the relationships among the various qualities of literature in their larger meanings to culture and civilization. It is not surprising, therefore, to find critical studies of the relationships of literature to society, to industrialization, to present and past institutions, to history and philosophy, to the daily life of man.

Sometimes criticism is described in terms of its emphases: formalistic criticism emphasizes the literary work, psychological criticism emphasizes the psychic life of the author, biographical criticism the place of the work of art in the life of the author, humanistic criticism the values to civilization, comparative criticism the relationships of literature, authors, works, philosophies, traditions, and techniques. In turn, each critical emphasis requires certain understandings of the history, traditions, forms, and scholarship of literature.

Thus, you will employ, as a formalistic critic of a poem, certain assumptions and techniques in your examination that you will not employ in your examination of novels and plays, and vice versa. So too, when you examine a lyric poem, as distinguished from narrative and dramatic poems, you will employ somewhat different techniques of analysis and interpretation.

The questions you ask, in part, determine the answers you find and the assumptions and techniques you employ. You may wish to ask the question: what are the meanings of a specific poem? "Meanings" may be interpreted as themes only, but themes are dependent upon the language of the poem, the structure, the symbols and patterns, the figures and images, the logics, the emotions, the sounds including rhythm and rhyme, the points of view, and even the syntax and printed appearance of the words. An effective critical interpretation, analysis, evaluation, judgment, or comparison of a literary work will require a detailed and systematic study of the work and integration of the results of your technical analysis. Throughout these critical steps you should maintain the integrity of your experience with literature and the work under consideration.

In *The Armed Vision* Stanley Hyman has described the critical method of modern literary criticism as "the organized use of non-literary techniques and bodies of knowledge to obtain insights into literature." As a critic you will derive critical ideas from the social sciences (for example, psychology, sociology, history, anthropology), the sciences (for example, physics, chemistry, biology, astronomy), and the humanities (for example, religion, philosophy, art, architecture) to assist you in your critical thought. A knowledge of Freud, Jung, Adler, Piaget, and Skinner may assist you in your critical study of the psychological aspects of literature; a knowledge of political thought—Jefferson, Hamilton, Marx—may aid you in your study of the relation of literature to the state and political institutions; a knowledge of the sciences, including such concepts as evolution and organicism, will provide methods of critical examination of literary works.

Meaningful criticism, your best intellectual engagement with literature, is the result of hard and exact thinking. You must analyze carefully, integrate the results of your analyses, construct hypotheses, draw conclusions. And then you write.

HAMLET

T. S. Eliot

Few critics have ever admitted that *Hamlet* the play is the primary problem, and Hamlet the character only secondary. And Hamlet the character has had an especial temptation for that most dangerous type of critic: the critic with a mind which is naturally of the creative order, but which through some weakness in creative power exercises itself in criticism instead. These minds often find in Hamlet a vicarious existence for their own artistic realization. Such a mind had Goethe, who made of Hamlet a Werther; and such had Coleridge, who made of Hamlet a Coleridge; and probably neither of these men in writing about Hamlet remembered that his first business was to study a work of art. The kind of criticism that Goethe and Coleridge produced, in writing of Hamlet, is the most misleading kind possible. For they both possessed unquestionable critical insight, and both make their critical aberrations the more plausible by the substitution—of their own Hamlet for Shakespeare's—which their creative gift effects. We should be thankful that Walter Pater did not fix his attention on this play.

Two writers of our time, Mr. J. M. Robertson and Professor Stoll of the University of Minnesota, have issued small books which can be praised for moving in the other direction. Mr. Stoll performs a service in recalling

---

to our attention the labours of the critics of the seventeenth and eighteenth centuries,[1] observing that

> "they knew less about psychology than more recent Hamlet critics, but they were nearer in spirit to Shakespeare's art; and as they insisted on the importance of the effect of the whole rather than on the importance of the leading character, they were nearer, in their old-fashioned way, to the secret of dramatic art in general."

Qua work of art, the work of art cannot be interpreted; there is nothing to interpret; we can only criticize it according to standards, in comparison to other works of art; and for "interpretation" the chief task is the presentation of relevant historical facts which the reader is not assumed to know. Mr. Robertson points out, very pertinently, how critics have failed in their "interpretation" of *Hamlet* by ignoring what ought to be very obvious: that *Hamlet* is a stratification, that it represents the efforts of a series of men, each making what he could out of the work of his predecessors. The *Hamlet* of Shakespeare will appear to us very differently if, instead of treating the whole action of the play as due to Shakespeare's design, we perceive his *Hamlet* to be superposed upon much cruder material which persists even in the final form.

We know that there was an older play by Thomas Kyd; that extraordinary dramatic (if not poetic) genius who was in all probability the author of two plays so dissimilar as *The Spanish Tragedy* and *Arden of Feversham*; and what this play was like we can guess from three clues: from *The Spanish Tragedy* itself, from the tale of Belleforest upon which Kyd's *Hamlet* must have been based, and from a version acted in Germany in Shakespeare's lifetime which bears strong evidence of having been adapted from the earlier, not from the later, play. From these three sources it is clear that in the earlier play the motive was a revenge-motive simply; that the action or delay is caused, as in *The Spanish Tragedy*, solely by the difficulty of assassinating a monarch surrounded by guards; and that the "madness" of Hamlet was feigned in order to escape suspicion, and successfully. In the final play of Shakespeare, on the other hand, there is a motive which is more important than that of revenge, and which explicitly "blunts" the latter; the delay in revenge is unexplained on grounds of necessity or expediency; and the effect of the "madness" is not to lull but to arouse the king's suspicion. The alteration is not complete enough, however, to be convincing. Furthermore, there are verbal parallels so close to *The Spanish Tragedy* as to leave no doubt that in places Shakespeare was merely *revising* the text of Kyd. And finally there are unexplained scenes—the Polonius-Laertes and the Polonius-Reynaldo scenes—for which there is little

---

[1] I have never, by the way, seen a cogent refutation of Thomas Rymer's objections to *Othello*.

excuse; these scenes are not in the verse style of Kyd, and not beyond doubt in the style of Shakespeare. These Mr. Robertson believes to be scenes in the original play of Kyd reworked by a third hand, perhaps Chapman, before Shakespeare touched the play. And he concludes, with very strong show of reason, that the original play of Kyd was, like certain other revenge plays, in two parts of five acts each. The upshot of Mr. Robertson's examination is, we believe, irrefragable: that Shakespeare's *Hamlet*, so far as it is Shakespeare's, is a play dealing with the effect of a mother's guilt upon her son, and that Shakespeare was unable to impose this motive successfully upon the "intractable" material of the old play.

Of the intractability there can be no doubt. So far from being Shakespeare's masterpiece, the play is most certainly an artistic failure. In several ways the play is puzzling, and disquieting as is none of the others. Of all the plays it is the longest and is possibly the one on which Shakespeare spent most pains; and yet he has left in it superfluous and inconsistent scenes which even hasty revision should have noticed. The versification is variable. Lines like

> Look, the morn, in russet mantle clad,
> Walks o'er the dew of yon high eastern hill,

are of the Shakespeare of *Romeo and Juliet*. The lines in Act v, sc. ii,

> Sir, in my heart there was a kind of fighting
> That would not let me sleep . . .
> Up from my cabin,
> My sea-gown scarf'd about me, in the dark
> Grop'd I to find out them: had my desire;
> Finger'd their packet;

are of his quite mature. Both workmanship and thought are in an unstable position. We are surely justified in attributing the play, with that other profoundly interesting play of "intractable" material and astonishing versification, *Measure for Measure*, to a period of crisis, after which follow the tragic successes which culminate in *Coriolanus*. *Coriolanus* may be not as "interesting" as *Hamlet*, but it is, with *Antony and Cleopatra*, Shakespeare's most assured artistic success. And probably more people have thought *Hamlet* a work of art because they found it interesting, than have found it interesting because it is a work of art. It is the "Mona Lisa" of literature.

The grounds of *Hamlet's* failure are not immediately obvious. Mr. Robertson is undoubtedly correct in concluding that the essential emotion of the play is the feeling of a son towards a guilty mother:

> "[Hamlet's] tone is that of one who has suffered tortures on the score of his mother's degradation. . . . The guilt of a mother is an almost intolerable motive for drama, but it had to be maintained and emphasized to supply a psychological solution, or rather a hint of one."

This, however, is by no means the whole story. It is not merely the "guilt of a mother" that cannot be handled as Shakespeare handled the suspicion of Othello, the infatuation of Antony, or the pride of Coriolanus. The subject might conceivably have expanded into a tragedy like these, intelligible, self-complete, in the sunlight. *Hamlet*, like the sonnets, is full of some stuff that the writer could not drag to light, contemplate, or manipulate into art. And when we search for this feeling, we find it, as in the sonnets, very difficult to localize. You cannot point to it in the speeches; indeed, if you examine the two famous soliloquies you see the versification of Shakespeare, but a content which might be claimed by another, perhaps by the author of the *Revenge of Bussy d'Ambois*, Act v, sc. i. We find Shakespeare's Hamlet not in the action, not in any quotations that we might select, so much as in an unmistakable tone which is unmistakably not in the earlier play.

The only way of expressing emotion in the form of art is by finding an "objective correlative"; in other words, a set of objects, a situation, a chain of events which shall be the formula of that *particular* emotion; such that when the external facts, which must terminate in sensory experience, are given, the emotion is immediately evoked. If you examine any of Shakespeare's more successful tragedies, you will find this exact equivalence; you will find that the state of mind of Lady Macbeth walking in her sleep has been communicated to you by a skilful accumulation of imagined sensory impressions; the words of Macbeth on hearing of his wife's death strike us as if, given the sequence of events, these words were automatically released by the last event in the series. The artistic "inevitability" lies in this complete adequacy of the external to the emotion; and this is precisely what is deficient in *Hamlet*. Hamlet (the man) is dominated by an emotion which is inexpressible, because it is in *excess* of the facts as they appear. And the supposed identity of Hamlet with his author is genuine to this point: that Hamlet's bafflement at the absence of objective equivalent to his feelings is a prolongation of the bafflement of his creator in the face of his artistic problem. Hamlet is up against the difficulty that his disgust is occasioned by his mother, but that his mother is not an adequate equivalent for it; his disgust envelops and exceeds her. It is thus a feeling which he cannot understand; he cannot objectify it, and it therefore remains to poison life and obstruct action. None of the possible actions can satisfy it; and nothing that Shakespeare can do with the plot can express Hamlet for him. And it must be noticed that the very nature of the *données* of the problem precludes objective equivalence. To have heightened the criminality of Gertrude would have been to provide the formula for a totally different emotion in Hamlet; it is just *because* her character is so negative and insignificant that she arouses in Hamlet the feeling which she is incapable of representing.

The "madness" of Hamlet lay to Shakespeare's hand; in the earlier play a simple ruse, and to the end, we may presume, understood as a ruse by the audience. For Shakespeare it is less than madness and more than feigned. The levity of Hamlet, his repetition of phrase, his puns, are not part of a deliberate plan of dissimulation, but a form of emotional relief. In the character Hamlet it is the buffoonery of an emotion which can find no outlet in action; in the dramatist it is the buffoonery of an emotion which he cannot express in art. The intense feeling, ecstatic or terrible, without an object or exceeding its object, is something which every person of sensibility has known; it is doubtless a subject of study for pathologists. It often occurs in adolescence: the ordinary person puts these feelings to sleep, or trims down his feelings to fit the business world; the artist keeps them alive by his ability to intensify the world to his emotions. The Hamlet of Laforgue is an adolescent; the Hamlet of Shakespeare is not, he has not that explanation and excuse. We must simply admit that here Shakespeare tackled a problem which proved too much for him. Why he attempted it at all is an insoluble puzzle; under compulsion of what experience he attempted to express the inexpressibly horrible, we cannot ever know. We need a great many facts in his biography; and we should like to know whether, and when, and after or at the same time as what personal experience, he read Montaigne, II. xii, *Apologie de Raimond Sebond*. We should have, finally, to know something which is by hypothesis unknowable, for we assume it to be an experience which, in the manner indicated, exceeded the facts. We should have to understand things which Shakespeare did not understand himself.

QUESTIONS

1. In Eliot's "Hamlet" we find a literary critic who "analyzes, interprets, evaluates, judges, and compares." For example, in the opening paragraph he analyzes various approaches to Shakespeare's *Hamlet*; in the second paragraph he evaluates the significance of the works of Robertson and Stoll; in the third paragraph he explains his particular understanding of the meaning of "interpretation"; in the fourth paragraph he compares and judges earlier versions of the Hamlet story in their relationships to Shakespeare's *Hamlet*. After performing these critical acts, Eliot, in the fifth paragraph, states the purpose of his essay, a judgment: "the play is most certainly an artistic failure." Examine a literary work, such as a short poem, by performing critical acts comparable to Eliot's, make a judgment concerning the work, and prepare a sentence outline of the arguments you will use to support your judgment.

2. Outline the argument Eliot presents in support of his judgment. What details are crucial to Eliot's argument? Prepare a second sentence outline in which you include the selected details you will use to

support your arguments. Are any of the details crucial or central to your purpose?

3.   In the opening sentence of this essay Eliot is critical of literary critics. "Few critics," he writes, "have ever admitted that *Hamlet* the play is the primary problem, and Hamlet the character only secondary." Write a brief essay in which you argue that either the central character or the entire play is the "primary problem" confronting the literary critic.

4.   Use Eliot's idea of the "objective correlative" as a critical tool for examining the expression of emotion in a literary work. Keep a notebook record of the steps you take in making this analysis.

5.   Prepare a critical article, based on the examination above and the notebook record, in which you support or attack the idea of the "objective correlative" as a helpful critical tool.

DEEP READERS OF THE WORLD, BEWARE!

Saul Bellow

Interviewed as he was getting on a train for Boston, E. M. Forster was asked how he felt on the eve of his first visit to Harvard. He replied that he had heard that there were some particularly deep readers of his books to be found in Cambridge. He expected to be questioned closely by them, and this worried him. The reason is perfectly understandable.

In this age of ours serious people are more serious than they ever were, and lightness of heart like Mr. Forster's is hard to find. To the serious a novel is a work of art; art has a role to play in the drama of civilized life; civilized life is set upon a grim and dangerous course—and so we may assume if we are truly serious that no good novelist is going to invite us to a picnic merely to eat egg salad and chase butterflies over the English meadows or through the Tuscan woods. Butterflies are gay, all right, but in them lies the secret of metamorphosis. As for eggs, life's mystery hides in the egg. We all know that. So much for butterflies and egg salad.

It would be unjust to say that the responsibility for this sort of thing belongs entirely to the reader. Often the writer himself is at fault. He doesn't mind if he *is* a little deeper than average. Why not?

Nevertheless deep reading has gone very far. It has become dangerous to literature.

"Why, sir," the student asks, "does Achilles drag the body of Hector around the walls of Troy?" "That sounds like a stimulating question. Most interesting. I'll bite," says the professor. "Well, you see, sir, the 'Iliad' is

---

© 1959 by The New York Times Company. Reprinted by permission.

full of circles—shields, chariot wheels and other round figures. And you know what Plato said about circles. The Greeks were all mad for geometry." "Bless your crew-cut head," says the professor, "for such a beautiful thought. You have exquisite sensibility. Your approach is both deep and serious. Still I always believed that Achilles did it because he was so angry."

It would take an unusual professor to realize that Achilles *was* angry. To many teachers he would represent much, but he would not *be* anything in particular. To be is too obvious. Our professor however is a "square," and the bright student is annoyed with him. Anger! What good is anger? Great literature is subtle, dignified, profound. Homer is as good as Plato anytime; and if Plato thought, Homer must surely have done so, too, thought just as beautifully circle for circle.

Things are not what they seem. And anyway, unless they represent something large and worthy, writers will not bother with them. Any deep reader can tell you that picking up a bus transfer is the *reisemotif* (journey motif) when it happens in a novel. A travel folder signifies Death. Coal holes represent the Underworld. Soda crackers are the Host. Three bottles of beer are—it's obvious. The busy mind can hardly miss at this game, and every player is a winner.

Are you a Marxist? Then Herman Melville's Pequod in "Moby Dick" can be a factory, Ahab the manager, the crew the working class. Is your point of view religious? The Pequod sailed on Christmas morning, a floating cathedral headed south. Do you follow Freud or Jung? Then your interpretations may be rich and multitudinous. I recently had a new explanation of "Moby Dick" from the young man in charge of an electronic brain. "Once and for all," he said. "That whale is everybody's mother wallowing in her watery bed. Ahab has the Oedipus complex and wants to slay the hell out of her."

This is deep reading. But it is only fair to remember that the best novelists and poets of the century have done much to promote it. When Mairy (in James Joyce's "Ulysses") loses the pin of her drawers, she doesn't know what to do to keep them up; the mind of Bloom goes from grammar to painting, from painting to religion. It is all accomplished in a few words. Joyce's genius holds all the elements in balance.

The deep reader, however, is apt to lose his head. He falls wildly on any particle of philosophy or religion and blows it up bigger than the Graf Zeppelin. Does Bloom dust Stephen's clothes and brush off the wood shavings? They are no ordinary shavings but the shavings from Stephen's cross.

What else? All the little monkish peculiarities at which Robert Browning poked fun in the "Soliloquy in a Spanish Cloister," crossing knife and fork on the platter at the end of a meal and the rest of it, have become the pillars of the new system.

Are we to attach meaning to whatever is grazed by the writer? Is modern literature Scripture? Is criticism Talmud, theology? Deep readers of the world, beware! You had better be sure that your seriousness is indeed high seriousness and not, God forbid, low seriousness.

A true symbol is substantial, not accidental. You cannot avoid it, you cannot remove it. You can't take the handkerchief from "Othello," or the sea from "The Nigger of the Narcissus," or the disfigured feet from "Oedipus Rex." You can, however, read "Ulysses" without suspecting that wood shavings have to do with the Crucifixion or that the name Simon refers to the sin of Simony or that the hunger of the Dubliners at noon parallels that of the Lestrigonians. These are purely peripheral matters; fringe benefits, if you like. The beauty of the book cannot escape you if you are any sort of reader, and it is better to approach it from the side of naïveté than from that of culture-idolatry, sophistication and snobbery. Of course it's hard in our time to be as naïve as one would like. Information does filter through. It leaks, as we have taken to saying. Still the knowledge of even the sophisticated is rather thin, and even the most wised-up devils, stuffed to the ears with arcana, turned out to be fairly simple.

Perhaps the deepest readers are those who are least sure of themselves. An even more disturbing suspicion is that they prefer meaning to feeling. What again about the feelings? Yes, it's too bad. I'm sorry to have to ring in this tiresome subject, but there's no help for it. The reason why the schoolboy takes refuge in circles is that the wrath of Achilles and the death of Hector are too much for him. He is doing no more than most civilized people do when confronted with passion and death. They contrive somehow to avoid them.

The practice of avoidance is so widespread that it is probably not fair to single out any group for blame. But if nothing is to be said or done, we might as well make ready to abandon literature altogether. Novels are being published today which consist entirely of abstractions, meanings, and while our need for meanings is certainly great our need for concreteness, for particulars, is even greater. We need to see how human beings act after they have appropriated or assimilated the meanings. Meanings themselves are a dime a dozen. In literature humankind becomes abstract when we begin to dislike it. And . . .

Interruption by a deep reader: Yes, yes, we know all that. But just look at the novels of the concrete and the particular, people opening doors and lighting cigarettes. Aren't they boring? Besides, do you want us to adopt a program to curtail the fear of feeling and to pretend to *like* the creature of flesh and bone?

Certainly not. No programs.

A pretty pass we have come to!

We must leave it to inspiration to redeem the concrete and the particular and to recover the value of flesh and bone. Meanwhile, let Plato have his circles and let the soda crackers be soda crackers and the wood shavings wood shavings. They are mysterious enough as it is.

QUESTIONS

1. Bellow, in his attack on a certain kind of critical reading, states his purpose in the fourth paragraph: "deep reading . . . has become dangerous to literature." Prepare a sentence outline of the arguments that Bellow advances in support of this thesis. Select a literary work: a novel, poem, play, or short story; then write a thesis statement concerning a particular critical view you hold concerning this literary work, make a list of the arguments you would advance in support of this critical view, and select relevant illustrations.

2. "Things are not what they seem," writes Bellow, and attacks arbitrary and impressionistic interpretations of symbols. "A true symbol," he adds, "is substantial, not accidental." Write a carefully thought-out critical essay in which you define and illustrate the meanings of a literary symbol.

3. Is "great" literature "subtle, dignified, profound"? Bellow ironically makes this assertion. Prepare a carefully phrased sentence outline in which you argue that "great" literature is something other than "subtle, dignified, profound."

4. Experiment with a single literary work from your critical viewpoint. Select a particular work and examine the qualities and characteristics of the work. For example, examine a familiar, short poem, one by Frost or a similar writer, for meanings, structure, symbols and patterns, figures and images, the logics, the emotions, the sounds including rhythm and rhyme, the points of view, the syntax and the printed appearance of the words. Then write a critical interpretation of the work, supporting each statement through specific references to the poem.

5. Now examine the same poem from a second critical viewpoint, based on an idea from biography, psychology, philosophy, or ethics. What are the strengths and weaknesses of this critical approach? Write a brief paper describing your experience.

THE FORMALIST CRITIC
Cleanth Brooks

Here are some articles of faith I could subscribe to:

That literary criticism is a description and an evaluation of its object.

Reprinted by permission of Cleanth Brooks, from *The Kenyon Review*, Volume 13, Number 1, Winter, 1957.

That the primary concern of criticism is with the problem of unity—the kind of whole which the literary work forms or fails to form, and the relation of the various parts to each other in building up this whole.

That the formal relations in a work of literature may include, but certainly exceed, those of logic.

That in a successful work, form and content cannot be separated.

That form is meaning.

That literature is ultimately metaphorical and symbolic.

That the general and the universal are not seized upon by abstraction, but got at through the concrete and the particular.

That literature is not a surrogate for religion.

That, as Allen Tate says, "specific moral problems" are the subject matter of literature, but that the purpose of literature is not to point a moral.

That the principles of criticism define the area relevant to literary criticism; they do not constitute a method for carrying out the criticism.

Such statements as these would not, however, even though greatly elaborated, serve any useful purpose here. The interested reader already knows the general nature of the critical position adumbrated—or, if he does not, he can find it set forth in writings of mine or of other critics of like sympathy. Moreover, a condensed restatement of the position here would probably beget as many misunderstandings as have past attempts to set it forth. It seems much more profitable to use the present occasion for dealing with some persistent misunderstandings and objections.

In the first place, to make the poem or the novel the central concern of criticism has appeared to mean cutting it loose from its author and from his life as a man, with his own particular hopes, fears, interests, conflicts, etc. A criticism so limited may seem bloodless and hollow. It will seem so to the typical professor of literature in the graduate school, where the study of literature is still primarily a study of the ideas and personality of the author as revealed in his letters, his diaries, and the recorded conversations of his friends. It will certainly seem so to literary gossip columnists who purvey literary chitchat. It may also seem so to the young poet or novelist, beset with his own problems of composition and with his struggles to find a subject and a style and to get a hearing for himself.

In the second place, to emphasize the work seems to involve severing it from those who actually read it, and this severance may seem drastic and therefore disastrous. After all, literature is written to be read. Wordsworth's poet was a man speaking to men. In each Sunday *Times*, Mr. J. Donald Adams points out that the hungry sheep look up and are not fed; and less strenuous moralists than Mr. Adams are bound to feel a proper revulsion against "mere aestheticism." Moreover, if we neglect the audience which reads the work, including that for which it was presumably written, the literary historian is prompt to point out that the kind of audience that

Pope had did condition the kind of poetry that he wrote. The poem has its roots in history, past or present. Its place in the historical context simply cannot be ignored.

I have stated these objections as sharply as I can because I am sympathetic with the state of mind which is prone to voice them. Man's experience is indeed a seamless garment, no part of which can be separated from the rest. Yet if we urge this fact of inseparability against the drawing of distinctions, then there is no point in talking about criticism at all. I am assuming that distinctions are necessary and useful and indeed inevitable.

The formalist critic knows as well as anyone that poems and plays and novels are written by men—that they do not somehow happen—and that they are written as expressions of particular personalities and are written from all sorts of motives—for money, from a desire to express oneself, for the sake of a cause, etc. Moreover, the formalist critic knows as well as anyone that literary works are merely potential until they are read—that is, that they are recreated in the minds of actual readers, who vary enormously in their capabilities, their interests, their prejudices, their ideas. But the formalist critic is concerned primarily with the work itself. Speculation on the mental processes of the author takes the critic away from the work into biography and psychology. There is no reason, of course, why he should not turn away into biography and psychology. Such explorations are very much worth making. But they should not be confused with an account of the work. Such studies describe the process of composition, not the structure of the thing composed, and they may be performed quite as validly for the poor work as for the good one. They may be validly performed for any kind of expression—non-literary as well as literary.

On the other hand, exploration of the various readings which the work has received also takes the critic away from the work into psychology and the history of taste. The various imports of a given work may well be worth studying. I. A. Richards has put us all in his debt by demonstrating what different experiences may be derived from the same poem by an apparently homogeneous group of readers; and the scholars have pointed out, all along, how different Shakespeare appeared to an 18th Century as compared with a 19th Century audience; or how sharply divergent are the estimates of John Donne's lyrics from historical period to historical period. But such work, valuable and necessary as it may be, is to be distinguished from a criticism of the work itself. The formalist critic, because he wants to criticize the work itself, makes two assumptions: (1) he assumes that the relevant part of the author's intention is what he got actually into his work; that is, he assumes that the author's intention *as realized* is the "intention" that counts, not necessarily what he was conscious of trying to do, or what he now remembers he was then trying to do. And (2) the formalist critic assumes an ideal reader: that is, instead of focusing on the varying spectrum of possible readings, he attempts to find a central point of reference from which he can focus upon the structure of the poem or novel.

But there *is* no ideal reader, someone is prompt to point out, and he will probably add that it is sheer arrogance that allows the critic, with his own blindsides and prejudices, to put himself in the position of that ideal reader. There is no ideal reader, of course, and I suppose that the practising critic can never be too often reminded of the gap between his reading and the "true" reading of the poem. But for the purpose of focusing upon the poem rather than upon his own reactions, it is a defensible strategy. Finally, of course, it is the strategy that all critics of whatever persuasion are forced to adopt. (The alternatives are desperate: either we say that one person's reading is as good as another's and equate those readings on a basis of absolute equality and thus deny the possibility of any standard reading. Or else we take a lowest common denominator of the various readings that have been made; that is, we frankly move from literary criticism into socio-psychology. To propose taking a consensus of the opinions of "qualified" readers is simply to split the ideal reader into a group of ideal readers.) As consequences of the distinction just referred to, the formalist critic rejects two popular tests for literary value. The first proves the value of the work from the author's "sincerity" (or the intensity of the author's feelings as he composed it). If we heard that Mr. Guest testified that he put his heart and soul into his poems, we would not be very much impressed, though I should see no reason to doubt such a statement from Mr. Guest. It would simply be critically irrelevant. Ernest Hemingway's statement in a recent issue of *Time* magazine that he counts his last novel his best is of interest for Hemingway's biography, but most readers of *Across the River and Into the Trees* would agree that it proves nothing at all about the value of the novel—that in this case the judgment is simply pathetically inept. We discount also such tests for poetry as that proposed by A. E. Housman—the bristling of his beard at the reading of a good poem. The intensity of his reaction has critical significance only in proportion as we have already learned to trust him as a reader. Even so, what it tells us is something about Housman—nothing decisive about the poem.

It is unfortunate if this playing down of such responses seems to deny humanity to either writer or reader. The critic may enjoy certain works very much and may be indeed intensely moved by them. I am, and I have no embarrassment in admitting the fact; but a detailed description of my emotional state on reading certain works has little to do with indicating to an interested reader what the work is and how the parts of it are related.

Should all criticism, then, be self-effacing and analytic? I hope that the answer is implicit in what I have already written, but I shall go on to spell it out. Of course not. That will depend upon the occasion and the audience. In practice, the critic's job is rarely a purely critical one. He is much more likely to be involved in dozens of more or less related tasks, some of them trivial, some of them important. He may be trying to get a hearing for a new author, or to get the attention of the freshman sitting in the back row. He may be comparing two authors, or editing a text; writing a brief newspaper review or reading a paper before the Modern Language Association. He may even be simply talking with a friend, talking about literature for the hell of it. Parable, anecdote, epigram, metaphor—these and a hundred other devices may be thoroughly legitimate for his varying purposes. He is certainly not to be asked to suppress his personal enthusiasms or his interest in social history or in politics. Least of all is he being asked to *present* his criticisms as the close reading of a text. Tact, common sense, and uncommon sense if he has it, are all requisite if the practising critic is to do his various jobs well.

But it will do the critic no harm to have a clear idea of what his specific job as a critic is. I can sympathize with writers who are tired of reading rather drab "critical analyses," and who recommend brighter, more amateur, and more "human" criticism. As ideals, these are excellent; as recipes for improving criticism, I have my doubts. Appropriate vulgarizations of these ideals are already flourishing, and have long flourished—in the class room presided over by the college lecturer of infectious enthusiasm, in the gossipy Book-of-the-Month Club bulletins, and in the columns of the *Saturday Review of Literature*.

I have assigned the critic a modest, though I think an important, role. With reference to the help which the critic can give to the practising artist, the role is even more modest. As critic, he can give only negative help. Literature is not written by formula: he can have no formula to offer. Perhaps he can do little more than indicate whether in his opinion the work has succeeded or failed. Healthy criticism and healthy creation do tend to go hand in hand. Everything else being equal, the creative artist is better off for being in touch with a vigorous criticism. But the other considerations are never equal, the case is always special, and in a given case the proper advice *could* be: quit reading criticism altogether, or read political science or history or philosophy—or join the army, or join the church.

There is certainly no doubt that the kind of specific and positive help that someone like Ezra Pound was able to give to several writers of our time is in one sense the most important kind of criticism that there can be. I think that it is not unrelated to the kind of criticism that I have described: there is the same intense concern with the text which is being built up, the same concern with "technical problems." But many other things are involved—matters which lie outside the specific ambit of criticism altogether, among them a knowledge of the personality of the particular writer, the ability to stimulate, to make positive suggestions.

A literary work is a document and as a document can be analysed in terms of the forces that have produced it, or it may be manipulated as a force in its own right. It mirrors the past, it may influence the future. These facts it would be futile to deny, and I know of no critic who does deny them. But the reduction of a work of literature to its causes does not constitute literary criticism; nor does an estimate of its effects. Good literature is more than effective rhetoric applied to true ideas—even if we could agree upon a philosophical yardstick for measuring the truth of ideas and even if we could find some way that transcended nose-counting for determining the effectiveness of the rhetoric.

A recent essay by Lionel Trilling bears very emphatically upon this point. (I refer to him the more readily because Trilling has registered some of his objections to the critical position that I maintain.) In the essay entitled "The Meaning of a Literary Idea," Trilling discusses the debt to Freud and Spengler of four American writers, O'Neill, Dos Passos, Wolfe, and Faulkner. Very justly, as it seems to me, he chooses Faulkner as the contemporary writer who, along with Ernest Hemingway, best illustrates the power and importance of ideas in literature. Trilling is thoroughly aware that his choice will seem shocking and perhaps perverse, "because," as he writes, "Hemingway and Faulkner have insisted on their indifference to the conscious intellectual tradition of our time and have acquired the reputation of achieving their effects by means that have the least possible connection with any sort of intellectuality or even with intelligence."

Here Trilling shows not only acute discernment but an admirable honesty in electing to deal with the hard cases—with the writers who do not clearly and easily make the case for the importance of ideas. I applaud the discernment and the honesty, but I wonder whether the whole discussion in his essay does not indicate that Trilling is really much closer to the so-called "new critics" than perhaps he is aware. For Trilling, one notices, rejects any simple one-to-one relation between the truth of the idea and the value of the literary work in which it is embodied. Moreover, he does not claim that "recognizable ideas of a force or weight are 'used' in the work," or "new ideas of a certain force or weight are 'produced' by the work." He praises rather the fact that we feel that Hemingway and Faulkner are "intensely at work upon the recalcitrant stuff of life." The last point is made the matter of real importance. Whereas Dos Passos, O'Neill, and Wolfe make us "feel that *they* feel that they have said the last word," "we seldom have the sense that [Hemingway and Faulkner] . . . have misrepresented to themselves the nature and the difficulty of the matter they work on."

Trilling has chosen to state the situation in terms of the writer's activity (Faulkner is intensely at work, etc.). But this judgment is plainly an inference from the quality of Faulkner's novels—Trilling has not simply heard Faulkner say that he has had to struggle with his work. (I take it Mr. Hemingway's declaration about the effort he put into the last novel impresses Trilling as little as it impresses the rest of us.)

Suppose, then, that we tried to state Mr. Trilling's point, not in terms of the effort of the artist, but in terms of the structure of the work itself. Should we not get something very like the terms used by the formalist critics? A description in terms of "tensions," of symbolic development, of ironies and their resolution? In short, is not the formalist critic trying to describe in terms of the dynamic form of the work itself how the recalcitrancy of the material is acknowledged and dealt with?

Trilling's definition of "ideas" makes it still easier to accommodate my position to his. I have already quoted a passage in which he repudiates the notion that one has to show how recognizable ideas are "used" in the work, or new ideas are "produced" by the work. He goes on to write: "All that we need to do is account for a certain aesthetic effect as being in some important part achieved by a mental process which is not different from the process by which discursive ideas are conceived, and which is to be judged by some of the criteria by which an idea is judged." One would have to look far to find a critic "formal" enough to object to this. What some of us have been at pains to insist upon is that literature does not simply "exemplify" ideas or "produce" ideas—as Trilling acknowledges. But no one claims that the writer is an inspired idiot. He uses his mind and his reader ought to use his, in processes "not different from the process by which discursive ideas are conceived." Literature is not inimical to ideas. It thrives upon ideas, but it does not present ideas patly and neatly. It involves them with the "recalcitrant stuff of life." The literary critic's job is to deal with that involvement.

The mention of Faulkner invites a closing comment upon the critic's specific job. As I have described it, it may seem so modest that one could take its performance for granted. But consider the misreadings of Faulkner now current, some of them the work of the most brilliant critics that we have, some of them quite wrong-headed, and demonstrably so. What is true of Faulkner is only less true of many another author, including many writers of the past. Literature has many "uses"—and critics propose new uses, some of them exciting and spectacular. But all the multiform uses to which literature can be put rest finally upon our knowing what a given work "means." That knowledge is basic.

QUESTIONS

1. One of the first questions a reader asks about literature involves meaning: What does the poem, play, short story, or novel mean? To answer such a question requires some knowledge of how to seek "meaning." In "The Formalist Critics" Brooks enumerates one way of finding "meaning," in a broad sense of the term. Examine carefully the ten "articles" Brooks enumerates. Then write a brief essay in which you agree with or challenge one of his statements; support your position through specific references to literature you have read.

2. In his remarks Brooks rejects the biographical approach to a literary work as not a "central concern of criticism." Outline the arguments you would advance in support of the biographical approach as the "central concern of criticism."

3.   Douglas Bush, in an essay entitled "The Humanist Critic," argues that the critic has the "function of actively conserving the ethical and cultural inheritance that we are in danger of losing altogether"; Brooks argues that "specific moral problems" "are the subject matter of literature, but that the purpose of literature is not to point a moral." Take a stand in this argument. Prepare a sentence outline in support of one of these positions or a third that you may wish to propose.

4.   In an article entitled "Psychoanalysis and Criticism" Herbert Read explains the position of the psychological-psychoanalytic critic: "Psychoanalysis finds in art a system of symbols, representing a hidden reality, and by analysis it can testify to the purposive genuineness of the symbols; it can also testify to the faithfulness, the richness, and the range of the mind behind the symbols." Examine the symbols in a short poem. Do these symbols indicate to you any qualities of the character and personality behind the literary work? Based on your analysis, write a brief interpretation of one quality of the author's mind and life.

5.   Select an idea from your major field of study or interest—the social studies area, the sciences, the humanities—and apply this idea critically to a work of art. For example, take the idea that a work of art should be an organic entity, an idea derived from the sciences, and apply it to a specific short story. What are the advantages and disadvantages of such a method? Write a brief essay in which you describe the process you followed and explain the values of such a critical method.

XIV

Research Paper

A research paper, the result of systematic inquiry into a specific subject, may provide answers to questions such as the following: what are the facts? is a specific hypothesis valid? does it conform to the facts? what is the support to a question? what is the truth about a given historical event? A researcher may ask, as did Walter Lord, why did the Titanic sink? and then devote thirty years to reading every detail available on the event, to interviewing every person who had any direct or remote connection with the event, to attempting to reconstruct in exact detail each facet of the conditions—human, naval, engineering, climatic—of that eventful day, and then to draw conclusions based on his research. In outline Lord's experience illustrates the purpose and procedure the honest and sound researcher must follow. Several dangers are apparent: the purpose of the research must be clearly conceived, which will require the student to have some preliminary information about the subject before he postulates the question he wishes to examine; second, the research method must be honestly and systematically carried out, but the method must not be allowed to take the place of the purpose of the research; third, the research paper must honestly and clearly present the results of the research.

In any overview of the research paper certain steps are necessary: first, the choice of a subject, and subsequently a specific purpose for research, is the result of your interest in the subject itself; second, once a purpose has been selected and limited, you acquire all of the facts resources make available; third, you evaluate the meanings of these facts as they are related to your purpose; and, finally, you interpret these facts and write out your interpretations through your research paper. The commonplace emphasis on documentation—footnoting and bibliography—has misplaced the value of research; documentation is a form of verification, nothing more. The object of research is the increase of human understanding.

Research papers may be little more than brief reports of facts gathered concerning a specific question or problem, a short article in which facts have been evaluated and interpreted, or a book in which the author attempts to argue and support a specific thesis. The limitations you place on your purpose will determine the length of the research paper you write. In general a research paper for a lower division university course is approximately 2000 to 2500 words.

Other characteristics of the standard research paper include the following: 1) a paragraph or several are devoted to the background of the subject and purpose of the research; 2) the point of view is usually impersonal; 3) the style is formal or semi-formal but not informal; 4) the organization is logically constructed and coherently developed; 5) the assumptions and limitations are stated exactly; 6) intellectual honesty is the *sine qua non.*

When you decide to undertake a research project, choose a subject in which you have a genuine interest. Then begin the rewarding process of posing a question and finding the best answers available.

INSIDE THE TWENTIETH CENTURY
John Gunther

Sixty-five years ago, when this most turbulent, unpredictable and fruitful of centuries began, nobody had ever flown in an airplane, read a Geiger counter or argued about the welfare state. Nobody in 1900 listened to radio, looked at a newsreel, read a tabloid, stayed in a motel, watched a striptease, rode in the New York subway (which wasn't built until 1904), washed with hard-water soap or traversed the Panama Canal (opened in 1914).

Things that we take utterly for granted today were unknown when this, our century, began—things like frozen foods, the theory of the self-determination of nations, nylon, the organization man, national public-opinion polls and penicillin. The Diesel engine was three years old in 1900, the Kodak camera 12, and the fountain pen 16, but still to come were the permanent wave and air conditioning. Nobody had ever heard of radar, the urbanization of suburbs, plastics or automation. Newspaper headlines in 1900 dealt with the Galveston flood, the Boxer Rebellion in Peking and Carry Nation, the Prohibitionist zealot who broke saloon windows with an ax. And, of course, there was a Presidential election in which William McKinley and Theodore Roosevelt were the winning Republican candidates against William Jennings Bryan and Adlai E. Stevenson, Democrats.

Nineteen-hundred was the birth year of today's Adlai E. Stevenson, who is thus a true child of the century. It was also the birth year of the first rigid airship known as the Zeppelin, and of cellophane, invented by a Swiss. Sam Goldwyn was 18 in 1900, Walter Lippmann 11, and Mao Tsetung 7. Unborn were LBJ, DDT, Harold Wilson, urban renewal, Garbo and the Federal income-tax amendment.

Almost everywhere in the world in 1900, the prevailing characteristics were stability, placidity and comforting Victorian beliefs such as that virtue is its own reward. Sharp political crises occurred, but these were mostly absorbed by the prevailing atmosphere of acquiescence and tranquillity. There had been no major war since 1870. Queen Victoria, an imperiously venerable mother hen, entered the last year of her fantastically long reign (1837–1901), and an imperturbable British Navy ruled the seas.

Enormous quadrants of the earth's surface belonged to the German, Dutch, French, Spanish, Belgian and, above all, British empires, as if by divine right. The anticolonial revolution, like several other cataclysmic revolutions of our time, was still to come. Negroes were mostly serfs in the American South or the lowest-class labor in our Northern towns. Women did not have the vote in national elections.

On the German throne sat Kaiser Wilhelm II, who was to make much mischief before his days were done. Nicholas II was Czar of all the Russias; few men had ever heard the names of Nikolai Lenin and Leon Trotsky, but 1900 was the date when Lenin left Russia to become an international revolutionist. The Emperor Franz Josef had ruled the crazy patchwork of Austria-Hungary since 1848. France was ruled by a stagnant old parliamentarian, Emile Loubet, and Victor Emmanual III became King of Italy the year the century turned, 1900.

China growled and wriggled under the Manchu dynasty, while Western imperialists set out to consolidate their "concessions" on the coast and elsewhere. Even then, Japan was on the march, and it became a first-class power for the first time when, in 1904–05, to the amazement of the world, it soundly trounced the Russians with all their prestige, immensity and hallowed power.

Troubles afflicted the world in the early 1900's, yes, but they were troubles limited, shallow and capable of being circumscribed or covered up. By and large, both America and Europe basked in rosy optimism, based on the rationalist ideas of the nineteenth century. The ruling classes were prosperous and packed with privilege, and the poor were dealt with by charity, if at all. Capitalist society and the established order seemed unshakable, and revolutionists were generally dismissed as long-haired cranks.

Now, that primitive and remote old world has been almost totally obliterated, blasted out of history forever. New social, political and economic forces of acute and comprehensive violence have wiped the old slate clean. Institutions, traditions, folkways, kingly regimes, philosophies have vanished. How? Why?

Answers lie largely in the sphere of scientific breakthrough, political advance and the unquenchable desire of men and women everywhere to better themselves and their condition.

The twentieth century does not remotely resemble the nineteenth or any other century. There have been more changes in the past 65 years than in all other centuries put together. No longer do most people believe in the orderly progression of cause and effect; no longer do they believe in the natural goodness of man and the inevitability of progress. Stability is gone.

This is an era of quibble, doubt and qualm. Science, technology, art, architecture, music, literature have all acquired new values, and revolutionary conflicts rage.

No century has ever been so rich as ours, rich particularly in variety and change. We have gone from the horse and buggy to outer space. We have seen unimaginable advances in the standard of living and education of people almost everywhere. We have also progressed, if "progressed" is the proper word, from battles decided by cavalry charges and men in scarlet uniforms to an age dominated by thermonuclear bombs. Never before in history has the possibility existed that most of the known world could be incinerated, carbonized, in a matter of minutes, by the push of a button —or maybe two buttons, one ours, one theirs.

This, our century, has suffered the greatest economic crash and the worst depression ever known, but it has also seen unprecedented material progress. Wealth, moreover, has been shared as never before. Our century has endured three major revolutions—the Chinese (1911), the Mexican (1910) and the Russian (1917), as well as the two greatest wars in history. It has seen the breakup of the world into two competing ideological systems and the unleashing of unutterably vast social forces. Women have been "emancipated," and Negroes both at home and abroad are on the march.

Violence, tumult, catastrophe, despair are hallmarks of our century, but so are hope and liberation. Advances of almost inconceivable weight and scope have taken place in medicine, social affairs, communications, transportation, the freedom of peoples, the position of labor and every cranny of the world of science. Above all, this has been a century of conflict, change and emancipation. People everywhere resist exploitation and demand a better break.

Centuries can be measured by men, and great men and women by the score have distinguished the twentieth century thus far. Consider personalities, plucked at random, as outstanding in several categories as Theodore Roosevelt, Georges Clemenceau, David Lloyd George, Sun Yat-sen, Eleanor Roosevelt, J. M. Keynes, Dag Hammarskjöld, Eamon de Valera, Jawaharlal Nehru and at least three popes, Leo XIII ("the workingman's pope"), Pius XII and John XXIII.

We have had movie stars (Rudolph Valentino, Marilyn Monroe), clowns (Charlie Chaplin, Cantinflas), saints (Edith Cavell, Albert Schweitzer), adventurers (Gabriele D'Annunzio), men and women of the theater (Sarah Bernhardt, Constantin Stanislavsky, Eleonora Duse, the Barrymores), notable women in many walks of life (Marie Curie, Isadora Duncan, Madame Chiang Kai-shek, Jane Addams, Helen Keller), iconoclasts (H. L. Mencken) and fathers of their countries (Thomas Masaryk, Chaim Weizmann).

We have had historians like Oswald Spengler, traitors like Pierre Laval and martyrs like Roger Casement. We have had conservationists (Roosevelt I, Gifford Pinchot), benefactors (Alfred Nobel, the Rockefellers) plotters (Franz von Papen), philosophers (John Dewey, Bertrand Russell), patriots (Joseph Pilsudski, Kemal Ataturk) and statesmen of the corridors (Eleutherios Venizelos). We have had military leaders in profusion (Foch, Ludendorff, Smuts, Rommel, Patton) dictators (Joseph Stalin, Benito Mussolini, Juan Perón), public servants (Earl Warren, Ralph Bunche, Lord Attlee), fashion designers (Dior), figures in folklore (Will Rogers, Damon Runyan), figures in sport (Jack Dempsey, Man o'War, Babe Ruth, Knute Rockne, William Tatem Tilden II and Bobby Jones) and heroes galore (Lord Kitchener, Albert, King of the Belgians, Hindenburg, Lawrence of Arabia, Charles A. Lindbergh, Haile Selassie, Douglas MacArthur, Dwight D. Eisenhower).

There also lived and worked in this century men like Igor Stravinsky (b. 1882), Pablo Picasso (b. 1881) and James Joyce (1882–1941). No matter how briefly, these giants must be mentioned, too, because this has been a revolutionary period in art as well as politics and science. Stravinsky, Picasso, Joyce—and architects like Mies van der Rohe—have importance far beyond their own significant achievements in music, painting and literature, because they have drastically changed basic patterns, liberalized old ideas and contributed more stimulus to the imagination than most statesmen. Scores of other writers, artists and musicians might be mentioned—Arturo Toscanini, H. G. Wells, Bernard Shaw, T. S. Eliot, Jean Sibelius, Henri Matisse, Frank Lloyd Wright, Thomas Mann, Henry Moore, Marcel Proust, Franz Kafka, Sinclair Lewis and Ernest Hemingway.

But we have not yet reached the top of the heap. Several men listed in this roster might have lived in any era. There have been patriots, warriors and men of genius who established new modes in politics, art, or literature in previous centuries. Characteristic of *this* century is a small knot of men without whom the contemporary world simply would not be what it is at all. Their influence has been so cardinal, so deep and all-embracing that it is impossible to conceive of the modern world without them. They are the epoch makers who made our convulsed century different from any that has ever gone before.

There was born in Simbirsk, Russia, in 1870 a man named Vladimir Ilyich Ulyanov, known as Lenin. He was the greatest revolutionist of the modern world, perhaps of all time. Carrying on the sultry flame lit by Karl Marx, he organized and led the Bolshevik Revolution (October, 1917), probably the most germinal event in history since the French Revolution 128 years before. Lenin was largely responsible for setting up the Soviet state, a new kind of state built on concepts never known before, based, in theory at least, on the ideal of an egalitarian society, and he was the founder of the Communist party. Moreover, he created the Communist International, or world association of Communist parties, hoping to make communism an insurrectionary world movement. Few men of this or any time have left a stronger mark on the history of mankind, or so influenced events.

There was born in Freiberg, Moravia, in 1856 a man named Sigmund Freud. He put forward concepts that have taken root in almost all Western societies and have irreversibly changed the character of modern thought. Freud, even if he is out of fashion in some circles now, was a major innovator in the intellectual history of mankind, and is responsible for many of the changes in attitude that distinguish this century from any other. He founded the science—or call it pseudo-science—of psychoanalysis and made it clear that the mysteries of human behavior depend not merely on will and reason, but on elements buried in the unconscious. Freud died in 1939.

There was born in Ulm, Württemberg, in 1879 a man named Albert Einstein. Einstein, who postulated the special theory of relativity in 1905, is another true father of the modern epoch. Out of Einstein came the magic and terrifying formula $E = mc^2$; out of this came the atomic bomb and much of the paraphernalia of the space age. But Einstein himself, wandering down lanes in Princeton, N. J., with his baffled look, was one of the gentlest of men. He died in his adopted country, the United States, in 1955.

There was born in Staunton, Va., in 1856 a man named Woodrow Wilson. Wilson, who also spent part of his life at Princeton, was one of the pivotal creators of both nationalism and internationalism as contemporary political forces, and as such marked our century indelibly. His Fourteen Points (1918) led to the birth or resuscitation of half a dozen nations—e.g., Czechoslovakia and Poland—but also he gave reality to the idea of an effective world organization to keep the peace and was the principal inspirer of the League of Nations (1919), of which our United Nations today is the successor. He died in 1924.

There was born on a farm near Dearborn, Mich., in 1863 a homely genius with tools and figures named Henry Ford, who perfected mass production, opened the automobile age and transformed the face of the nation. Ford, in his own quirky way, has had almost as profound a revolutionary effect on the world as Lenin, though in a totally different direction. He was the first large-scale American manufacturer to grasp the idea that if you made goods cheap rather than expensive, the total volume of your sales and profits would expand, not diminish. Then, too, he raised wages on the theory that the more money consumers had, the more goods would they be able to buy, a doctrine thought to be wacky by the general business community of the time, but which made Ford one of the richest men in the world. Only the oldest among us today will remember the sensation caused by Ford's announcement in 1914 that he would pay labor the unprecedented wage of $5 for an eight-hour day, instead of $2.40 for a nine-hour day. Once he said that history was bunk, but he helped to make it. He died in 1947.

There was born in Porbandar, India, in 1869 a man named Mohandas Karamchand Gandhi, known as the Mahatma. Gandhi was an incredible combination of God, Tammany Hall and your father. He was not only an indisputable man of genius as well as saint, but a towering political innovator. His moral and spiritual quality, and the glowing searchlight of goodness that came out of his frail body (he weighed 104 pounds), assisted him to his supreme goal—freedom for the great subcontinent of India—but so did his extraordinary astuteness. India gained its freedom on August 15, 1947, one of the great dates of the century, but the Mahatma himself was assassinated in 1948 by one of those he had liberated.

There was born in the Austrian village of Braunau-am-Inn in 1889 a man named Adolf Hitler. This frustrated and distorted little man was probably the greatest murderer in history. Not only did he ignite the flame that brought World War II, but his was the responsibility for the death of some six million Jews. Hitler combined in his person the two dominant forces that give this century its chief political configuration—nationalism and socialism. Of course, his brand of socialism was a fraud, a fake—bait for the masses. Hitler's armies once stood from the Arctic Circle in Norway to the gates of Stalingrad, from the crests of the Pyrenees to the Caucasus. Beaten to a pulp, he killed himself ignominiously in Berlin in 1945.

There was born in Blenheim Palace, Oxfordshire, in 1874 a man named Winston Leonard Spencer Churchill, who has just turned 90. Of few men can it be said that, almost singlehanded, he saved a nation. Moreover, it can fairly be said that Churchill saved a whole world, our world. He flung the Nazis back in the Battle of Britain during his service as the greatest wartime Prime Minister in British history, and has found time in an incredibly versatile as well as stirring career to be a successful soldier, parliamentarian, orator, war correspondent, painter, bricklayer, prophet and historian. Some of his ideas were—and are—antediluvian, but his heroic imprint on the life of his times will never be effaced.

There was born in 1882 at Hyde Park, N. Y., a man named Franklin Delano Roosevelt, who had little use of his legs after the age of 39, but who nevertheless became President of the United States four times, led the nation out of the most catastrophic depression in its history, and directed the American war effort in World War II. He died in 1945, and is still a hotly controversial character. The chief landmark associated with him is, of course, the New Deal, the vast, interlocked series of social reforms that not only saved the country in the 1930's, but transformed its economic structure and vastly influenced governments all over the world to experiments with managed economies and the welfare state.

These are among the great movers and shakers who have given our era its special texture, spirit and configuration.

The 65 years of the twentieth century we have survived so far have been unprecedentedly rich in events, as well as men. We have had great explorations (Robert Peary to the North Pole, Roald Amundsen to the South), heroic feats (the conquest of Everest), advances in entertainment (the talkies, TV) tragic assassinations (from Archduke Franz Ferdinand in Sarajevo in 1914 to John F. Kennedy in Dallas in 1963), natural disasters (the San Francisco earthquake) and such man-made disasters as the torpedoing of the *Lusitania.*

There have been celebrated romances (King Edward VIII and Mrs. Wallis Simpson), celebrated scandals (the Dreyfus Affair in France, Teapot Dome in the United States) and celebrated crimes (the murder of Rasputin, the Landru murders, the Leopold-Loeb case). We have had weird social "experiments" (Prohibition), outrages (the Sacco-Vanzetti case), abominations (the McCarthy hearings) and social ameliorations such as the establishment of the Tennessee Valley Authority, the reforms of the Popular Front government in France and the introduction of socialized medicine in Britain. In the fields of national and world affairs, we have suffered such events as the 1929 Wall Street crash, the sellout at Munich and several fancy blunders such as the division of Germany into zones, Suez and the invasion at the Bay of Pigs in Cuba.

Two or three enormous events or developments outshadow all others and make our epoch essentially what it is. One is scientific breakthrough; another is the convulsion caused by two world wars.

Never before has there been such an advance in science, invention, technology, medicine and communications. Lee De Forest invented the three-electrode vacuum tube in 1906, opening the way for radio, radar and TV. In 1910, Dr. Ivan Pavlov announced in St. Petersburg the theory of the conditioned reflex. The endless-chain tractor was produced in 1906, the gyro compass was first used on a ship in 1911, the cyclotron was developed in 1931, and sulfanilimide in 1935. Insulin was discovered in 1922, and Sir Alexander Fleming opened the way in 1929 to the use of penicillin. The Salk vaccine came in 1953, and Dr. Selman Waksman discovered streptomycin in 1943. Margaret Sanger and her courageous associates began in the 1920's to propagate the idea of birth control—one of the significant developments of modern times.

Never before in the more advanced centuries have standards of public health been so high as today. New methods of diagnosis, new techniques in therapy have saved millions of lives. We have discovered vitamins and hormones. The ancient scourge of tuberculosis has been virtually wiped out in the Western world. Surgical operations on blood vessels, the chest, the heart, inconceivable in former days, are commonplace. Of *all* drugs used in today's pharmacopoeia, over 70 percent are new since World War II. New discoveries in genetics ("breaking the genetic code") and the new sciences like microbiology and astrophysics are fomidable. But progress also creates problems. Our lakes and streams have been polluted by chemical wastes and detergents, our fields and woodlands poisoned by insecticides.

Lord Rutherford, perhaps the greatest modern physicist after Einstein, reached in 1919 a goal pursued ever since the days of the medieval alchemists—the transmutation of elements—and opened the way to the atomic age. The first nuclear chain reaction in history took place at the University of Chicago in 1942.

Back in 1901, Guglielmo Marconi sent a radio signal across the Atlantic for the first time, and in 1903, two daring pioneers made the first automobile trip across the United States. The Wright brothers became the first men ever to fly in a mechanically propelled airplane, and in 1909, Louis Blériot flew the English Channel. Transcontinental air mail was inaugurated in the U.S. in 1920, and in 1927, Charles A. Lindbergh flew the Atlantic solo. A piloted airplane flew faster than the speed of sound for the first time in 1947. The first jazz record—another form of communication—was put out in 1916 or 1917, and the first licensed broadcasting station—KDKA in Pittsburgh—went on the air in 1920. The first man-made satellite, Sputnik I, rose sensationally into the heavens on October 4, 1957, and in 1961, Maj. Yuri Gagarin of the Soviet Union became the first space traveler in history. His feat of circling the globe in orbit has since been repeated and amplified by both Russians and Americans a number of times. Meantime, research on missiles gave both the United States and Russia the ICBM. The space age began—and with it, the era of nuclear deadlock, or balance of terror between the two chief powers on earth.

So, with this disconcerting development, unique in the world's history, we reach politics and international affairs. The list of distinctive events ranges from the decision of the Turks to push a railway into Arabia in 1900 to the test-ban treaty in 1963 and quarrels over NATO in 1964. At random, one may mention such momentous happenings as the Japanese conquest of Manchuria in 1931 and the Spanish Civil War in 1936. Out of Russia came not merely purges, terror and privation, but the concept of the Five Year Plan, which has been imitated all over the world. Roosevelt II inaugurated a Good Neighbor Policy for Latin America in the 1930's. Austria fell to Hitler in 1938, and Marshal Tito of Yugoslavia was tossed out into the cold by the Kremlin in 1948, an event presaging the breakup of the monolithic solidarity of the Communist empire. Israel became a free nation in the same year. The Marshall Plan helped put war-racked Europe on its feet. In 1950 came the American decision, made largely by Dean Acheson under the courageous eye of President Harry S. Truman, to stand up against Communist aggression in Korea. President John F. Kennedy carried on its implications by standing up against Nikita Khrushchev and imposing a blockade on Cuba in 1962.

Meantime—in other parts of the world—the Chinese invaded Tibet, the Congo exploded, the Berlin Wall was built, dramatizing the continuing Cold War between Russia and the United States, and every known kind of trouble descended on Southeast Asia. But above and beyond all these occurrences were World Wars I and II, the paramount cataclysms of our time. Breaking it down to the simplest terms, World War I(1914–18) was set off when Germany invaded Belgium. It started out as a romantic old-style war, symbolized by the poems of Rupert Brooke, and then developed into the horror of deadlocked trench warfare with such unprecedented weapons as tanks and poison gas. It was distinguished by mass slaughters like Verdun, and 8.5 million soldiers died. It was the first truly *world* war in history, and the Central Powers came within a squeak of winning.

Basically, the cause of the war was the conflict of competing old-style imperialisms, and it is a significant irony that one of the war's important consequences was the disappearance from history of four major dynasties—Hohenzollern, Hapsburg, Romanov and Ottoman. One historic result was to bring U. S. troops into Europe for the first time. The old world died with World War I, and no integrated, secure new world has yet arisen to replace it.

World War II (1939–1945), the most frightful in history, probably cost at least 40 million lives, directly or indirectly. It was not merely a clash of dynasties, but of ideologies. Poland, France, the Low Countries, Denmark, Norway, most of the Balkans were crushed by the Nazi onslaught. Hitler totally changed the character and tempo of the war by repudiating the Russo-German pact and invading the Soviet Union in June, 1941, and the Japanese attack on Pearl Harbor followed on December 7, 1941. Armies, navies and air forces were locked in battles as titanic and decisive as the Coral Sea, El Alamein and Stalingrad before the spectacular invasion of Normandy.

World War II, although we won it, came near to wrecking what was left of established order in the world. The rickety structure built up precariously on the ruins of World War I came close to disintegrating under the shocks and distresses imposed by World War II. An Iron Curtain made a prison out of Eastern Europe, and China went Communist. The world became almost equally split into giant thirds—roughly 900 million people on our side, 900 million people on the Communist side, 900 million people neutralist. The war killed American isolationism once and for all, which meant that America must accept responsibilities unknown before. The age of foreign aid began. The war also produced the atom bomb, and indeed it was this fierce and unprecedented weapon that brought the Japanese to their knees in 1945. We killed 78,150 men, women and children in one blast on Hiroshima, 73,884 in another at Nagasaki. But these bombs were lilliputian compared to those that might be used today.

To sound a more positive note, we should remember that the League of Nations came out of World War I. It didn't work, but this was partly because the U. S. did not join. Most of the new nations liberated or set up after 1919 did not last long, but that wasn't their fault. World War II produced the UN as well as the atomic bomb.

These then are some of the men, events and forces that have shaped our age, and have carved the twentieth century so far into its distinctive shape and form. What has been the result? What do we look like? What are the principal characteristics and qualities of the modern era? Generalizations of such scope are hard to make, but one thing to say is that dominating notes in most of our lives are pace, stress and change.

One principal change has been the shrinkage of the twentieth-century world. This, in the main, has been the product of two factors, air travel and electronic communication. None of us are ever going to get over whatever devil invented the internal combustion engine, to say nothing of electricity. Years ago, China, let us say, and Japan were distant countries. Places like Saudi Arabia, Bechuanaland, or even Paraguay were hard to reach. There was a considerable problem in transportation. If a man had visited India in the days when I grew up, he was thought to be a somewhat extraordinary character. He could dine out for months on what the Taj Mahal really looked like in moonlight. Today, friends of mine pop off for casual weekends in Bangkok, Capetown or Rio de Janeiro without more nuisance than calling a travel bureau. The great coin of the globe has become a dime.

But while the world has become much smaller, it has become bigger as well, and this makes for trouble. Today, we find ourselves enmeshed in situations boiling up here, there and everywhere—Saigon, Cyprus, or La Paz. It becomes progressively more difficult for any single human being, from the Secretary of State up or down, to gather in and absorb the whole picture. In the old days, we could deal with political affairs sector by sector. We could confront crises one at a time. Now, everything is inextricably conjoined and interlocked, and the sheer mass of what we have to take in is overwhelming.

Then consider pace. Not only is the century distinguished above all others by trenchant change, but the pace of change is more rapid, more sweeping, than ever before. Changes pile up on changes with incredible velocity. Not only are we supposed, as citizens of the world, to keep ourselves informed on all sorts of impossible levels, but to make judgment on forces of bewildering complexity moving at an insane rate of speed. As a result, people become confused, and this confusion is reflected not merely in political, but in moral and individual terms. The world seems topsy-turvey as old taboos disappear; people lose emotional stability, emotional security.

Flux, worry, unrest, mobility have all contributed to another characteristic of the modern age, a radical shift in modes and standards. Puritanism in literature is dead. As to other forms of entertainment, think of the movies, and consider the difference between *The Birth of a Nation* and *La Dolce Vita*. Social patterns have altered vastly. We have juvenile delinquency on a new and savage level, vulgarization in many patterns of behavior, political irresponsibility and fantastic libertarianism in sex. Religious observance has declined, and one out of every 3.8 marriages in the U. S. ends in divorce.

Here, in 1965, are some other distinguishing and more specific characteristics of our century:

1. It is an age of big government, big business and, a more novel factor, big labor. In 1901, the giant hands of J. P. Morgan put together the U. S. Steel Corporation, the first billion-dollar corporation in history. The CIO was founded by John L. Lewis in 1935, and merged with the older AFL in 1955. Prolonged strikes attended labor's rise to a successful bargaining position. Good pay 50 years ago was 29 cents an hour for ten hours' work a day. Think what your plumber or carpenter would say today if you followed this scale and offered him $17.40 a week!

2. It is also the age of the Common Man. This was symbolized after World War I, when various governments erected monuments not merely to heroes, but to an "unknown" soldier. The common man, the average man, the little man is probably the outstanding hero of the century. He thrives today because of the spread of education, social legislation, greater economic opportunity and the redistribution of wealth through taxation. Nor will he tolerate being pushed around. Exploitation of man by man is on the way out.

3. This is an age of managed economies and the welfare state, if only because the old laissez-faire system has broken down. Governments today prop up the economy, go in for vast exercises in paternalism and deficit spending, regulate industry, support agriculture, administer scientific research, sponsor education and housing, and exercise wide regulatory powers over banking, the stock exchanges, transportation, power and communications. Few governments in the world today would dare to deny that they have responsibility for the general well-being of citizens, and few indeed could survive without elaborate mechanisms like unemployment insurance, old-age pensions and social security in general. (Germany had social security under Bismarck in the nineteenth century, but the process has been enormously amplified and speeded up.)

4. This is an age of almost limitless abundance and economic well-being, but a disgraceful amount of poverty remains. Our Gross National Product has risen from $104 billion in 1929 to $554.9 billion in 1962, but between 40 and 50 million Americans are still classified as "poor." There are more than 79,000,000 cars and trucks on the roads in the United States today, but a substantial segment of the nation is still inadequately housed, clothed and fed. The national budget stands near $100 billion (half of it for defense), but a lot of us still have trouble paying the grocery bill. Also,

there have come tremendous changes in industrial management and production, including the new role of computers, a fantastic growth in sales and the influence of Madison Avenue on merchandising—something unknown in 1900. Roughly 4,000 passenger automobiles were sold in the United States in 1900, and almost 7,000,000 in 1962. Then, too, women play a role in the national economy overwhelmingly greater than before.

5.   This era has been distinguished also by the most formidable educational advance in history, partly because the rank and file of people almost everywhere demand education as a natural right. It is no longer something doled out or reserved for the privileged.

6.   This is the century in which the Negro problem has become the most gravid, difficult and cancerous in the nation, one that can only be solved by full civil rights for our Negro population.

7.   This is the age in which colonialism (except in a few isolated areas) disappeared. Thirteen Asian countries have become free since World War II, including such giants as India, Indonesia and Pakistan (respectively the second, fifth and sixth biggest nations in the world in population), and no fewer than 33 nations in Africa. The British Empire has become the British Commonwealth. When the UN was inaugurated in San Francisco in 1945, it had 50 members; today, it has 115, several of which could not have come into being except for the UN. Many of the new nations are painfully poor and underdeveloped; to assist them is a major world responsibility. That several are handling their affairs badly and are sensitive and parochial does not make the problem easier.

8.   The principal imponderable in today's political picture is the position of Communist China, with its 686,400,000 people—particularly since 1964 when it exploded its first nuclear device. China has attacked India and still threatens it. Much in the general international field will depend on future developments between China and the Soviet Union, which are in a puzzling flux. Meanwhile, relations between the U. S. and U. S. S. R., pivotal to everything, have eased a bit, but they may not stay eased for long.

9.   An encouraging factor in world affairs is the steep and powerful recovery of Western Europe that symbolizes the end of the immediate postwar period. The tragic feud across the Rhine, which has caused wars since Charlemagne, may have been patched up for good. But the Western Alliance as a whole has been subjected in the last years to difficult stresses and strains, largely because of the abrasive policies of Gen. Charles de Gaulle. This will be one of the first problems that President Lyndon B. Johnson will have to face in 1965.

10.   This is the era in which, atop everything, above everything, is poised dangerously the supreme question of peace or war. A paradox brings hope. It is that the nuclear stalemate prevailing today makes full-scale nuclear war impossible (except by egregious blunder or accident), if only be-

cause no nation can reasonably hope to win. Absolute military power did not come with the bomb, but went out.

Our twentieth-century lives are assailed by a variety of challenges and problems, from the "war on poverty" to the maintenance of world peace. As Adlai Stevenson said in a recent speech, "For the first time in history, the world is being changed radically within the span of an average lifetime." We are entering "a world in which the myth of monolithic blocs is giving way to a bewildering diversity among nations, one in which realities are eroding the once-rigid political dogmas, one in which the old trading systems, monetary systems and market systems . . . are being . . . changed, one which is both fabulously rich and desperately poor, and, finally, one in which fundamental issues of human rights, which have been hidden in closets down the long corridor of history, are out in the open and high on the agenda of human affairs."

Our present era has been distinguished by war, threat of more war, revolution and collapse. It has been an era of high hopes dashed, illusions shattered and dreams turned into nightmares. It has been called an "Age of Longing," an "Age of Frustration" and an "Age of Apprehension." But if I were asked to label this tremendous period of history with just one phrase, I would call it the "Age of Liberation." This has been the most volatile century in history, with crises and difficulties aplenty, but it has also brought intellectual as well as material advance beyond measure, and has given us such power over the forces of the universe as has never been dreamed of before. The question remains what we will do with it. Man has gone a long way toward conquering the totality of his environment, but we do not know as yet whether or not he has conquered himself.

What a 65 years! What a century!

Questions

A. Type

1. Richard D. Altick, in *The Art of Literary Research*, states: "Research is the means, scholarship the end; research is an occupation, scholarship is a habit of mind and a way of life." Research includes the collecting and interpreting of facts. To what extent is Gunther's "Inside the Twentieth Century" a collection of facts? To what extent is it an interpretation of facts?

2. Using the second paragraph only, list the facts mentioned and explain the significance of each in terms of Gunther's contrast between the nineteenth and twentieth centuries.

3. From the facts gathered, the researcher draws the logical conclusions inherently present. Gunther makes a series of generalizations about both the nineteenth and twentieth centuries: to what extent do

the facts presented support the generalizations? You may wish to consider such statements as the following: "Things that we take utterly
for granted today were unknown when this, our century, began. . . .";
"Almost everywhere in the world in 1900, the prevailing characteristics
were stability, placidity, and comforting Victorian beliefs. . . ."; "The
anticolonial revolution . . . was still to come"; "No century has ever
been so rich as ours, rich particularly in variety and change"; "Never
before has there been such an advance in science, invention, technology, medicine, and communications"; "One principal change has been
the shrinkage of the twentieth century"; "It [century] is an age of big
government, big business and . . . big labor."

B. Purpose and Content

1. John Gunther asks the question, "What is the character or quality
of human life in the twentieth century?" And he poses four related
questions that lead to answering the primary one: who and what are
the forces, men, events, and characteristics that shaped the twentieth
century? How are his answers to these related questions pertinent to
his purpose?

2. What specific statement indicates Gunther's purpose in "Inside
the Twentieth Century"? Normally you can expect to find such a
statement early in the research paper; if you do not, assume the writer
is using details, cases, examples, to build up a clear purpose.

3. In the first section of the research paper Gunther asks, "What are
some of the primary forces of the period 1900–1965?" What are some
of these forces?

C. Techniques

1. Herbert Read, in *English Prose Style*, an examination of the techniques of composition and rhetoric used by writers of the English language, asserts that most writers have "a rhythm of thought." Some
writers present ideas in rapid-fire order; others introduce one idea at a
time, examine it carefully, and then more to a second; still other writers begin with details or parts of larger ideas, developing gradually in
the reader's mind the extent of the idea under consideration. Your
"rhythm of thought" is your first principle of organization; in order to
write effectively you should examine carefully the "rhythm," slow or
rapid, through which you present your ideas. In what way does the
"rhythm" of Gunther's thought provide the organization of "Inside
the Twentieth Century"?

2. What kind of effect is gained by Gunther in his opening sentence
through his description of the first sixty-five years of the century as
"turbulent, unpredictable and fruitful"?

3. What tone is established through choice of such details as "welfare state," "Geiger counter," "newsreel," "motel," "striptease," and
"hard-water soap"?

4. After the two introductory paragraphs Gunther contrasts the nineteenth century world of Queen Victoria with the twentieth century world shaped by new social, political, economic, and scientific forces. What contrasts between the two centuries are established?

5. In the second section of his essay Gunther states that he has "plucked at random" outstanding personalities of the twentieth century. In what way does his "random" selection of names prepare the reader for his later selection of the "small knot of men without whom the contemporary century would not be what it is at all"?

6. Using parallel structure Gunther briefly mentions the names and contributions of this "small knot of men." Does parallel structure contribute to the coherence of the research paper?

7. Later Gunther enumerates the "specific characteristics of our century." Can you find any principle of order governing the sequence of Gunther's choices, extending from "big government, big business and . . . big labor" to "the supreme question of peace or war"?

D. Writing

1. Using Gunther's selection of great men as a basis for your position, do you agree with Carlyle's view that history is "a study of the lives of great men"? Do your research carefully.

2. Write a brief research paper on one of the following major figures of the twentieth century: Lenin, Freud, Einstein, Woodrow Wilson, Henry Ford, Gandhi, Hitler, Churchill, Franklin Delano Roosevelt. You must ask a specific question and seek a specific answer.

3. Write a brief research paper on one of the following individuals: Eleanor Roosevelt, John XXIII, J. M. Keynes, Albert Schweitzer, Igor Stravinsky, Pablo Picasso, James Joyce. For example, what is Albert Schweitzer's conception of the "holy"?

4. In the third section of his research paper Gunther briefly mentions major events of the first sixty-five years of the twentieth century. Trace the influence of one aspect of one of these events on a particular twentieth-century issue. For example, you may wish to discuss the impact of the Pavlovian "conditioned reflex" on George Orwell's *1984.*

5. A critical reader will not be circumscribed by the material he reads. Gunther, in the fourth section of his paper, proposes ten specific characteristics of the twentieth century. Propose an eleventh and support your position through careful research and documentation.

6. In conclusion Gunther affirms, "This has been the most volatile century in history." Using another century as the basis of your research, argue that that particular century—the first, the fourth, the seventeenth—is the "most volatile century in history."

Index of Authors and Titles

215

DATE DUE